THE FIVE SCROLLS

חמש
מגלות

THE FIVE SCROLLS

Hebrew texts, English translations,
introductions, and new liturgies

Translations edited by
Rabbi Albert H. Friedlander

Introductions co-edited by
Rabbi Herbert Bronstein
and
Rabbi Albert H. Friedlander

Liturgies edited by
Rabbi Herbert Bronstein

Research, development, and editorial services
by Dr. Yehiel Hayon

Illustrated and designed by
Leonard Baskin

CCAR PRESS
Central Conference of American Rabbis
New York, New York
1984 / 5744

LIBRARY OF CONGRESS CATALOGING IN PUBLICATION DATA

Bible. O.T. Five Scrolls. Hebrew. 1984.
    The Five Scrolls.

    English and Hebrew.
    Bibliography: p.
    1. Pilgrimage Festivals (Judaism)—Liturgy—Texts. 2. Maḥzorim
—Texts. 3. Reform Judaism—Liturgy—Texts. I. Friedlander,
Albert H. II. Bronstein, Herbert. III. Central Conference of
American Rabbis. IV. Bible. O.T. Five Scrolls. English. Friedlander.
1984. V. Maḥzor. Pilgrim Festivals (Reform, Central Conference of
American Rabbis) Selections. 1984. VI. Title.
BS1309.A3F75 1984   221'.044   84–12183
ISBN 0–916694–80–1 (hardbound)
ISBN 0–916694–81–X (cloth art ed.)
ISBN 0–916694–82–8 (leather ltd. ed.)

CONTENTS

INTRODUCTION TO
THE FIVE SCROLLS

This presentation of the Five Scrolls, with liturgies for the festivals, is intended as a contribution to the process of the religious renewal of American Jewry.

For a long time Western Jewry had suffered a process of spiritual disruption and debilitation. In the course of scarcely a century and a half, Jewry experienced the upheaval of the great migrations from Europe to America. As great as were the physical disruptions, the cultural devastation was greater still. American society was a frontier world. American society was preoccupied with establishing the *material* basis of life. Isaac Mayer Wise, a founder of Reform Judaism, could not find on the entire continent, when he first arrived here in the mid-nineteenth century, even a single copy of a basic book of Jewish law, the Mishnah. There were large numbers of unlearned Jews without the basic knowledge or skills to understand or to express Jewish spirituality.

Furthermore, even among some scholars, Jewish learning was no longer *Torah,* the kind of learning which would enable Jews "to learn and to teach, to observe and to do in love." Many books about Judaism were written in a debunking spirit. They explained religion away as a psychological aberration, or shadowy superstition to be dispelled by the light of a kind of rationalism that has proved, alas, to be sterile and soul-destroying. Some Jewish scholars were resigned to the disappearance of religion altogether.

Now there is an increasingly well-educated and highly intelligent community of Jews looking for the kind of Jewish books which can communicate *Torah* in a way that endows life with value and meaning. An increasing number of Jews want not to diminish but to amplify the religious content of their lives.

If a dispassionate observer were to look at a host of Jewish books being published now (the *New Torah Commentary*, the educational materials on classical rabbinic texts, anthologies of Jewish literature, but above all those books which present Judaic worship and observance: prayerbooks, Haggadot, Holy Day guides)—that observer would, if perceptive, realize that whatever the differences, all of these books reveal a great community united by a single commonality of purpose: to rejuvenate, to create, to raise the level of spirituality among an entire people.

This edition of the Five Scrolls is meant to be such *Torah*. It reflects an ardent didactic mission. It is born of a passionate desire to raise the level of Jewish observance, to recover in this particular case that richness of color, motif, sound, and story, the fullness (to coin a phrase) of spiritual sensuality in our festival observance; and thus to strengthen Jewish consciousness, to give greater content to Jewish identity. Out of the liturgical glories of our heritage we hope to provide not only content and meaning, but direction as well in the lives of Jews; in sum, to restore and rebuild the reality of Jewish religious community: *kehila kedosha*.

This text is intended as a part of the recovery among liberal Jewry of festival observance. The premise of this edition of the Five Scrolls is that there is a Jewry ready and waiting for this renewal. And, in fact, American Jewry is now a vast craft studio, a spiritual *atelier,* in which numerous teachers, rabbis, poets, artists of all kinds, with utter dedication, are engaged in bringing into being the most beautiful of works of art: a religious way of life.

That is why it is so appropriate that this edition of the Five Scrolls should be enhanced by the work of one of the finest Jewish artists of our time, Leonard Baskin. This is an act of *hidur mitzvah:* the holiness of beauty expressing the beauty of holiness. His work is itself a midrash, a commentary on the biblical Five Scrolls.

The Five Scrolls were once, throughout Jewry, an intrinsic element of our way of life. The books were familiar to the people and beloved by them. In recent years, these five books of the Bible have been read, and studied and analyzed by scholars as if under a microscope, but too often in isolation, as if they were

objects in themselves and divorced from the ongoing daily life of a larger community.

In the living Jewish religious community each of these books is assigned to one of the festivals. Read in the synagogue on these holidays, they become an organic part of the round of the seasons as seed time and harvest, blossom and fruit. In this way they become part and parcel of the personal life and mentality of every Jew. They become part of one's growth, one's personal history, a component of one's own identity.

The editors of *The Five Scrolls* hope to make these books live again in the religious life of our people, as part of observance in home and synagogue.

Because the book is meant to be a part of festival worship, special liturgies have been prepared for each of the scrolls which link the text to the distinctive mood, themes, and images of the day. The liturgies which accompany the scrolls are meant for communal worship. As frankly creative as they are, the liturgies are nevertheless deeply rooted in the texts, in the symbols, and in the observances of our tradition. They are drawn from many Judaic sources, both old and new. The liturgies can be considered as preludes and postludes to the biblical texts. They are also commentaries. In liturgical fashion they reveal the themes of the festival days and why each particular scroll was assigned to the particular holy day on which it is read.

Our Hebrew text addresses itself to a generation which has relearned or is relearning the ancient language of its soul. And in the Hebrew text we have provided the cantillation marks for the words, which make it possible for congregations to recover the rich musical leitmotifs which are a part of festival observance.

A note on the translation is in order here. A number of excellent new translations of the Bible have appeared in recent years, and this text is not intended to compete with them. Much of our translation is built upon the *Jewish School and Family Bible* translation, presented by Dr. A. Benisch to Sir Anthony de Rothschild in London in 1851. It is a Victorian text of some elegance and scholarship. The calm rationalism of its introduction anticipated some of Darwin's ideas on evolution (*The Origin of Species* appeared in 1859). We can be comfortable with the text; although it has been brought up to date and modernized, the

style and charm of the older English text endures and blends with the illustrations. It is true that new words are needed by every age, even for the old experiences. Yet we still rejoice that "his banner over me was love"; Ruth will not be entreated to "return from following after" Naomi; and "that which is crooked cannot be made straight." An old love is not easily set aside; and if this English version shows extra respect to the Masorites and to the older translators, it is a self-indulgence that may be accepted by readers and condoned by scholars, even though a number of words can be challenged by experts. The Jerusalem *Koren Tanach* similarly uses the old Friedlander version of 1881 because "it was faithful to the Mesora . . . and retained much . . . of the unsurpassed language and rhythm of the 1611 (King James) text."

In Germany, the Buber-Rosenzweig Bible was created to be read aloud. But that generation died; its speech was silenced, its golden age could not be achieved. American Jewry, moving towards a time of great creativity, is served by Bible scholars bringing the Hebrew word into the center of its cultural and spiritual life. The Hebrew text is at the center of our edition of the Five Scrolls also. Yet the English words also unite us with parents and grandparents who might have muttered that "all is vanity" and that "of the making of books there is no end"—but who also made that English text part of their daily conversation. If only we can regain that sense of belonging to the everlasting world of the Bible, this knowledge that we share our text with all of the past and with the future as well, because in some mysterious way they bind us to the God of the eternal covenant!

Let these scrolls be part of the recurring springtimes of our life, helping us to reflect both on the times of light and darkness and to express the full exuberance of joy as well as the abysmal depths of sorrow, and to provide more content to our lives as Jews.

Many American Jews know the "forest tale" of the Chasidim. The story reflects the very sense of depletion, decay, and debilitation that many "Jews of modernity" were feeling. According to this story, the Baal Shem Tov was able, in his generation, to go to a certain place at a certain time and perform a certain ritual which brought wholeness, meaning, content and fulfillment to life. The next generation of Jews had forgotten the observance,

but they knew of the time and the place. That had to suffice. In the next generation, they forgot the place, but they could tell the story, and that had to suffice. Many American Jews could well have added: "And we do not even know the story!"

We can no longer accept this surrender to despair, this spiritual depletion. There is a renewed sense of the power not only to recover the old but to create new observances, even the new "times and places" of fullness and meaning in behalf of a renewed Jewish community.

We must again provide, teach, learn, and come to know the great "stories" told in the Five Scrolls.

The followers of the Baal Shem Tov liked to say that while other rabbis left us books, the Baal Shem Tov left us Jews. But the need for our time is exactly for books which will make better Jews. And Franz Rosenzweig, confronting the disruption and depletion of Jewish spirituality and of religious community for modern Jews, echoed this when he argued that the need of the hour, the need for the Jews of modernity, was not for more books of mere dry scholarship, but for more real Jews.

Now we need Jewish books which will help us to be Jews. We hope that this edition of the Five Scrolls is such a book.

We can again become Jews: the People of the Book.

Herbert Bronstein   שבת הגדול, תשמ"ד
Albert H. Friedlander   April 13, 1984

Chicago and London

A NOTE ON USAGE

As indicated in the Introduction, this presentation of the Five Scrolls is intended to enrich festival worship and to contribute to the revitalization of festival observance among our people.

Brief liturgies, in accord with the mood and "color" of each of the holy days, have been prepared both to precede and to follow the readings from the biblical texts. The prayers before the readings, as preludes, are intended to prepare our minds and our spirits for themes of the readings; in instances, to highlight aspects of the scrolls; and to reveal, in part, the relationship of each of the biblical books to the motifs, the ethos, and the pathos of the holy day to which each book is assigned by our tradition.

In this edition, then, each of the biblical books is placed like a jewel in a setting. It follows, of course, that one finds the prayers which are intended to precede the biblical readings just before each of the books; and those which should follow, just after the books.

There are two exceptions. For both Purim and Tish-ah Be-Av, there is included a *complete* service. These are printed as a whole, respectively, before the Scroll of Esther and the Scroll of Lamentations. We read from each of those biblical works at the place indicated in those services, and then return to the service itself.

For the convenience of the congregation, a complete new Festival Service has been prepared, along with a new Hallel Service, which, like the liturgies for the scrolls, is original. The Hallel Service is intended to convey, with creative fidelity to our heritage, the theme of life over death, cosmos triumphant over chaos, a motif deeply rooted in the festivals.

The Hallel is presented separately that it might be used on various occasions. Its place for recitation during the Festival Service is indicated in the text.

THE SCROLL OF ECCLESIASTES

INTRODUCTION TO
THE SCROLL OF ECCLESIASTES

Wisdom literature does not necessarily make us wiser, and in no book is this more readily apparent than in the Scroll of Ecclesiastes. Yet this most brilliant exposition of the futility of human strivings and of the inevitability of death will not convince us that life has no meaning. Resignation is an attitude born of one kind of response to life experience. It is a response of the whole being and is not a result of reason or logic alone. Yet our horizons are enlarged by the skeptics and the rebels whose thoughts fill the pages of the Bible. The authors of the Scroll of Ecclesiastes and the Book of Job explore areas of our life which have moved to the forefront of our awareness in this Age of Brutality.

An Italian commentary to the Bible notes that:

> Ecclesiastes concludes the work of limiting wisdom which Job had begun; it deprives man of the vain hope of being able to recognize the supposed order of the universe. He only knows one thing, that we must all die and that here the wise man and the fool are on the same level.
>
> (J. Alberto Soggin, *Introduction to the Old Testament*, p. 400)

Nevertheless, the text also suggests that if wisdom fails as a human attempt to dominate existence, an unconditional faith remains which banishes all insecurity. In this respect Job's great celebration of wisdom (chapter 28) must be kept in mind:

> Reverence for the Lord, that is wisdom;
> And to depart from evil is understanding.

Our scroll ends on the same note: "Fear God and keep His commandments; for this is the whole man." But there is far more

to our text than this. Leo Baeck, writing in the concentration camp, compared the volcanic text of Job with the coolness of Kohelet, "the speaker of the assembly," the calm scholar who spins, weaves, and unravels questions, who philosophizes about the world and God in measured words:

> [Fear God and keep His commandments . . .] This is his final word, the word of *hokhmah*. It is not just that this man philosophizes and believes, head and heart, a precursor of that romanticism which is derived from scepticism; for he remained, with all his rationality, one of this people, which is unable to understand itself or the world without the law of God, indeed, cannot live without it. This people can have its members who, like Koheleth, can cast doubt on all else, because they never doubt the law of God . . .
>
> (Leo Baeck, *This People Israel,* p. 99)

Where Job storms the heaven of heavens, Kohelet, from the vantage point of a person who knows his limitations and has no false illusions, addresses himself to his fellow human beings. As Baeck pointed out, Kohelet observes only what he is able to see. Everything is therefore in motion for him, in flux; it comes and goes. Only the world abides, but nothing is certain. Measurement and clear knowledge are unattainable. Time is the framework for all things: "There is a time for everything under the sun." But one hour is as the next and "there is nothing new under the sun." The cycle repeats itself, without change. Yet this knowledge can lead the human being to the wisdom, the *chochma,* of that which unites humanity with the cosmos, with one another; the experience of the moment joined to the awareness of the universality of human fate. Even the knowledge that we do not know links us to all others. And the Scroll of Ecclesiastes, placed within the full expression of faith and experience reaching from Sinai into our own time, is totally expressive of Jewish fate and faith which must incorporate scepticism and doubt within the dynamic polarities of its religion.

The wisdom of the "speaker of the assembly" is presented to us in the form of maxims, reflections, confessions, and poetic meditations. Often, it speaks in autobiographical terms, and the

reference to being "the son of David, king of Jerusalem" led tradition to identify the author as Solomon. The very language, the ideas, and the literary structure argue against this.

As Robert Gordis has said, if the author wanted this work identified as the words of Solomon, he would have said so, instead of using the name Kohelet. And the consensus of modern scholarship would see the grammar, expressions, and ideas of the Hebrew text as arguments placing the author into the third century B.C.E. Who and what he was cannot be totally deduced from the text, although a vast array of conflicting ideas exist in scholarly tomes—which calls to mind Baeck's translation of the text: "Be admonished, my son: to make many books is not a goal!" It must suffice us that we have here a sparkling array of ideas about the nature of life and the reality of death which have rarely been surpassed in literature. As the rabbis saw it, even the contradictions and challenges to faith must not be used to exclude this scroll from the canon, for "its beginning is religious teaching and its end is religious teaching" (*Shabbat* 30b).

We read this scroll on Sukkot, which is additional evidence that the rabbis saw something profoundly religious in this sceptical approach to life. There is, of course, the recognition of the rhythmic pattern of time which brings season and harvest. The acknowledgment of insecurity is not strange to those who depend upon the harvest and know how powerless the farmer is when a harsh wind bites into the summer crop. But it may well be the farmer, tied to the seasons and understanding how little chance planning and hard work have against the inexorable rhythm of nature, who will feel most at home with Kohelet.

We follow this teacher through the metamorphoses of life: the futility of the ruler, the rich man, the scholar, and the sybarite— all appear before us in turn. We rediscover the seasons of life, and feel the sad beauty of old age described in poetic passages which are rediscovered by every generation. Ultimately, the negations become affirmations; recognition of our limitations does not lead to despair but to acceptance. With Leo Baeck, we come to understand the wisdom, the *chochma* of Kohelet:

> *Hokhmah* is that in which the revelation and therefore the creation prove true, that which speaks out of everything, out of

the world and its laws, out of human life, and its laws too. It is that which testifies to the permanence of the creation, to the permanence of the revelation.

(Leo Baeck, *This People Israel*, p. 100)

Practical piety might also have found it wise to contrast the season of harvest with the ironies and anomalies of life expressed in Ecclesiastes. Just as the New Year period is a time of joy comingled with deep introspection and prayer, we seek a balance between the self-satisfaction produced by the abundance of flocks, fields or commerce, and on the other hand, an awareness of life's pain, anxiety and fragility.

This is analogous to the balance induced by the commandment to enjoy life, and the demand, at the same time, that we care for the poor, the widow, the helpless in society. This dialectic of enjoyment of our well-being and realism about the insecurities of life has given a tensile strength to our national character that is close to what we mean in Judaic heritage by "wisdom." All of this is linked with the deeply rooted practice, in Judaism, particularly at this season, of giving *tzedakah,* charity, "according to the gifts of God's hand," which is a fine expression of that reverence for God which is wisdom.

SERVICE FOR THE READING OF
THE SCROLL OF ECCLESIASTES

חַג הַסֻּכּוֹת תַּעֲשֶׂה לְךָ שִׁבְעַת יָמִים בְּאָסְפְּךָ מִגָּרְנְךָ וּמִיִּקְבֶךָ. וְשָׂמַחְתָּ בְּחַגֶּךָ.

After the ingathering from your threshing floor and your vat, you shall hold the Feast of Booths for seven days. You shall rejoice in your festival, in that God will bless you in the work of your hands. And you shall be altogether joyful.

    𝄞 וְשָׂמַחְתָּ בְּחַגֶּךָ

וְהָיִיתָ אַךְ שָׂמֵחַ.

(You shall rejoice in your festival . . .
You shall have nothing but joy.)

It is written:

וְשָׂמַחְתָּ בְּחַגֶּךָ וְהָיִיתָ אַךְ שָׂמֵחַ.

Rejoice in your festival, and be altogether joyous!
On this day of celebration we rejoice.
And on this day a book of wisdom is set before us.
On this day we enjoy the gifts of harvest goodness.
And on this day we ponder teachings
with which we can dower all our days with joy.

*O God who commands rejoicing, we seek the wisdom
which can bless our days with joy.*

כִּי יֵשׁ לַכֶּסֶף מוֹצָא

וּמָקוֹם לַזָּהָב יָזֹקּוּ.

בַּרְזֶל מֵעָפָר יֻקָּח

וְאֶבֶן יָצוּק נְחוּשָׁה.

וְהַחָכְמָה מֵאַיִן תִּמָּצֵא,

וְאֵי־זֶה מְקוֹם בִּינָה?

אֱלֹהִים הֵבִין דַּרְכָּהּ,

וְהוּא יָדַע אֶת־מְקוֹמָהּ.

הֵן יִרְאַת אֲדֹנָי הִיא חָכְמָה,

וְסוּר מֵרָע בִּינָה.

For there is a mine for silver,
and a source for gold which is then refined.
Iron is taken out of the dust,
and brass is molten out of the stone.
Humankind sets an end to darkness,
and searches to the furthest bound—
overturning mountains by the roots,
cutting out channels among the rocks,
and seeing every precious thing;
binding the streams that they trickle not;
and the thing that is hidden bringing forth to light.
But wisdom, where shall it be found?
And where is the place of understanding?

Even while rejoicing in our festivals,
even while dancing and singing our joy,
our beings are burdened by knowledge of suffering.
The glories of nature dazzle our eyes;
yet injustice and brute pain still daily confront us.
As our minds puzzle the mystery of God's ways—
hovering between pitch darkness and celestial light,
our spirits yearn for a resolving peace.

קִדְּשָׁנוּ בְּמִצְוֹתֶיךָ,

וְתֶן חֶלְקֵנוּ בְּתוֹרָתֶךָ.

שַׂמְּחֵנוּ בִּישׁוּעָתֶךָ,
וְטַהֵר לִבֵּנוּ לְעָבְדְּךָ בֶּאֱמֶת.

Hallow us through Thy commandments,
endow us with the inheritance of Thy Torah.
Gladden us with Thy redemption,
refine our spirits that we may serve Thee with truth.

Bless God, O my soul.
My God, Thou art very great;
Thou art clothed with glory and majesty.
Thou stretchest out the heavens like a curtain;
Thou maketh the clouds Thy chariot.

The earth is full of the fruit of Thy works.
Thou causest the grass to spring up for the cattle,
and herb for the service of humankind;
to bring forth bread out of the earth,
and wine that maketh glad the human heart.

Vanity of vanities, saith Kohelet,
Vanity of vanities, all is vanity.

The wind goeth toward the south,
and turneth about unto the north;
it turneth about continually in its circuit,
and the wind returneth again to its circuits.
All rivers run into the sea,
yet the sea is not full.
That which hath been is that which shall be,
and that which hath been done
is that which shall be done;
and there is nothing new under the sun.

The end of the matter, all having been heard:
Revere God, and keep the commandments.
For this applies to all humankind.

When I behold Thy heavens, the work of Thy fingers,
the moon and the stars, which Thou hast established—
What is humankind, that Thou art mindful of us?
A human being, to whom one should pay heed?
Yet Thou hast made us but little lower than the divine,
and hast crowned us with glory and honor.

Vanity of vanities, saith Kohelet,
Vanity of vanities, all is vanity.

O God!
What are human beings
that Thou shouldst acknowledge and take notice of us!
A person is like a vain breath of air;
one's days a passing shadow;
in the morning budding,
by evening faded and dry.
Are not all the mighty heroes
as nought before Thee,
the famous as though they had never been,
the wisest as if without knowledge at all,
the understanding bereft of counsel?
For most of their works are void;
their entire lives a breath;
and the pre-eminence
of the human over the beast
is as nothing.

The end of the matter, all having been heard:
Revere God and keep the commandments.
For this applies to all humankind.

Do not be vexed because of evil-doers,
neither be Thou envious against them
that work unrighteousness,
for they soon wither like grass,
and fade as the green herb.
Give up anger, abandon fury,
do not be vexed;

it can only do harm.
For evil-doers will be cut off,
but those who look to God—
they shall inherit the land.

Vanity of vanities, saith Kohelet,
Vanity of vanities, all is vanity.

I returned, and saw under the sun,
that the race is not to the swift,
nor the battle to the strong,
nor bread to the wise,
nor even riches to those of understanding,
nor even favor to those of skill;
but time and chance
happeneth to them all.

The end of the matter all having been heard:
Revere God, and keep the commandments.
For this is the whole of humankind.

I made great works for myself;
I built myself houses.
I planted vineyards for myself;
I made myself gardens and parks,
and I planted trees in them of all kinds of fruit.
I constructed for myself pools of water . . .
Also, I had great possessions . . .
I withheld not myself from any pleasure,
for I derived great pleasure from all of my labor.

Vanity of vanities, saith Kohelet,
Vanity of vanities, all is vanity.

You shall give as you are able,
according to the measure of the blessing
which God has given you.

The end of the matter all having been heard:
Revere God and keep the commandments.
For this applies to all humankind.

How fortunate, how good our portion!
How pleasant our lot!
How beautiful our heritage!

אַשְׁרֵינוּ, מַה־טּוֹב חֶלְקֵנוּ! ¶
וּמַה־נָּעִים גּוֹרָלֵנוּ!
וּמַה־יָּפָה יְרוּשָׁתֵנוּ!

Blessings before reading from the Scroll of Ecclesiastes

בָּרוּךְ אַתָּה, יְיָ אֱלֹהֵינוּ, מֶלֶךְ הָעוֹלָם, אֲשֶׁר קִדְּשָׁנוּ בְּמִצְוֹתָיו
וְצִוָּנוּ עַל מִקְרָא מְגִלָּה.

Ba-ruch a-ta, A-do-nai E-lo-hei-nu, me-lech ha-o-lam, a-sher ki-de-sha-nu be-mits-vo-tav ve-tsi-va-nu al mik-ra me-gi-la.

We praise Thee, O God, Sovereign of existence, who has hallowed our lives with commandments and commanded us to read this scroll.

בָּרוּךְ אַתָּה, יְיָ אֱלֹהֵינוּ, מֶלֶךְ הָעוֹלָם, שֶׁהֶחֱיָנוּ וְקִיְּמָנוּ
וְהִגִּיעָנוּ לַזְּמַן הַזֶּה.

Ba-ruch a-ta, A-do-nai E-lo-hei-nu, me-lech ha-olam, she-he-che-ya-nu ve-ki-ye-ma-nu ve-hi-gi-a-nu la-ze-man ha-zeh.

We praise Thee, O God, Sovereign of existence, who has kept us alive, sustained us, and enabled us to perform this Mitzvah in joy.

READING FROM
THE SCROLL OF ECCLESIASTES

א א דִּבְרֵי קֹהֶלֶת בֶּן־דָּוִד מֶלֶךְ בִּירוּשָׁלָ͏ִם:
ב הֲבֵל הֲבָלִים אָמַר קֹהֶלֶת
הֲבֵל הֲבָלִים הַכֹּל הָבֶל:
ג מַה־יִּתְרוֹן לָאָדָם
בְּכָל־עֲמָלוֹ
שֶׁיַּעֲמֹל תַּחַת הַשָּׁמֶשׁ:
ד דּוֹר הֹלֵךְ וְדוֹר בָּא
וְהָאָרֶץ לְעוֹלָם עֹמָדֶת:
ה וְזָרַח הַשֶּׁמֶשׁ וּבָא הַשָּׁמֶשׁ
וְאֶל־מְקוֹמוֹ
שׁוֹאֵף זוֹרֵחַ הוּא שָׁם:
י הוֹלֵךְ אֶל־דָּרוֹם
וְסוֹבֵב אֶל־צָפוֹן
סוֹבֵב ׀ סֹבֵב הוֹלֵךְ הָרוּחַ
וְעַל־סְבִיבֹתָיו שָׁב הָרוּחַ:
ז כָּל־הַנְּחָלִים הֹלְכִים אֶל־הַיָּם
וְהַיָּם אֵינֶנּוּ מָלֵא
אֶל־מְקוֹם שֶׁהַנְּחָלִים הֹלְכִים
שָׁם הֵם שָׁבִים לָלָכֶת:
ח כָּל־הַדְּבָרִים יְגֵעִים
לֹא־יוּכַל אִישׁ לְדַבֵּר
לֹא־תִשְׂבַּע עַיִן לִרְאוֹת
וְלֹא־תִמָּלֵא אֹזֶן מִשְּׁמֹעַ:
ט מַה־שֶּׁהָיָה הוּא שֶׁיִּהְיֶה
וּמַה־שֶּׁנַּעֲשָׂה

1 ¹The words of Kohelet, son of David, king of Jerusalem.
²"Vanity of vanities," said Kohelet;
"Vanity of vanities—all is vanity."
³What profit has a man
From all his labor
Which he labors under the sun?
⁴One generation goes, and another generation comes;
But the earth abides forever.
⁵The sun also rises, and the sun goes down,
And hastens to the place
From whence it rose.
⁶Going towards the South,
Returning to the North,
The wind whirls about continually;
And the wind returns again to its rounds.
⁷All rivers run to the sea,
But the sea is never full.
To the place from which the rivers come,
There they return again.
⁸All things are wearisome;
No one can recount them.
The eye is not satisfied with seeing,
Nor is the ear filled with hearing.
⁹What has been is that which will be.
What has been done

Kohelet, Son of David   1:1

דברי חכמים בנחת
נשמעים מזעקת

הוּא שֶׁיֵּעָשֶׂה
וְאֵין כָּל־חָדָשׁ תַּחַת הַשָּׁמֶשׁ:
יֵשׁ דָּבָר שֶׁיֹּאמַר רְאֵה־זֶה חָדָשׁ הוּא כְּבָר הָיָה
לְעֹלָמִים אֲשֶׁר הָיָה מִלְּפָנֵנוּ: יֹא אֵין זִכְרוֹן
לָרִאשֹׁנִים וְגַם לָאַחֲרֹנִים שֶׁיִּהְיוּ לֹא־יִהְיֶה לָהֶם
זִכָּרוֹן עִם שֶׁיִּהְיוּ לָאַחֲרֹנָה:
יֹב אֲנִי קֹהֶלֶת הָיִיתִי מֶלֶךְ עַל־יִשְׂרָאֵל בִּירוּשָׁלָם:
יֹג וְנָתַתִּי אֶת־לִבִּי לִדְרוֹשׁ וְלָתוּר בַּחָכְמָה עַל כָּל־
אֲשֶׁר נַעֲשָׂה תַּחַת הַשָּׁמָיִם הוּא | עִנְיַן רָע נָתַן
אֱלֹהִים לִבְנֵי הָאָדָם לַעֲנוֹת בּוֹ: יֹד רָאִיתִי אֶת־כָּל־
הַמַּעֲשִׂים שֶׁנַּעֲשׂוּ תַּחַת הַשָּׁמֶשׁ וְהִנֵּה הַכֹּל הֶבֶל
וּרְעוּת רוּחַ:
טֹו מְעֻוָּת לֹא־יוּכַל לִתְקֹן
וְחֶסְרוֹן לֹא־יוּכַל לְהִמָּנוֹת:
טֹז דִּבַּרְתִּי אֲנִי עִם־לִבִּי לֵאמֹר אֲנִי הִנֵּה הִגְדַּלְתִּי
וְהוֹסַפְתִּי חָכְמָה עַל כָּל־אֲשֶׁר־הָיָה־לְפָנַי עַל־
יְרוּשָׁלָם וְלִבִּי רָאָה הַרְבֵּה חָכְמָה וָדָעַת: יֹז וָאֶתְּנָה
לִבִּי לָדַעַת חָכְמָה וְדַעַת הֹלֵלוֹת וְשִׂכְלוּת יָדַעְתִּי
שֶׁגַּם־זֶה הוּא רַעְיוֹן רוּחַ:
יֹח כִּי בְּרֹב חָכְמָה רָב־כָּעַס
וְיוֹסִיף דַּעַת יוֹסִיף מַכְאוֹב:
ב אָמַרְתִּי אֲנִי בְּלִבִּי לְכָה־נָּא אֲנַסְּכָה בְשִׂמְחָה
וּרְאֵה בְטוֹב וְהִנֵּה גַם־הוּא הָבֶל:
ב לִשְׂחוֹק אָמַרְתִּי מְהוֹלָל
וּלְשִׂמְחָה מַה־זֹּה עֹשָׂה:

Is that which will be done again.
And there is nothing new under the sun.
[10]If there is a thing of which it is said: "See, this is new!"
It has been already, in the ages which were before us.
[11]There is no remembrance of former things, neither will
there be any remembrance of things which are to come
with those who shall come afterwards.
[12]I, Kohelet, was king over Israel in Jerusalem. [13]And I
applied my mind to seek and search out through
wisdom everything that is done under heaven. It is a
sore task that God has given to the sons of man to keep
them occupied. [14]I have seen all the works that are done
under the sun; and behold, all is vanity, a feeding on
wind.
[15]That which is crooked cannot be made straight,
And that which is wanting cannot be numbered.
[16]I said to myself: "I have grown great and have amassed
more wisdom than all who were before me in
Jerusalem. Yes, my mind has acquired much wisdom
and knowledge." [17]And so I set my mind to know
wisdom, and to know madness and folly. I perceived
that this also is a striving after wind.
[18]For in much wisdom is much grief;
And he who increases knowledge increases pain.
2 [1]I said to myself: "Come, I will test you with mirth;
therefore, enjoy pleasure." And behold, this also was
vanity.
[2]I said of laughter: "It is mad";
And of mirth: "What does it do?"

גתַּרְתִּי בְלִבִּי לִמְשׁוֹךְ בַּיַּיִן אֶת־בְּשָׂרִי וְלִבִּי נֹהֵג
בַּחָכְמָה וְלֶאֱחֹז בְּסִכְלוּת עַד אֲשֶׁר־אֶרְאֶה אֵי־זֶה
טוֹב לִבְנֵי הָאָדָם אֲשֶׁר יַעֲשׂוּ תַּחַת הַשָּׁמַיִם מִסְפַּר
יְמֵי חַיֵּיהֶם: דהִגְדַּלְתִּי מַעֲשָׂי בָּנִיתִי לִי בָּתִּים
נָטַעְתִּי לִי כְּרָמִים: העָשִׂיתִי לִי גַּנּוֹת וּפַרְדֵּסִים
וְנָטַעְתִּי בָהֶם עֵץ כָּל־פֶּרִי: ועָשִׂיתִי לִי בְּרֵכוֹת מָיִם
לְהַשְׁקוֹת מֵהֶם יַעַר צוֹמֵחַ עֵצִים: זקָנִיתִי עֲבָדִים
וּשְׁפָחוֹת וּבְנֵי־בַיִת הָיָה לִי גַּם מִקְנֶה בָקָר וָצֹאן
הַרְבֵּה הָיָה לִי מִכֹּל שֶׁהָיוּ לְפָנַי בִּירוּשָׁלָ͏ִם:
חכָּנַסְתִּי לִי גַּם־כֶּסֶף וְזָהָב וּסְגֻלַּת מְלָכִים
וְהַמְּדִינוֹת עָשִׂיתִי לִי שָׁרִים וְשָׁרוֹת וְתַעֲנֻגוֹת בְּנֵי
הָאָדָם שִׁדָּה וְשִׁדּוֹת: טוְגָדַלְתִּי וְהוֹסַפְתִּי מִכֹּל
שֶׁהָיָה לְפָנַי בִּירוּשָׁלָ͏ִם אַף חָכְמָתִי עָמְדָה לִי:
יוְכֹל אֲשֶׁר שָׁאֲלוּ עֵינַי לֹא אָצַלְתִּי מֵהֶם לֹא־
מָנַעְתִּי אֶת־לִבִּי מִכָּל־שִׂמְחָה כִּי־לִבִּי שָׂמֵחַ מִכָּל־
עֲמָלִי וְזֶה־הָיָה חֶלְקִי מִכָּל־עֲמָלִי:
יאוּפָנִיתִי אֲנִי בְּכָל־מַעֲשַׂי שֶׁעָשׂוּ יָדַי וּבֶעָמָל
שֶׁעָמַלְתִּי לַעֲשׂוֹת וְהִנֵּה הַכֹּל הֶבֶל וּרְעוּת רוּחַ
וְאֵין יִתְרוֹן תַּחַת הַשָּׁמֶשׁ: יבוּפָנִיתִי אֲנִי לִרְאוֹת
חָכְמָה וְהוֹלֵלוֹת וְסִכְלוּת כִּי | מֶה הָאָדָם שֶׁיָּבוֹא
אַחֲרֵי הַמֶּלֶךְ אֵת אֲשֶׁר־כְּבָר עָשׂוּהוּ:
יגוְרָאִיתִי אָנִי
שֶׁיֵּשׁ יִתְרוֹן לַחָכְמָה מִן־הַסִּכְלוּת
כִּיתְרוֹן הָאוֹר מִן־הַחֹשֶׁךְ:

³I searched in my mind how to pamper my flesh with wine and to grasp folly, even while my mind conducted itself with wisdom, till I might see what is better for the sons of man to do under the heavens all the days of their life. ⁴I made myself great works; I built myself houses. I planted vineyards for myself. ⁵I made myself gardens and parks, and I planted trees in them of all kinds of fruit. ⁶I made myself water pools, to water with them the wood bringing forth trees. ⁷I acquired manservants and maidservants, and had servants born in my house. Also, I had great possessions of herds and flocks, more than any who had been in Jerusalem before me. ⁸I gathered for myself silver and gold, the treasure of kings and provinces. And I got myself men singers and women singers, and the sons of man, a wife and concubines. ⁹So I was great, and increased more than any that were before me in Jerusalem. Yet my wisdom stayed with me. ¹⁰Whatever my eyes desired I kept not from them. I denied myself no enjoyment. I found pleasure in all my labor; and this was my reward for all my work.

¹¹Then I looked on all the works that my hands had accomplished, and on the labor which I had expended in making them; and behold: all was vanity and a striving after wind, and there was no profit under the sun. ¹²So I turned again to look at wisdom, madness, and folly: for what can the man do who comes after the king? Only that which has already been done.

¹³Then I saw
That wisdom is better than folly,
Even as light is better than darkness.

"As it is with the fool, so it is with me.
How, then, was I wiser? This also is vanity." 2:15

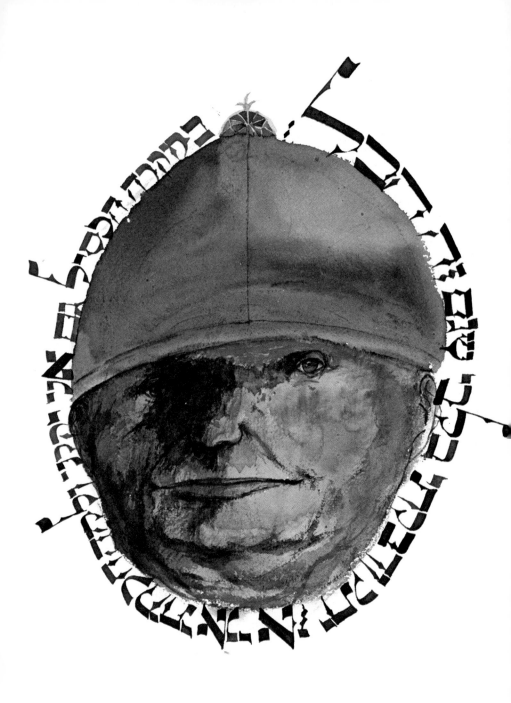

יד הֶחָכָם עֵינָיו בְּרֹאשׁוֹ
וְהַכְּסִיל בַּחֹשֶׁךְ הוֹלֵךְ
וְיָדַעְתִּי גַם־אָנִי
שֶׁמִּקְרֶה אֶחָד יִקְרֶה אֶת־כֻּלָּם: טו וְאָמַרְתִּי אֲנִי בְּלִבִּי כְּמִקְרֵה הַכְּסִיל גַּם־אֲנִי
יִקְרֵנִי וְלָמָּה חָכַמְתִּי אֲנִי אָז יֹתֵר וְדִבַּרְתִּי בְלִבִּי
שֶׁגַּם־זֶה הָבֶל: טז כִּי אֵין זִכְרוֹן לֶחָכָם עִם־הַכְּסִיל
לְעוֹלָם בְּשֶׁכְּבָר הַיָּמִים הַבָּאִים הַכֹּל נִשְׁכָּח וְאֵיךְ
יָמוּת הֶחָכָם עִם־הַכְּסִיל:
יז וְשָׂנֵאתִי אֶת־הַחַיִּים כִּי רַע עָלַי הַמַּעֲשֶׂה
שֶׁנַּעֲשָׂה תַּחַת הַשָּׁמֶשׁ כִּי־הַכֹּל הֶבֶל וּרְעוּת רוּחַ:
יח וְשָׂנֵאתִי אֲנִי אֶת־כָּל־עֲמָלִי שֶׁאֲנִי עָמֵל תַּחַת
הַשָּׁמֶשׁ שֶׁאַנִּיחֶנּוּ לָאָדָם שֶׁיִּהְיֶה אַחֲרָי: יט וּמִי
יוֹדֵעַ הֶחָכָם יִהְיֶה אוֹ סָכָל וְיִשְׁלַט בְּכָל־עֲמָלִי
שֶׁעָמַלְתִּי וְשֶׁחָכַמְתִּי תַּחַת הַשָּׁמֶשׁ גַּם־זֶה הָבֶל:
כ וְסַבּוֹתִי אֲנִי לְיַאֵשׁ אֶת־לִבִּי עַל כָּל־הֶעָמָל
שֶׁעָמַלְתִּי תַּחַת הַשָּׁמֶשׁ: כא כִּי־יֵשׁ אָדָם שֶׁעֲמָלוֹ
בְּחָכְמָה וּבְדַעַת וּבְכִשְׁרוֹן וּלְאָדָם שֶׁלֹּא עָמַל־בּוֹ
יִתְּנֶנּוּ חֶלְקוֹ גַּם־זֶה הֶבֶל וְרָעָה רַבָּה: כב כִּי
מֶה־הֹוֶה לָאָדָם בְּכָל־עֲמָלוֹ וּבְרַעְיוֹן לִבּוֹ שְׁהוּא
עָמֵל תַּחַת הַשָּׁמֶשׁ: כג כִּי כָל־יָמָיו מַכְאֹבִים וָכַעַס
עִנְיָנוֹ גַּם־בַּלַּיְלָה לֹא־שָׁכַב לִבּוֹ גַּם־זֶה הֶבֶל הוּא:
כד אֵין־טוֹב בָּאָדָם שֶׁיֹּאכַל וְשָׁתָה וְהֶרְאָה אֶת־
נַפְשׁוֹ טוֹב בַּעֲמָלוֹ גַּם־זֹה רָאִיתִי אָנִי כִּי מִיַּד
הָאֱלֹהִים הִיא: כה כִּי מִי יֹאכַל וּמִי יָחוּשׁ חוּץ

¹⁴The wise man's eyes are in his head,
And the fool walks in darkness.
Nevertheless, I came to understand
That the same fate overtakes them all.
¹⁵And I said to myself: "As it happens to the fool, so will
it happen to me; how, then, was I wiser?" Then I said
to myself: "This also is vanity." ¹⁶For there is no
enduring remembrance of the wise more than of the
fool. In the coming days, everything that was shall be
forgotten. Oh, the wise man dies just like the fool.
¹⁷Therefore, I hated life. For everything that is done
under the sun was grievous to me; for everything is
vanity and a striving after wind.
¹⁸I hated all my labor at which I had labored under the
sun; because I must leave it to the man who shall come
after me. ¹⁹Who knows whether he will be a wise man
or a fool; but he will rule over all my labor at which I
have labored, and in which I have shown myself wise
under the sun. This also is vanity. ²⁰And so I despaired
within myself regarding all the labor at which I had
labored under the sun. ²¹For if there is a man whose labor
is done with wisdom, with knowledge, and with skill,
it will yet go as an inheritance to a man who has spent
no labor on it. This also is vanity and a great evil. ²²For
what does a man have of all his labor, and of the
striving of his mind, in which he labors under the sun?
²³For all his days are pain, and his occupation is grief, and
at night his mind finds no rest. This also is vanity.
²⁴There is nothing better for a man than that he should
eat and drink, and make his soul enjoy good in his
labor. This too I have seen, that it is from the hand of

"To everything there is a season..." 3:1

עֵת לָלֶדֶת וְעֵת לָמוּת

עֵת לָטַעַת וְעֵת לַעֲקוֹר נָטוּעַ

עֵת לַהֲרוֹג וְעֵת לִרְפּוֹא

עֵת לִפְרוֹץ וְעֵת לִבְנוֹת

עֵת לִבְכּוֹת וְעֵת לִשְׂחוֹק

עֵת סְפוֹד וְעֵת רְקוֹד

עֵת לְהַשְׁלִיךְ אֲבָנִים וְעֵת כְּנוֹס אֲבָנִים

עֵת לַחֲבוֹק וְעֵת לִרְחֹק מֵחַבֵּק

עֵת לְבַקֵּשׁ וְעֵת לְאַבֵּד

עֵת לִשְׁמוֹר וְעֵת לְהַשְׁלִיךְ

עֵת לִקְרוֹעַ וְעֵת לִתְפּוֹר

עֵת לַחֲשׁוֹת וְעֵת לְדַבֵּר

עֵת לֶאֱהֹב וְעֵת לִשְׂנֹא

עֵת מִלְחָמָה וְעֵת שָׁלוֹם:

מִמֶּֽנִּי: ^{כו} כִּי לְאָדָם שֶׁטּוֹב לְפָנָיו נָתַן חָכְמָה וְדַעַת
וְשִׂמְחָה וְלַחוֹטֶא נָתַן עִנְיָן לֶאֱסֹף וְלִכְנוֹס לָתֵת
לְטוֹב לִפְנֵי הָאֱלֹהִים גַּם־זֶה הֶבֶל וּרְעוּת רֽוּחַ:

ג ^א לַכֹּל זְמָן
וְעֵת לְכָל־חֵפֶץ תַּחַת הַשָּׁמָֽיִם:
^ב עֵת לָלֶדֶת וְעֵת לָמוּת
עֵת לָטַעַת
וְעֵת לַעֲקוֹר נָטֽוּעַ:
^ג עֵת לַהֲרוֹג וְעֵת לִרְפּוֹא
עֵת לִפְרוֹץ וְעֵת לִבְנֽוֹת:
^ד עֵת לִבְכּוֹת וְעֵת לִשְׂחוֹק
עֵת סְפוֹד וְעֵת רְקֽוֹד:
^ה עֵת לְהַשְׁלִיךְ אֲבָנִים
וְעֵת כְּנוֹס אֲבָנִים
עֵת לַחֲבוֹק
וְעֵת לִרְחֹק מֵחַבֵּֽק:
^ו עֵת לְבַקֵּשׁ וְעֵת לְאַבֵּד
עֵת לִשְׁמוֹר וְעֵת לְהַשְׁלִֽיךְ:
^ז עֵת לִקְרוֹעַ וְעֵת לִתְפּוֹר
עֵת לַחֲשׁוֹת וְעֵת לְדַבֵּֽר:
^ח עֵת לֶאֱהֹב וְעֵת לִשְׂנֹא
עֵת מִלְחָמָה וְעֵת שָׁלֽוֹם:
^ט מַה־יִּתְרוֹן הָעוֹשֶׂה בַּאֲשֶׁר הוּא עָמֵל: ^י רָאִיתִי
אֶת־הָעִנְיָן אֲשֶׁר נָתַן אֱלֹהִים לִבְנֵי הָאָדָם לַעֲנוֹת
בּֽוֹ: ^{יא} אֶת־הַכֹּל עָשָׂה יָפֶה בְעִתּוֹ גַּם אֶת־הָעֹלָם

God. [25]For who should eat, and who should enjoy, if not
I? [26]God gives wisdom, and knowledge, and joy to a man
who is good in His sight; but to the sinner He gives the
task to gather and to heap up, so that he may give that
to him who is good before God. This also is vanity and
a striving after wind.

3 [1]To everything there is a season,
And a time to every purpose under the heaven.
[2]A time to be born, and a time to die;
A time to plant,
And a time to pluck up that which is planted;
[3]A time to kill, and a time to heal,
A time to break down, and a time to build up;
[4]A time to weep, and a time to laugh;
A time to mourn, and a time to dance.
[5]A time to cast away stones,
and a time to gather stones;
A time to embrace,
And a time to refrain from embracing.
[6]A time to seek, and a time to lose;
A time to keep, and a time to cast away.
[7]A time to rend, and a time to sew;
A time to keep silent, and a time to speak;
[8]A time to love, and a time to hate;
A time for war, and a time for peace.
[9]What profit has the worker from his labor? [10]I have seen
the tasks which God has given to the sons of man to
keep them occupied. [11]He has made everything beautiful

נָתַן בְּלִבָּם מִבְּלִי אֲשֶׁר לֹא־יִמְצָא הָאָדָם אֶת־
הַמַּעֲשֶׂה אֲשֶׁר־עָשָׂה הָאֱלֹהִים מֵרֹאשׁ וְעַד־סוֹף:
יָדַעְתִּי כִּי אֵין טוֹב בָּם כִּי אִם־לִשְׂמוֹחַ וְלַעֲשׂוֹת
טוֹב בְּחַיָּיו: וְגַם כָּל־הָאָדָם שֶׁיֹּאכַל וְשָׁתָה וְרָאָה
טוֹב בְּכָל־עֲמָלוֹ מַתַּת אֱלֹהִים הִיא:
יָדַעְתִּי כִּי כָּל־אֲשֶׁר יַעֲשֶׂה הָאֱלֹהִים הוּא יִהְיֶה
לְעוֹלָם
עָלָיו אֵין לְהוֹסִיף
וּמִמֶּנּוּ אֵין לִגְרֹעַ
וְהָאֱלֹהִים עָשָׂה
שֶׁיִּרְאוּ מִלְּפָנָיו:
מַה־שֶּׁהָיָה כְּבָר הוּא
וַאֲשֶׁר לִהְיוֹת כְּבָר הָיָה
וְהָאֱלֹהִים יְבַקֵּשׁ אֶת־נִרְדָּף:
וְעוֹד רָאִיתִי תַּחַת הַשָּׁמֶשׁ
מְקוֹם הַמִּשְׁפָּט שָׁמָּה הָרֶשַׁע
וּמְקוֹם הַצֶּדֶק שָׁמָּה הָרָשַׁע:
אָמַרְתִּי אֲנִי בְּלִבִּי אֶת־הַצַּדִּיק וְאֶת־הָרָשָׁע
יִשְׁפֹּט הָאֱלֹהִים כִּי־עֵת לְכָל־חֵפֶץ וְעַל כָּל־
הַמַּעֲשֶׂה שָׁם: אָמַרְתִּי אֲנִי בְּלִבִּי עַל־דִּבְרַת בְּנֵי
הָאָדָם לְבָרָם הָאֱלֹהִים וְלִרְאוֹת שְׁהֶם־בְּהֵמָה
הֵמָּה לָהֶם: כִּי מִקְרֶה בְנֵי־הָאָדָם וּמִקְרֶה
הַבְּהֵמָה וּמִקְרֶה אֶחָד לָהֶם כְּמוֹת זֶה כֵּן מוֹת זֶה
וְרוּחַ אֶחָד לַכֹּל וּמוֹתַר הָאָדָם מִן־הַבְּהֵמָה אָיִן כִּי
הַכֹּל הָבֶל: הַכֹּל הוֹלֵךְ אֶל־מָקוֹם אֶחָד הַכֹּל הָיָה

in its time; also, He has planted eternity into their minds, yet even then man cannot find out the work which God has made from the beginning to the end. [12]I know that there is nothing better for man than to rejoice, and to do good in his life. [13]And also, that every man should eat and drink and enjoy the good of all his labor; it is the gift of God.

[14]I know that whatever God does shall be forever;
Nothing can be added to it,
Nor anything taken away from it.
God has ordained it so
That they shall be in awe of Him.
[15]Whatever is, has been long ago;
And what is to be has been long ago;
And God summons every event back in its turn.
[16]Moreover, I saw under the sun
That iniquity was there alongside of justice,
And that iniquity was there alongside of righteousness.
[17]I said to myself: God will judge the righteous and the wicked, for He has set a time for every purpose and for every work. [18]I said to myself: It is because of the sons of men, that God may test them, and that they may see that they themselves are no more than beasts. [19]For there is one fate for both man and beast, and it is the same fate: as the one dies, so dies the other; yes, they all breathe the same, and man has no pre-eminence above the beast; for all is vanity. [20]All go to one place. All are

מִן־הֶעָפָ֔ר וְהַכֹּ֖ל שָׁ֣ב אֶל־הֶעָפָֽר: כא מִ֣י יוֹדֵ֗עַ ר֤וּחַ
בְּנֵ֣י הָאָדָ֔ם הָעֹלָ֥ה הִ֖יא לְמָ֑עְלָה וְר֨וּחַ֙ הַבְּהֵמָ֔ה
הַיֹּרֶ֥דֶת הִ֖יא לְמַ֥טָּה לָאָֽרֶץ: כב וְרָאִ֗יתִי כִּ֣י אֵ֥ין טוֹב֙ מֵאֲשֶׁ֤ר יִשְׂמַח֙ הָאָדָ֣ם
בְּמַעֲשָׂ֔יו כִּי־ה֖וּא חֶלְק֑וֹ כִּ֣י מִ֤י יְבִיאֶ֨נּוּ֙ לִרְא֔וֹת
בְּמֶ֖ה שֶׁיִּהְיֶ֥ה אַחֲרָֽיו:
ד א וְשַׁ֣בְתִּֽי אֲנִ֗י וָאֶרְאֶה֙ אֶת־כָּל־הָ֣עֲשׁוּקִ֔ים אֲשֶׁ֥ר
נַעֲשִׂ֖ים תַּ֣חַת הַשָּׁ֑מֶשׁ וְהִנֵּ֣ה ׀ דִּמְעַ֣ת הָעֲשׁוּקִ֗ים
וְאֵ֤ין לָהֶם֙ מְנַחֵ֔ם וּמִיַּ֤ד עֹֽשְׁקֵיהֶם֙ כֹּ֔חַ וְאֵ֥ין לָהֶ֖ם
מְנַחֵֽם: ב וְשַׁבֵּ֧חַ אֲנִ֛י אֶת־הַמֵּתִ֖ים שֶׁכְּבָ֣ר מֵ֑תוּ מִן־
הַ֣חַיִּ֔ים אֲשֶׁ֛ר הֵ֥מָּה חַיִּ֖ים עֲדֶֽנָה: ג וְטוֹב֙ מִשְּׁנֵיהֶ֔ם
אֵ֥ת אֲשֶׁר־עֲדֶ֖ן לֹ֣א הָיָ֑ה אֲשֶׁ֤ר לֹֽא־רָאָה֙ אֶת־
הַמַּעֲשֶׂ֣ה הָרָ֔ע אֲשֶׁ֥ר נַעֲשָׂ֖ה תַּ֥חַת הַשָּֽׁמֶשׁ: ד וְרָאִ֨יתִֽי אֲנִ֜י אֶת־כָּל־עָמָ֗ל וְאֵת֙ כָּל־כִּשְׁר֣וֹן
הַֽמַּעֲשֶׂ֔ה כִּ֣י הִ֥יא קִנְאַת־אִ֖ישׁ מֵרֵעֵ֑הוּ גַּם־זֶ֥ה הֶ֖בֶל
וּרְע֥וּת רֽוּחַ: ה הַכְּסִיל֙ חֹבֵ֣ק אֶת־יָדָ֔יו
וְאֹכֵ֖ל אֶת־בְּשָׂרֽוֹ: ו ט֕וֹב מְלֹ֥א כַ֖ף נָ֑חַת
מִמְּלֹ֥א חָפְנַ֛יִם עָמָ֖ל וּרְע֥וּת רֽוּחַ: ז וְשַׁ֧בְתִּי אֲנִ֛י וָאֶרְאֶ֥ה הֶ֖בֶל תַּ֣חַת הַשָּֽׁמֶשׁ: ח יֵ֣שׁ אֶחָד֩
וְאֵ֨ין שֵׁנִ֜י גַּ֣ם בֵּ֧ן וָאָ֣ח אֵֽין־ל֗וֹ וְאֵ֥ין קֵץ֙ לְכָל־עֲמָל֔וֹ
גַּם־עֵינוֹ* לֹֽא־תִשְׂבַּ֣ע עֹ֔שֶׁר וּלְמִ֣י ׀ אֲנִ֣י עָמֵ֗ל

(עיניו כתיב)

of the dust, and all return to dust again. ²¹Who knows of the spirit of man whether it goes upward, and of the spirit of the beast whether it goes downward to the earth?

²²Wherefore, I perceived that there is nothing better than that a man should rejoice in his own works; for that is his portion. For who shall bring him to see what shall be after him?

4 ¹So I returned, and considered all the oppressions that are done under the sun; and behold, the tears of those who are oppressed—and they had no comforter. On the side of the oppressors there was power; but there was no comforter for them. ²Therefore, I praised the dead who were already dead more than the living who are still alive. ³But better than both of them is he who has not yet been, who has not seen the evil work that is done under the sun.

⁴Again I saw that all labor and hard work rises out of man's jealousy against his neighbor. This also is a jealousy and a striving after wind.

⁵The fool folds his hands together,
And eats his own flesh.

⁶Better is a handful of quietness,
Than both hands full of labor and striving after wind.

⁷Then I returned, and I saw vanity under the sun. ⁸There is a person, alone, without a companion; he has neither son nor brother, but there is no end to all his labor, neither is his eye satisfied with riches. He may say: "For

וּמְחַסֵּר אֶת־נַפְשִׁי מִטּוֹבָה גַּם־זֶה הֶבֶל וְעִנְיַן רָע
הוּא:
ט טוֹבִים הַשְּׁנַיִם מִן־הָאֶחָד אֲשֶׁר יֵשׁ־לָהֶם שָׂכָר
טוֹב בַּעֲמָלָם: י כִּי אִם־יִפֹּלוּ הָאֶחָד יָקִים אֶת־
חֲבֵרוֹ וְאִילוֹ הָאֶחָד שֶׁיִּפּוֹל וְאֵין שֵׁנִי לַהֲקִימוֹ:
יא גַּם אִם־יִשְׁכְּבוּ שְׁנַיִם וְחַם לָהֶם וּלְאֶחָד אֵיךְ
יֵחָם: יב וְאִם־יִתְקְפוֹ הָאֶחָד הַשְּׁנַיִם יַעַמְדוּ נֶגְדּוֹ
וְהַחוּט הַמְשֻׁלָּשׁ לֹא בִמְהֵרָה יִנָּתֵק:
יג טוֹב יֶלֶד מִסְכֵּן וְחָכָם מִמֶּלֶךְ זָקֵן וּכְסִיל אֲשֶׁר
לֹא־יָדַע לְהִזָּהֵר עוֹד: יד כִּי־מִבֵּית הָסוּרִים יָצָא
לִמְלֹךְ כִּי גַּם בְּמַלְכוּתוֹ נוֹלַד רָשׁ: טו רָאִיתִי אֶת־
כָּל־הַחַיִּים הַמְהַלְּכִים תַּחַת הַשָּׁמֶשׁ עִם הַיֶּלֶד
הַשֵּׁנִי אֲשֶׁר יַעֲמֹד תַּחְתָּיו: טז אֵין־קֵץ לְכָל־הָעָם
לְכֹל אֲשֶׁר־הָיָה לִפְנֵיהֶם גַּם הָאַחֲרוֹנִים לֹא
יִשְׂמְחוּ־בוֹ כִּי־גַם־זֶה הֶבֶל וְרַעְיוֹן רוּחַ: יז שְׁמוֹר
רַגְלְךָ* כַּאֲשֶׁר תֵּלֵךְ אֶל־בֵּית הָאֱלֹהִים וְקָרוֹב
לִשְׁמֹעַ מִתֵּת הַכְּסִילִים זָבַח כִּי־אֵינָם יוֹדְעִים
לַעֲשׂוֹת רָע:
ה א אַל־תְּבַהֵל עַל־פִּיךָ וְלִבְּךָ אַל־יְמַהֵר לְהוֹצִיא
דָבָר לִפְנֵי הָאֱלֹהִים כִּי הָאֱלֹהִים בַּשָּׁמַיִם וְאַתָּה
עַל־הָאָרֶץ עַל־כֵּן יִהְיוּ דְבָרֶיךָ מְעַטִּים: ב כִּי בָּא
הַחֲלוֹם בְּרֹב עִנְיָן וְקוֹל כְּסִיל בְּרֹב דְּבָרִים:
ג כַּאֲשֶׁר תִּדֹּר נֶדֶר לֵאלֹהִים אַל־תְּאַחֵר לְשַׁלְּמוֹ

(רגליך כתיב)

whom then do I labor and deprive my soul of pleasure?" This also is vanity and an evil matter. [9]Two are better than one; for they receive a good reward for their labor. [10]For, if they fall, one can lift up his comrade. But woe to him who is alone when he falls, and has no one to lift him up. [11]Also, if two lie together, then they have heat; but how can one get warm alone? [12]And, if a man is alone, an attacker may overpower him, but two can withstand him; and a threefold cord is not quickly broken.

[13]Better is a poor and wise child than an old and foolish king who will no longer take advice. [14]For out of prison he may come forth to be a king, even if he was born poor in his future kingdom. [15]I saw all the living who walk under the sun, with yet a second child to supplant the other one. [16]There was no end of all the people, all those whom he did lead; but those who came afterwards will not rejoice in him. Surely this also is vanity and a feeding on wind. [17]Guard your foot when you go to the house of God, for He is more ready to hear than when fools bring sacrifices, for they do not know that they do evil.

5 [1]Be not rash with your mouth, and let not your heart be hasty to utter anything before God. For God is in heaven and you are upon earth; therefore let your words be few. [2]For the dream comes with much ado; and a fool's voice with a multitude of words. [3]When you vow a vow to God, do not delay to pay it, for He

"The sleep of a laboring man is sweet..." 5:11

מתוקה שנת העבד אם מעט ואם הרבה יאכל

והשבע לעשיר איננו מניח לו לישון:

כִּי אֵין חֵפֶץ בַּכְּסִילִים אֵת אֲשֶׁר־תִּדֹּר שַׁלֵּם: ⁴טוֹב
אֲשֶׁר לֹא־תִדֹּר מִשֶּׁתִּדּוֹר וְלֹא תְשַׁלֵּם: ⁵אַל־תִּתֵּן
אֶת־פִּיךָ לַחֲטִיא אֶת־בְּשָׂרֶךָ וְאַל־תֹּאמַר לִפְנֵי
הַמַּלְאָךְ כִּי שְׁגָגָה הִיא לָמָה יִקְצֹף הָאֱלֹהִים עַל־
קוֹלֶךָ וְחִבֵּל אֶת־מַעֲשֵׂה יָדֶיךָ: ⁶כִּי בְרֹב חֲלֹמוֹת
וַהֲבָלִים וּדְבָרִים הַרְבֵּה כִּי אֶת־הָאֱלֹהִים יְרָא:
⁷אִם־עֹשֶׁק רָשׁ וְגֵזֶל מִשְׁפָּט וָצֶדֶק תִּרְאֶה בַמְּדִינָה
אַל־תִּתְמַהּ עַל־הַחֵפֶץ כִּי גָבֹהַּ מֵעַל גָּבֹהַּ שֹׁמֵר
וּגְבֹהִים עֲלֵיהֶם: ⁸וְיִתְרוֹן אֶרֶץ בַּכֹּל הוּא* מֶלֶךְ
לְשָׂדֶה נֶעֱבָד:
⁹אֹהֵב כֶּסֶף לֹא־יִשְׂבַּע כֶּסֶף וּמִי־אֹהֵב בֶּהָמוֹן לֹא
תְבוּאָה גַּם־זֶה הָבֶל: ¹בִּרְבוֹת הַטּוֹבָה רַבּוּ
אוֹכְלֶיהָ וּמַה־כִּשְׁרוֹן לִבְעָלֶיהָ כִּי אִם־רְאוּת*
עֵינָיו: ¹¹מְתוּקָה שְׁנַת הָעֹבֵד אִם־מְעַט וְאִם־
הַרְבֵּה יֹאכֵל וְהַשָּׂבָע לֶעָשִׁיר אֵינֶנּוּ מַנִּיחַ לוֹ
לִישׁוֹן:
¹²יֵשׁ רָעָה חוֹלָה רָאִיתִי תַּחַת הַשָּׁמֶשׁ עֹשֶׁר שָׁמוּר
לִבְעָלָיו לְרָעָתוֹ: ¹³וְאָבַד הָעֹשֶׁר הַהוּא בְּעִנְיַן רָע
וְהוֹלִיד בֵּן וְאֵין בְּיָדוֹ מְאוּמָה:
¹⁴כַּאֲשֶׁר יָצָא מִבֶּטֶן אִמּוֹ עָרוֹם יָשׁוּב לָלֶכֶת
כְּשֶׁבָּא וּמְאוּמָה לֹא־יִשָּׂא בַעֲמָלוֹ שֶׁיֹּלֵךְ בְּיָדוֹ:
¹⁵וְגַם־זֹה רָעָה חוֹלָה כָּל־עֻמַּת שֶׁבָּא כֵּן יֵלֵךְ וּמַה־
יִּתְרוֹן לוֹ שֶׁיַּעֲמֹל לָרוּחַ: ¹⁶גַּם כָּל־יָמָיו בַּחֹשֶׁךְ

takes no pleasure in fools. Pay what you have vowed. [4]It is better for you not to vow, than to vow and not to pay. [5]Let not your mouth cause your flesh to sin, nor say before the messenger that it was an error: why should God be angry at your voice and destroy the work of your hands? [6]For as in the multitude of dreams so in many words are vanities. Therefore, fear God.

[7]If you see the oppression of the poor, and violent perverting of judgment and justice in the province, marvel not at the matter. Every official has a higher one set over him, and the highest keeps watch on them all. [8]And the advantage of a country is that he is everywhere; land that has a king is tilled.

[9]He who loves silver shall never be satisfied with silver, nor he who loves abundance with increase. This also is vanity. [10]When goods increase, so do those increase who eat them; and what profit is there to the owners, except seeing them with their eyes? [11]The sleep of a laboring man is sweet, whether he eats little or much; but the abundance of a rich man does not permit him to sleep.

[12]There is a sore evil which I have seen under the sun: riches kept for the owners to their own hurt. [13]And those riches perish in an unfortunate venture, and the son born to him has nothing in his hand.

[14]As he came forth of his mother's womb, naked shall he return, to go as he came, and shall take nothing for his labor which he may carry away in his hand. [15]And this also is a sore evil, that in all points, as he came so shall he go; and what profit has he who labors for the wind?

יֹאכֵ֣ל וְכָעַ֥ס הַרְבֵּ֖ה וְחָלְי֥וֹ וָקָֽצֶף׃

יֹ֣ז הִנֵּ֣ה אֲשֶׁר־רָאִ֣יתִי אָ֗נִי ט֣וֹב אֲשֶׁר־יָפֶ֣ה לֶֽאֱכ֣וֹל

וְֽלִשְׁתּ֡וֹת וְלִרְא֣וֹת טוֹבָ֣ה בְּכָל־עֲמָל֣וֹ ׀ שֶׁיַּעֲמֹ֣ל

תַּֽחַת־הַשֶּׁ֗מֶשׁ מִסְפַּ֥ר יְמֵי־חַיָּ֛ו אֲשֶׁר־נָֽתַן־ל֥וֹ

הָאֱלֹהִ֖ים כִּי־ה֥וּא חֶלְקֽוֹ׃ יֹ֣ח גַּ֣ם כָּֽל־הָאָדָ֡ם אֲשֶׁ֣ר

נָֽתַן־ל֣וֹ הָאֱלֹהִים֩ עֹ֨שֶׁר וּנְכָסִ֜ים וְהִשְׁלִיט֣וֹ לֶֽאֱכֹ֣ל

מִמֶּ֗נּוּ וְלָשֵׂ֤את אֶת־חֶלְקוֹ֙ וְלִשְׂמֹ֣חַ בַּעֲמָל֔וֹ זֹ֕ה

מַתַּ֥ת אֱלֹהִ֖ים הִֽיא׃ יֹ֣ט כִּ֛י לֹ֥א הַרְבֵּ֖ה יִזְכֹּ֣ר אֶת־יְמֵ֣י

חַיָּ֑יו כִּ֧י הָאֱלֹהִ֛ים מַעֲנֶ֖ה בְּשִׂמְחַ֥ת לִבּֽוֹ׃

ו יֹ֣א יֵ֣שׁ רָעָ֗ה אֲשֶׁ֤ר רָאִ֙יתִי֙ תַּ֣חַת הַשֶּׁ֔מֶשׁ וְרַבָּ֥ה הִ֖יא

עַל־הָאָדָֽם׃ יֹ֣ב אִ֣ישׁ אֲשֶׁ֣ר יִתֶּן־ל֣וֹ הָאֱלֹהִ֡ים עֹשֶׁר֩

וּנְכָסִ֨ים וְכָב֜וֹד וְֽאֵינֶ֥נּוּ חָסֵ֣ר לְנַפְשׁ֣וֹ ׀ מִכֹּ֣ל אֲשֶׁר־

יִתְאַוֶּ֗ה וְלֹֽא־יַשְׁלִיטֶ֤נּוּ הָֽאֱלֹהִים֙ לֶאֱכֹ֣ל מִמֶּ֔נּוּ כִּ֛י

אִ֥ישׁ נָכְרִ֖י יֹֽאכְלֶ֑נּוּ זֶ֥ה הֶ֛בֶל וָחֳלִ֥י רָ֖ע הֽוּא׃ יֹ֣ג אִם־

יוֹלִ֣יד אִ֣ישׁ מֵאָ֗ה וְשָׁנִים֙ רַבּ֣וֹת יִֽחְיֶ֔ה וְרַ֣ב ׀ שֶׁיִּהְי֣וּ

יְמֵֽי־שָׁנָ֗יו וְנַפְשׁוֹ֙ לֹא־תִשְׂבַּ֣ע מִן־הַטּוֹבָ֔ה וְגַם־

קְבוּרָ֖ה לֹא־הָ֣יְתָה לּ֑וֹ אָמַ֕רְתִּי ט֥וֹב מִמֶּ֖נּוּ הַנָּֽפֶל׃

יֹ֣ד כִּֽי־בַהֶ֥בֶל בָּ֖א וּבַחֹ֣שֶׁךְ יֵלֵ֑ךְ וּבַחֹ֖שֶׁךְ שְׁמ֥וֹ יְכֻסֶּֽה׃

יֹ֣ה גַּם־שֶׁ֥מֶשׁ לֹא־רָאָ֖ה וְלֹ֣א יָדָ֑ע נַ֥חַת לָזֶ֖ה מִזֶּֽה׃

יֹ֣ו וְאִלּ֣וּ חָיָ֗ה אֶ֤לֶף שָׁנִים֙ פַּעֲמַ֔יִם וְטוֹבָ֖ה לֹ֣א רָאָ֑ה

הֲלֹ֛א אֶל־מָק֥וֹם אֶחָ֖ד הַכֹּ֥ל הוֹלֵֽךְ׃ יֹ֣ז כָּל־עֲמַ֥ל

הָאָדָ֖ם לְפִ֑יהוּ וְגַם־הַנֶּ֖פֶשׁ לֹ֥א תִמָּלֵֽא׃ יֹ֣ח כִּ֣י מַה־

יוֹתֵ֤ר לֶֽחָכָם֙ מִֽן־הַכְּסִ֔יל מַה־לֶּעָנִ֣י יוֹדֵ֔עַ לַהֲלֹ֖ךְ נֶ֥גֶד

הַֽחַיִּֽים׃ יֹ֣ט ט֛וֹב מַרְאֵ֥ה עֵינַ֖יִם מֵֽהֲלָךְ־נָ֑פֶשׁ גַּם־זֶ֥ה

הֶ֖בֶל וּרְע֥וּת רֽוּחַ׃

[16]Besides, all his days he eats in darkness, and he has much grief, and resentment, and sickness. [17]Behold that which I have seen: it is good and comely for one to eat and to drink, and to enjoy himself in return for his labor, in which he labors under the sun all the days of his life which God has given him, for that is his portion. [18]Every man also to whom God has given riches and wealth, and has given him the power to eat of it, and to take his portion, and to rejoice in his labor: that is the gift of God. [19]Let him remember the days of his life—that they are not many, and that God fills his time with joy of heart.

6 [1]There is an evil which I have seen under the sun, and it is common among men: [2]A man to whom God has given riches, wealth, and honor, so that he lacks nothing for his soul of anything he desires—yet God does not give him the power to enjoy it, and an alien enjoys it instead; this is vanity, and an evil disease. [3]If a man begets a hundred children and lives many years, and, however numerous the days of his years are, if his soul is not filled with good and he does not even have a burial—then I say that a still-birth is better than he. [4]For it comes in vain, and departs in darkness, and its name shall be covered in darkness. [5]Moreoever, it has not seen the sun, nor known anything; yet its state is better than his. [6]Yea, though he live a thousand years twice told, but he has seen no good: do we not all go to the same place? [7]All the labor of man is for his mouth, and yet the appetite is not filled. [8]For what advantage has the wise man over the fool? Or the poor man, with his knowledge of experience, over the others living? [9]Better is what your

יᵉ מַה־שֶּׁהָיָה כְּבָר נִקְרָא שְׁמוֹ וְנוֹדָע אֲשֶׁר־הוּא
אָדָם וְלֹא־יוּכַל לָדִין עִם שֶׁתַּקִּיף* מִמֶּנּוּ: יאᵉ כִּי יֵשׁ־
דְּבָרִים הַרְבֵּה מַרְבִּים הָבֶל מַה־יֹּתֵר לָאָדָם: יבᵉ כִּי
מִי־יוֹדֵעַ מַה־טּוֹב לָאָדָם בַּחַיִּים מִסְפַּר יְמֵי־חַיֵּי
הֶבְלוֹ וְיַעֲשֵׂם כַּצֵּל אֲשֶׁר מִי־יַגִּיד לָאָדָם מַה־יִּהְיֶה
אַחֲרָיו תַּחַת הַשָּׁמֶשׁ:

ז אᵉ טוֹב* שֵׁם מִשֶּׁמֶן טוֹב וְיוֹם הַמָּוֶת מִיּוֹם הִוָּלְדוֹ:
בᵉ טוֹב לָלֶכֶת אֶל־בֵּית־אֵבֶל מִלֶּכֶת אֶל־בֵּית
מִשְׁתֶּה בַּאֲשֶׁר הוּא סוֹף כָּל־הָאָדָם וְהַחַי יִתֵּן אֶל־
לִבּוֹ:
גᵉ טוֹב כַּעַס מִשְּׂחוֹק כִּי־בְרֹעַ פָּנִים יִיטַב לֵב: דᵉ לֵב
חֲכָמִים בְּבֵית אֵבֶל וְלֵב כְּסִילִים בְּבֵית שִׂמְחָה:
הᵉ טוֹב לִשְׁמֹעַ גַּעֲרַת חָכָם מֵאִישׁ שֹׁמֵעַ שִׁיר
כְּסִילִים: וᵉ כִּי כְקוֹל הַסִּירִים תַּחַת הַסִּיר כֵּן שְׂחֹק
הַכְּסִיל וְגַם־זֶה הָבֶל: זᵉ כִּי הָעֹשֶׁק יְהוֹלֵל חָכָם
וִיאַבֵּד אֶת־לֵב מַתָּנָה:
חᵉ טוֹב אַחֲרִית דָּבָר מֵרֵאשִׁיתוֹ
טוֹב אֶרֶךְ־רוּחַ מִגְּבַהּ רוּחַ:
טᵉ אַל־תְּבַהֵל בְּרוּחֲךָ לִכְעוֹס כִּי כַעַס בְּחֵיק
כְּסִילִים יָנוּחַ:
יᵉ אַל־תֹּאמַר מֶה הָיָה שֶׁהַיָּמִים הָרִאשֹׁנִים הָיוּ
טוֹבִים מֵאֵלֶּה כִּי לֹא מֵחָכְמָה שָׁאַלְתָּ עַל־זֶה:

(שהתקיף כתיב)

(ט׳ רבתי)

eyes can see than what your desire wants; this also is vanity and feeding on wind. [10]That which has been is already named, and what man is, is already known; neither may he contend with him who is mightier than he. [11]Seeing that there are many words which increase vanity, where is the advantage to man? [12]For who knows what is good for a man in this life, all the days of his vain life which he spends as a shadow? For who can tell a man what shall be after him under the sun?

7 [1]A good name is better than fragrant ointment, and the day of death than the day of birth.

[2]It is better to go to the house of mourning, than to go to the house of feasting: for that is the end of all men; and the living shall lay it to his heart.

[3]Sorrow is better than idle games; for while the face is sad the heart may be glad. [4]The heart of the wise is in the house of mourning; but the heart of the fool is in the house of merriment.

[5]It is better to hear the rebuke of the wise, than for a man to hear praise-singing from fools. [6]For the laughter of the fool is as the crackling of thorns under the pot; this also is vanity. [7]Surely oppression makes a wise man mad, and a bribe destroys understanding.

[8]Better is the end of a matter than the beginning of it; And the patient in spirit is better than the proud in spirit.

[9]Be not hasty in your spirit to be angry, for anger lives on in the bosom of fools.

[10]Do not say: Why is it that the former days were better

יא טוֹבָ֥ה חָכְמָ֖ה עִֽם־נַחֲלָ֑ה וְיֹתֵ֖ר לְרֹאֵ֥י הַשָּֽׁמֶשׁ:

יב כִּ֛י בְּצֵ֥ל הַֽחָכְמָ֖ה בְּצֵ֣ל הַכָּ֑סֶף וְיִתְר֣וֹן דַּ֔עַת הַֽחָכְמָ֖ה תְּחַיֶּ֥ה בְעָלֶֽיהָ:

יג רְאֵ֖ה אֶת־מַֽעֲשֵׂ֣ה הָֽאֱלֹהִ֑ים כִּ֣י מִ֤י יוּכַל֙ לְתַקֵּ֔ן אֵ֖ת אֲשֶׁ֥ר עִוְּתֽוֹ: יד בְּי֤וֹם טוֹבָה֙ הֱיֵ֣ה בְט֔וֹב וּבְי֥וֹם רָעָ֖ה רְאֵ֑ה גַּ֣ם אֶת־זֶ֤ה לְעֻמַּת־זֶה֙ עָשָׂ֣ה הָֽאֱלֹהִ֔ים עַל־דִּבְרַ֗ת שֶׁלֹּ֨א יִמְצָ֧א הָֽאָדָ֛ם אַחֲרָ֖יו מְאֽוּמָה:

טו אֶת־הַכֹּ֥ל רָאִ֖יתִי בִּימֵ֣י הֶבְלִ֑י יֵ֤שׁ צַדִּיק֙ אֹבֵ֣ד בְּצִדְק֔וֹ וְיֵ֣שׁ רָשָׁ֔ע מַֽאֲרִ֖יךְ בְּרָֽעָתֽוֹ: טז אַל־תְּהִ֤י צַדִּיק֙ הַרְבֵּ֔ה וְאַל־תִּתְחַכַּ֖ם יוֹתֵ֑ר לָ֖מָּה תִּשּׁוֹמֵֽם:

יז אַל־תִּרְשַׁ֥ע הַרְבֵּ֖ה וְאַל־תְּהִ֣י סָכָ֑ל לָ֥מָּה תָמ֖וּת בְּלֹ֥א עִתֶּֽךָ: יח ט֚וֹב אֲשֶׁ֣ר תֶּֽאֱחֹ֣ז בָּזֶ֔ה וְגַם־מִזֶּ֖ה אַל־תַּנַּ֣ח אֶת־יָדֶ֑ךָ כִּֽי־יְרֵ֥א אֱלֹהִ֖ים יֵצֵ֥א אֶת־כֻּלָּֽם:

יט הַֽחָכְמָ֖ה תָּעֹ֣ז לֶֽחָכָ֑ם מֵֽעֲשָׂרָה֙ שַׁלִּיטִ֔ים אֲשֶׁ֥ר הָי֖וּ בָּעִֽיר:

כ כִּ֣י אָדָ֞ם אֵ֥ין צַדִּ֛יק בָּאָ֖רֶץ אֲשֶׁ֥ר יַֽעֲשֶׂה־טּ֖וֹב וְלֹ֥א יֶֽחֱטָֽא:

כא גַּ֤ם לְכָל־הַדְּבָרִים֙ אֲשֶׁ֣ר יְדַבֵּ֔רוּ אַל־תִּתֵּ֣ן לִבֶּ֑ךָ אֲשֶׁ֥ר לֹֽא־תִשְׁמַ֥ע אֶֽת־עַבְדְּךָ֖ מְקַלְלֶֽךָ: כב כִּ֚י גַּם־פְּעָמִ֣ים רַבּ֔וֹת יָדַ֖ע לִבֶּ֑ךָ אֲשֶׁ֥ר גַּם־*אַתְּ קִלַּ֥לְתָּ אֲחֵרִֽים:

כג כָּל־זֹ֖ה נִסִּ֣יתִי בַֽחָכְמָ֑ה אָמַ֣רְתִּי אֶחְכָּ֔מָה וְהִ֖יא רְחוֹקָ֥ה מִמֶּֽנִּי: כד רָח֥וֹק מַה־שֶּֽׁהָיָ֖ה וְעָמֹ֣ק ׀ עָמֹ֑ק מִ֖י

(את כתיב)

than these? For it is not wise of you to inquire concerning this.

[11]Wisdom is good with an inheritance, and a profit to those who see the sun. [12]For wisdom is a shelter, as money is a shelter; but the advantage of wisdom is that it preserves its possessors.

[13]Consider the work of God: for who can make straight what He has formed crooked? [14]In the day of prosperity be joyful, but in the days of adversity consider: God has made the one as well as the other, to the end that man should find nothing after it.

[15]I have seen everything in the days of my vanity: there is a righteous person who perishes in his righteousness, and there is a wicked person who prolongs his life in his wickedness. [16]Be not too righteous, nor make yourself too wise: why should you destroy yourself? [17]Be not too wicked, nor be foolish: why should you die before your time? [18]It is good that you take hold of the one, and that you do not let go of the other; for he who fears God will do his duty in all things.

[19]Wisdom is a stronghold to the wise, more than ten rulers who are in the city.

[20]For there is not a just man upon earth who does good and does not sin.

[21]Finally, take not heed of every word that is spoken, lest you hear your servant curse you. [22]For often you will remember that you yourself have cursed others.

[23]All this have I tried by wisdom: I said, I will be wise; but it was far from me. [24]That which is far off, and

"A man's wisdom lights up his face."   8:1

יִמְצָאֶנּוּ: ^{כה} סַבּוֹתִי אֲנִי וְלִבִּי לָדַעַת וְלָתוּר וּבַקֵּשׁ
חָכְמָה וְחֶשְׁבּוֹן וְלָדַעַת רֶשַׁע כֶּסֶל וְהַסִּכְלוּת
הוֹלֵלוֹת: ^{כו} וּמוֹצֵא אֲנִי מַר מִמָּוֶת אֶת־הָאִשָּׁה
אֲשֶׁר־הִיא מְצוֹדִים וַחֲרָמִים לִבָּהּ אֲסוּרִים יָדֶיהָ
טוֹב לִפְנֵי הָאֱלֹהִים יִמָּלֵט מִמֶּנָּה וְחוֹטֵא יִלָּכֶד
בָּהּ: ^{כז} רְאֵה זֶה מָצָאתִי אָמְרָה קֹהֶלֶת אַחַת לְאַחַת
לִמְצֹא חֶשְׁבּוֹן: ^{כח} אֲשֶׁר עוֹד־בִּקְשָׁה נַפְשִׁי וְלֹא
מָצָאתִי אָדָם אֶחָד מֵאֶלֶף מָצָאתִי וְאִשָּׁה בְּכָל־
אֵלֶּה לֹא מָצָאתִי: ^{כט} לְבַד רְאֵה־זֶה מָצָאתִי אֲשֶׁר
עָשָׂה הָאֱלֹהִים אֶת־הָאָדָם יָשָׁר וְהֵמָּה בִקְשׁוּ
חִשְּׁבֹנוֹת רַבִּים:
ח ^א מִי כְּהֶחָכָם
וּמִי יוֹדֵעַ פֵּשֶׁר דָּבָר
חָכְמַת אָדָם תָּאִיר פָּנָיו
וְעֹז פָּנָיו יְשֻׁנֶּא:
^ב אֲנִי פִּי־מֶלֶךְ שְׁמֹר וְעַל דִּבְרַת שְׁבוּעַת אֱלֹהִים:
^ג אַל־תִּבָּהֵל מִפָּנָיו תֵּלֵךְ אַל־תַּעֲמֹד בְּדָבָר רָע כִּי
כָּל־אֲשֶׁר יַחְפֹּץ יַעֲשֶׂה: ^ד בַּאֲשֶׁר דְּבַר־מֶלֶךְ שִׁלְטוֹן
וּמִי יֹאמַר־לוֹ מַה־תַּעֲשֶׂה:
^ה שׁוֹמֵר מִצְוָה לֹא יֵדַע דָּבָר רָע וְעֵת וּמִשְׁפָּט יֵדַע
לֵב חָכָם: ^ו כִּי לְכָל־חֵפֶץ יֵשׁ עֵת וּמִשְׁפָּט כִּי־רָעַת
הָאָדָם רַבָּה עָלָיו: ^ז כִּי־אֵינֶנּוּ יֹדֵעַ מַה־שֶּׁיִּהְיֶה כִּי
כַּאֲשֶׁר יִהְיֶה מִי יַגִּיד לוֹ: ^ח אֵין אָדָם שַׁלִּיט בָּרוּחַ
לִכְלוֹא אֶת־הָרוּחַ וְאֵין שִׁלְטוֹן בְּיוֹם הַמָּוֶת וְאֵין

exceeding deep—who can find it out? ²⁵I applied my mind to know, and to search, and to seek out wisdom and the reason of things, but only to understand that wickedness is folly, and folly madness. ²⁶I also find more bitter than death the woman, whose heart is snares and nets, and whose hands are fetters. He who pleases God shall escape from her, but the sinner shall be taken by her. ²⁷See, this I have found, says Kohelet, adding one thing to another to find out the account. ²⁸What my soul still seeks, but what I have not found: one man among a thousand have I found, but a woman among all those I have not found. ²⁹Lo, this only have I found: that God made man upright; but they have sought out many inventions.

8 ¹Who is a wise man?
And who knows the interpretation of a thing?
"A man's wisdom lights up his face,
And the harshness of his face is changed."
²I counsel you: keep the king's commandment, also in regard to an oath to God. ³Be not hasty to go out of his presence; stand not in an evil thing; for he does whatever pleases him. ⁴Where the word of a king is, there is power; and who may say to him: What are you doing? ⁵"One who obeys the commandment shall feel no evil thing, and the wise mind discerns the time of judgment."
⁶For to every matter there is time and judgment, and a man's calamity may be great upon him. ⁷For he knows not that which shall be: for who can tell him when it shall be? ⁸There is no man who has power over the breath of life to retain the breath of life, neither has he

מְשַׁלַּחַת בַּמִּלְחָמָה וְלֹא־יְמַלֵּט רֶשַׁע אֶת־בְּעָלָיו:
ⁱ אֶת־כָּל־זֶה רָאִיתִי וְנָתוֹן אֶת־לִבִּי לְכָל־מַעֲשֶׂה
אֲשֶׁר נַעֲשָׂה תַּחַת הַשָּׁמֶשׁ עֵת אֲשֶׁר שָׁלַט הָאָדָם
בְּאָדָם לְרַע לוֹ: ⁱ וּבְכֵן רָאִיתִי רְשָׁעִים קְבֻרִים
וָבָאוּ וּמִמְּקוֹם קָדוֹשׁ יְהַלֵּכוּ וְיִשְׁתַּכְּחוּ בָעִיר
אֲשֶׁר כֵּן־עָשׂוּ גַּם־זֶה הָבֶל:
 יא אֲשֶׁר אֵין־נַעֲשָׂה פִתְגָם מַעֲשֵׂה הָרָעָה מְהֵרָה
עַל־כֵּן מָלֵא לֵב בְּנֵי־הָאָדָם בָּהֶם לַעֲשׂוֹת רָע:
יב אֲשֶׁר חֹטֶא עֹשֶׂה רָע מְאַת וּמַאֲרִיךְ לוֹ כִּי גַּם־
יוֹדֵעַ אָנִי אֲשֶׁר יִהְיֶה־טּוֹב לְיִרְאֵי הָאֱלֹהִים אֲשֶׁר
יִירְאוּ מִלְּפָנָיו: יג וְטוֹב לֹא־יִהְיֶה לָרָשָׁע וְלֹא־
יַאֲרִיךְ יָמִים כַּצֵּל אֲשֶׁר אֵינֶנּוּ יָרֵא מִלִּפְנֵי אֱלֹהִים:
יד יֶשׁ־הֶבֶל אֲשֶׁר נַעֲשָׂה עַל־הָאָרֶץ אֲשֶׁר | יֵשׁ
צַדִּיקִים אֲשֶׁר מַגִּיעַ אֲלֵהֶם כְּמַעֲשֵׂה הָרְשָׁעִים
וְיֵשׁ רְשָׁעִים שֶׁמַּגִּיעַ אֲלֵהֶם כְּמַעֲשֵׂה הַצַּדִּיקִים
אָמַרְתִּי שֶׁגַּם־זֶה הָבֶל:
טו וְשִׁבַּחְתִּי אֲנִי אֶת־הַשִּׂמְחָה אֲשֶׁר אֵין־טוֹב
לָאָדָם תַּחַת הַשָּׁמֶשׁ כִּי אִם־לֶאֱכֹל וְלִשְׁתּוֹת
וְלִשְׂמוֹחַ וְהוּא יִלְוֶנּוּ בַעֲמָלוֹ יְמֵי חַיָּיו אֲשֶׁר־נָתַן־
לוֹ הָאֱלֹהִים תַּחַת הַשָּׁמֶשׁ:
טז כַּאֲשֶׁר נָתַתִּי אֶת־לִבִּי לָדַעַת חָכְמָה וְלִרְאוֹת
אֶת־הָעִנְיָן אֲשֶׁר נַעֲשָׂה עַל־הָאָרֶץ כִּי גַם בַּיּוֹם
וּבַלַּיְלָה שֵׁנָה בְּעֵינָיו אֵינֶנּוּ רֹאֶה: יז וְרָאִיתִי אֶת־
כָּל־מַעֲשֵׂה הָאֱלֹהִים כִּי לֹא יוּכַל הָאָדָם לִמְצוֹא
אֶת־הַמַּעֲשֶׂה אֲשֶׁר נַעֲשָׂה תַחַת־הַשָּׁמֶשׁ בְּשֶׁל

power over the day of death. There is no discharge in
that war; neither shall wickedness deliver those who are
given to it.

⁹All this have I seen, and applied my mind to every
work that is done under the sun, at a time when one
man ruled over another to his own hurt. ¹⁰And so I saw
the wicked buried and they entered into their rest; but
they that had done right went away from the holy
place, yet were they forgotten in the city: this also is
vanity.

¹¹Since sentence against an evil work is not carried out
speedily, human beings make up their minds to do evil.
¹²Though a sinner do evil a hundred times, and his days
may be prolonged, yet surely I know that it shall be
well with them who fear God, because they feared
Him. ¹³But it shall not be well with the wicked, neither
shall he prolong his days which are as a shadow,
because he does not fear God. ¹⁴There is a vanity which is
done upon the earth: that there are just ones, to whom
it happens according to the work of the wicked. Again,
there are wicked ones, to whom it happens according to
the work of the just. I said: this also is vanity.

¹⁵Then I commended mirth, because a man has no better
thing under the sun, than to eat, and to drink and to be
merry: for that shall accompany him in his labor the
days of his life which God gives him under the sun.
¹⁶When I applied my mind to know wisdom, and to see
the business that is done upon the earth (for neither day
nor night do men see sleep with their eyes), ¹⁷Then I
beheld all the work of God, that a man cannot find out
the work that is done under the sun. For though a man

אֲשֶׁר יַעֲמֹל הָאָדָם לְבַקֵּשׁ וְלֹא יִמְצָא וְגַם אִם־
יֹאמַר הֶחָכָם לָדַעַת לֹא יוּכַל לִמְצֹא:

ט כִּי אֶת־כָּל־זֶה נָתַתִּי אֶל־לִבִּי וְלָבוּר אֶת־כָּל־זֶה
אֲשֶׁר הַצַּדִּיקִים וְהַחֲכָמִים וַעֲבָדֵיהֶם בְּיַד
הָאֱלֹהִים גַּם־אַהֲבָה גַם־שִׂנְאָה אֵין יוֹדֵעַ הָאָדָם
הַכֹּל לִפְנֵיהֶם: ² הַכֹּל כַּאֲשֶׁר לַכֹּל מִקְרֶה אֶחָד
לַצַּדִּיק וְלָרָשָׁע לַטּוֹב וְלַטָּהוֹר וְלַטָּמֵא וְלַזֹּבֵחַ
וְלַאֲשֶׁר אֵינֶנּוּ זֹבֵחַ כַּטּוֹב כַּחֹטֶא הַנִּשְׁבָּע כַּאֲשֶׁר
שְׁבוּעָה יָרֵא: ³ זֶה ׀ רָע בְּכֹל אֲשֶׁר־נַעֲשָׂה תַּחַת
הַשֶּׁמֶשׁ כִּי־מִקְרֶה אֶחָד לַכֹּל וְגַם לֵב בְּנֵי־הָאָדָם
מָלֵא־רָע וְהוֹלֵלוֹת בִּלְבָבָם בְּחַיֵּיהֶם וְאַחֲרָיו אֶל־
הַמֵּתִים: ⁴ כִּי־מִי אֲשֶׁר יְחֻבַּר* אֶל כָּל־הַחַיִּים יֵשׁ
בִּטָּחוֹן כִּי־לְכֶלֶב חַי הוּא טוֹב מִן־הָאַרְיֵה הַמֵּת:
⁵ כִּי הַחַיִּים יוֹדְעִים שֶׁיָּמֻתוּ וְהַמֵּתִים אֵינָם יוֹדְעִים
מְאוּמָה וְאֵין־עוֹד לָהֶם שָׂכָר כִּי נִשְׁכַּח זִכְרָם: ⁶ גַּם
אַהֲבָתָם גַּם־שִׂנְאָתָם גַּם־קִנְאָתָם כְּבָר אָבָדָה
וְחֵלֶק אֵין־לָהֶם עוֹד לְעוֹלָם בְּכֹל אֲשֶׁר־נַעֲשָׂה
תַּחַת הַשָּׁמֶשׁ:
⁷ לֵךְ אֱכֹל בְּשִׂמְחָה לַחְמֶךָ וּשְׁתֵה בְלֶב־טוֹב יֵינֶךָ כִּי
כְבָר רָצָה הָאֱלֹהִים אֶת־מַעֲשֶׂיךָ: ⁸ בְּכָל־עֵת יִהְיוּ
בְגָדֶיךָ לְבָנִים וְשֶׁמֶן עַל־רֹאשְׁךָ אַל־יֶחְסָר: ⁹ רְאֵה
חַיִּים עִם־אִשָּׁה אֲשֶׁר־אָהַבְתָּ כָּל־יְמֵי חַיֵּי הֶבְלֶךָ
אֲשֶׁר נָתַן־לְךָ תַּחַת הַשֶּׁמֶשׁ כֹּל יְמֵי הֶבְלֶךָ כִּי הוּא

(יבחר כתיב)

labor to seek it out, yet shall he not find it. Even more: though a wise man think to know it, yet shall he not be able to find it.

9 ¹For I considered all this in my mind, to make it clear, that the righteous, and the wise, and their works, are in the hand of God: no man knows either love or hatred; it is marked out for them. ²All things come alike to all: there is one event to the righteous and to the wicked; to the good, and to the clean, and to the unclean; to one who sacrifices, and to one who does not sacrifice. As is the good, so is the sinner; one who takes an oath as one who avoids an oath. ³This is an evil among all things that are done under the sun: that there is one event for all (not only that, but the heart of the sons of man is full of evil, and madness is in their minds while they live, and after that they go to the dead). ⁴For to him that is joined to all the living there is hope: for a living dog is better than a dead lion. ⁵For the living know that they shall die; but the dead no longer know anything, neither have they any more a reward; for the memory of them is forgotten. ⁶Also their love, and their hatred, and their envy is now perished; neither do they evermore have a portion in anything that is done under the sun.

⁷Go your way, eat your bread with joy, and drink your wine with a merry heart; for God has long ago accepted your work. ⁸Let your garments always be white, and let your head lack no ointments. ⁹Live joyfully with the woman whom you love, all the days of the life of your vanity, which He has given you under the sun—all the

חֶלְקְךָ֙ בַּֽחַיִּ֔ים וּבַעֲמָֽלְךָ֙ אֲשֶׁר־אַתָּ֥ה עָמֵ֖ל תַּ֥חַת
הַשָּֽׁמֶשׁ: י כֹּ֠ל אֲשֶׁ֨ר תִּמְצָ֧א יָֽדְךָ֛ לַעֲשׂ֖וֹת בְּכֹחֲךָ֥
עֲשֵׂ֑ה כִּי֩ אֵ֨ין מַעֲשֶׂ֤ה וְחֶשְׁבּוֹן֙ וְדַ֣עַת וְחָכְמָ֔ה
בִּשְׁא֖וֹל אֲשֶׁ֥ר אַתָּ֖ה הֹלֵ֥ךְ שָֽׁמָּה:
יא שַׁ֣בְתִּי וְרָאֹ֣ה תַֽחַת־הַשֶּׁ֗מֶשׁ כִּ֣י לֹ֩א לַקַּלִּ֨ים
הַמֵּר֜וֹץ וְלֹ֧א לַגִּבּוֹרִ֣ים הַמִּלְחָמָ֗ה וְגַ֨ם לֹ֤א
לַחֲכָמִ֥ים לֶ֙חֶם֙ וְגַ֨ם לֹ֤א לַנְּבֹנִים֙ עֹ֔שֶׁר
וְגַ֛ם לֹ֥א לַיֹּדְעִ֖ים חֵ֑ן
כִּי־עֵ֥ת וָפֶ֖גַע יִקְרֶ֥ה אֶת־כֻּלָּֽם:
יב כִּ֣י גַּ֤ם לֹֽא־יֵדַע֙ הָֽאָדָם֙ אֶת־עִתּ֔וֹ כַּדָּגִים֙
שֶׁנֶּֽאֱחָזִים֙ בִּמְצוֹדָ֣ה רָעָ֔ה וְכַ֨צִּפֳּרִ֔ים הָאֲחֻז֖וֹת בַּפָּ֑ח
כָּהֵ֗ם יֽוּקָשִׁים֙ בְּנֵ֣י הָֽאָדָ֔ם לְעֵ֥ת רָעָ֖ה כְּשֶׁתִּפּ֥וֹל
עֲלֵיהֶ֖ם פִּתְאֹֽם:
יג גַּם־זֹ֛ה רָאִ֥יתִי חָכְמָ֖ה תַּ֣חַת הַשָּׁ֑מֶשׁ וּגְדוֹלָ֥ה הִ֖יא
אֵלָֽי: יד עִ֣יר קְטַנָּ֔ה וַאֲנָשִׁ֥ים בָּ֖הּ מְעָ֑ט וּבָא־אֵלֶ֜יהָ
מֶ֤לֶךְ גָּדוֹל֙ וְסָבַ֣ב אֹתָ֔הּ וּבָנָ֥ה עָלֶ֖יהָ מְצוֹדִ֥ים
גְּדֹלִֽים: טו וּמָ֣צָא בָ֗הּ אִ֤ישׁ מִסְכֵּן֙ חָכָ֔ם וּמִלַּט־ה֥וּא
אֶת־הָעִ֖יר בְּחָכְמָת֑וֹ וְאָדָם֙ לֹ֣א זָכַ֔ר אֶת־הָאִ֥ישׁ
הַמִּסְכֵּ֖ן הַהֽוּא:
טז וְאָמַ֖רְתִּי אָ֑נִי
טוֹבָ֥ה חָכְמָ֖ה מִגְּבוּרָ֑ה
וְחָכְמַ֤ת הַמִּסְכֵּן֙ בְּזוּיָ֔ה
וּדְבָרָ֖יו אֵינָ֥ם נִשְׁמָעִֽים:
יז דִּבְרֵ֣י חֲכָמִ֔ים בְּנַ֖חַת נִשְׁמָעִ֑ים מִזַּעֲקַ֖ת מוֹשֵׁ֥ל
בַּכְּסִילִֽים:

days of your vanity. For that is your portion in life and in your work which you do under the sun. ¹⁰Whatever your hand finds to do, do it with all your might. For there is no work, nor device, nor knowledge, nor wisdom in the grave where you are going.

¹¹I returned, and saw under the sun, that the race is not to the swift, nor the battle to the strong, nor bread to the wise, nor even riches to men of understanding,
Nor even favor to men of skill;
But time and chance happen to them all.
¹²For man does not know when his time will come: as fishes are taken in an evil net, and as birds caught in the snare, so are the sons of man snared in an evil time when it falls suddenly upon them.

¹³This wisdom I have also seen under the sun, and it seemed good to me: ¹⁴There was a little city, and few men within. And there came a great king against it, and besieged it, and built great bulwarks against it. ¹⁵Now there was found in it a poor wise man, and he by his wisdom might have delivered the city; but nobody remembered that poor man.

¹⁶Then I said:
Wisdom is better than strength,
But, "A poor man's wisdom is despised,
And his words are not heard."
¹⁷The words of the wise spoken quietly are heard more than the cry of a ruler among fools.

יח טוֹבָה חָכְמָה מִכְּלֵי קְרָב וְחוֹטֶא אֶחָד יְאַבֵּד
טוֹבָה הַרְבֵּה:

י א זְבוּבֵי מָוֶת יַבְאִישׁ יַבִּיעַ שֶׁמֶן רוֹקֵחַ יָקָר מֵחָכְמָה
מִכָּבוֹד סִכְלוּת מְעָט:

ב לֵב חָכָם לִימִינוֹ וְלֵב כְּסִיל לִשְׂמֹאלוֹ: ג וְגַם־
בַּדֶּרֶךְ כְּשֶׁסָּכָל* הֹלֵךְ לִבּוֹ חָסֵר וְאָמַר לַכֹּל סָכָל
הוּא:

ד אִם־רוּחַ הַמּוֹשֵׁל תַּעֲלֶה עָלֶיךָ מְקוֹמְךָ אַל־תַּנַּח
כִּי מַרְפֵּא יַנִּיחַ חֲטָאִים גְּדוֹלִים:

ה יֵשׁ רָעָה רָאִיתִי תַּחַת הַשָּׁמֶשׁ כִּשְׁגָגָה שֶׁיֹּצָא
מִלִּפְנֵי הַשַּׁלִּיט: ו נִתַּן הַסֶּכֶל בַּמְּרוֹמִים רַבִּים
וַעֲשִׁירִים בַּשֵּׁפֶל יֵשֵׁבוּ: ז רָאִיתִי עֲבָדִים עַל־
סוּסִים וְשָׂרִים הֹלְכִים כַּעֲבָדִים עַל־הָאָרֶץ:

ח חֹפֵר גּוּמָּץ בּוֹ יִפּוֹל וּפֹרֵץ גָּדֵר יִשְּׁכֶנּוּ נָחָשׁ:

ט מַסִּיעַ אֲבָנִים יֵעָצֵב בָּהֶם בּוֹקֵעַ עֵצִים יִסָּכֶן בָּם:

י אִם־קֵהָה הַבַּרְזֶל וְהוּא לֹא־פָנִים קִלְקַל וַחֲיָלִים
יְגַבֵּר וְיִתְרוֹן הַכְשֵׁיר חָכְמָה: יא אִם־יִשֹּׁךְ הַנָּחָשׁ
בְּלוֹא־לָחַשׁ וְאֵין יִתְרוֹן לְבַעַל הַלָּשׁוֹן:

יב דִּבְרֵי פִי־חָכָם חֵן וְשִׂפְתוֹת כְּסִיל תְּבַלְּעֶנּוּ:

יג תְּחִלַּת דִּבְרֵי־פִיהוּ סִכְלוּת וְאַחֲרִית פִּיהוּ
הוֹלֵלוּת רָעָה:

יד וְהַסָּכָל יַרְבֶּה דְבָרִים לֹא־יֵדַע הָאָדָם מַה־
שֶּׁיִּהְיֶה וַאֲשֶׁר יִהְיֶה מֵאַחֲרָיו מִי יַגִּיד לוֹ:

(כשהסכל כתיב)

[18]Wisdom is more than weapons of war, but one sinner destroys much good.

10 [1]Dead flies make the ointment of the perfumer fetid and putrid; so may a little folly do to one valued for wisdom and honor.

[2]A wise man's mind is at his right hand; but a fool's mind is at his left. [3]Also, when a fool walks by the way, his wisdom fails him, and he tells everyone that he is a fool.

[4]If the spirit of the ruler rises against you, do not leave your post; submissiveness pacifies for great offenses.

[5]There is an evil which I have seen under the sun, an error which proceeds from the ruler: [6]Folly is set in many high places, and the rich sit in the low place. [7]I have seen servants upon horses, and princes walking like servants upon the ground.

[8]He who digs a pit shall fall into it, and he who breaks through a fence may be bitten by a serpent. [9]He who quarries stones will be hurt by them, and he who cleaves wood will be endangered by it. [10]If the iron be blunt, and one does not whet the edge, then one must use more strength. But wisdom teaches the value of adaption. [11]If the serpent will bite before a charm is uttered, then there is no profit to the master of charms.

[12]The words of a wise man's mouth are gracious, but the lips of a fool will swallow him up. [13]The beginning of his talk is foolishness, and the end of his talk is mischievous madness.

[14]The fool is full of words: a person cannot tell what is coming, and who can tell what will come after that!

טו עֲמַל הַכְּסִילִים תְּיַגְּעֶנּוּ אֲשֶׁר לֹא־יָדַע לָלֶכֶת
אֶל־עִיר:

טז אִי־לָךְ אֶרֶץ שֶׁמַּלְכֵּךְ נָעַר וְשָׂרַיִךְ בַּבֹּקֶר יֹאכֵלוּ:

יז אַשְׁרֵיךְ אֶרֶץ שֶׁמַּלְכֵּךְ בֶּן־חוֹרִים וְשָׂרַיִךְ בָּעֵת
יֹאכֵלוּ בִּגְבוּרָה וְלֹא בַשְּׁתִי:

יח בַּעֲצַלְתַּיִם יִמַּךְ הַמְּקָרֶה
וּבְשִׁפְלוּת יָדַיִם יִדְלֹף הַבָּיִת:

יט לִשְׂחוֹק עֹשִׂים לֶחֶם וְיַיִן יְשַׂמַּח חַיִּים וְהַכֶּסֶף
יַעֲנֶה אֶת־הַכֹּל:

כ גַּם בְּמַדָּעֲךָ מֶלֶךְ אַל־תְּקַלֵּל
וּבְחַדְרֵי מִשְׁכָּבְךָ
אַל־תְּקַלֵּל עָשִׁיר
כִּי עוֹף הַשָּׁמַיִם יוֹלִיךְ אֶת־הַקּוֹל
וּבַעַל כְּנָפַיִם* יַגֵּיד דָּבָר:

יא א שַׁלַּח לַחְמְךָ עַל־פְּנֵי הַמָּיִם כִּי־בְרֹב הַיָּמִים
תִּמְצָאֶנּוּ: ב תֶּן־חֵלֶק לְשִׁבְעָה וְגַם לִשְׁמוֹנָה כִּי לֹא
תֵדַע מַה־יִּהְיֶה רָעָה עַל־הָאָרֶץ:

ג אִם־יִמָּלְאוּ הֶעָבִים גֶּשֶׁם עַל־הָאָרֶץ יָרִיקוּ וְאִם־
יִפּוֹל עֵץ בַּדָּרוֹם וְאִם בַּצָּפוֹן מְקוֹם שֶׁיִּפּוֹל הָעֵץ
שָׁם יְהוּא: ד שֹׁמֵר רוּחַ לֹא יִזְרָע וְרֹאֶה בֶעָבִים לֹא
יִקְצוֹר: ה כַּאֲשֶׁר אֵינְךָ יוֹדֵעַ מַה־דֶּרֶךְ הָרוּחַ
כַּעֲצָמִים בְּבֶטֶן הַמְּלֵאָה כָּכָה לֹא תֵדַע אֶת־
מַעֲשֵׂה הָאֱלֹהִים אֲשֶׁר יַעֲשֶׂה אֶת־הַכֹּל: ו בַּבֹּקֶר

(הכנפים כתיב)

¹⁵The fool's labor makes him utterly weary, and he does not even know how to get to the city.

¹⁶Woe to you, O land, when your king is a child, and your princes feast in the morning. ¹⁷Blessed are you, O land, when your king is the son of nobles, and your princes eat at the right time of day—with restraint, and not as drunkards.

¹⁸By much slothfulness the timber decays,
And through idleness of the hands the house falls down.

¹⁹A feast is made for laughter, and wine makes life glad; but money is the answer to everything.

²⁰Curse not the king, no, not in your thoughts;
And do not curse the rich
In your bed chambers.
For a bird of the air shall carry the voice,
And that which has wings shall tell the matter.

11 ¹Cast your bread upon the waters: for you shall find it after many days. ²Give a portion to seven, and even to eight; for you do not know what evil shall be upon the earth.

³If the clouds are full of rain, they empty themselves upon the earth; and if a tree falls towards the South or towards the North, the tree will remain where it fell. ⁴He who watches the wind will not sow, and he who observes the clouds will not reap. ⁵As you do not know the way of the spirit, or how the bones grow in the womb of her who is with child, even so you do not know the work of God Who does all things. ⁶In the

זְרַע אֶת־זַרְעֶ֫ךָ וְלָעֶ֫רֶב אַל־תַּנַּח יָדֶ֑ךָ כִּי אֵינְךָ֣ יוֹדֵ֫עַ
אֵי זֶ֣ה יִכְשָׁר֙ הֲזֶ֣ה אוֹ־זֶ֔ה וְאִם־שְׁנֵיהֶ֖ם כְּאֶחָ֥ד
טוֹבִֽים:
ז וּמָת֥וֹק הָא֖וֹר וְט֣וֹב לַֽעֵינַ֑יִם לִרְא֖וֹת אֶת־הַשָּֽׁמֶשׁ:
ח כִּ֣י אִם־שָׁנִ֥ים הַרְבֵּ֛ה יִֽחְיֶ֥ה הָֽאָדָ֖ם בְּכֻלָּ֣ם יִשְׂמָ֑ח
וְיִזְכֹּר֙ אֶת־יְמֵ֣י הַחֹ֔שֶׁךְ כִּֽי־הַרְבֵּ֥ה יִֽהְי֖וּ כָּל־שֶׁבָּ֥א
הָֽבֶל:
ט שְׂמַ֧ח בָּח֣וּר בְּיַלְדוּתֶ֗ךָ וִֽיטִֽיבְךָ֤ לִבְּךָ֙ בִּימֵ֣י
בְחוּרוֹתֶ֔יךָ וְהַלֵּךְ֙ בְּדַרְכֵ֣י לִבְּךָ֔ וּבְמַרְאֵ֖ה* עֵינֶ֑יךָ
וְדָ֕ע כִּ֧י עַל־כָּל־אֵ֛לֶּה יְבִֽיאֲךָ֥ הָאֱלֹהִ֖ים בַּמִּשְׁפָּֽט:
י וְהָסֵ֥ר כַּ֙עַס֙ מִלִּבֶּ֔ךָ וְהַֽעֲבֵ֥ר רָעָ֖ה מִבְּשָׂרֶ֑ךָ כִּֽי־
הַיַּלְד֥וּת וְהַֽשַּׁחֲר֖וּת הָֽבֶל:
יב וּזְכֹר֙ אֶת־בּֽוֹרְאֶ֔יךָ בִּימֵ֖י בְּחוּרֹתֶ֑יךָ עַ֣ד אֲשֶׁ֤ר לֹֽא־
יָבֹ֙אוּ֙ יְמֵ֣י הָֽרָעָ֔ה וְהִגִּ֣יעוּ שָׁנִ֔ים אֲשֶׁ֣ר תֹּאמַ֔ר אֵֽין־
לִ֥י בָהֶ֖ם חֵֽפֶץ: ב עַ֣ד אֲשֶׁ֤ר לֹֽא־תֶחְשַׁךְ֙ הַשֶּׁ֔מֶשׁ
וְהָא֕וֹר וְהַיָּרֵ֖חַ וְהַכּֽוֹכָבִ֑ים וְשָׁ֥בוּ הֶֽעָבִ֖ים אַחַ֥ר
הַגָּֽשֶׁם:
ג בַּיּ֗וֹם שֶׁיָּזֻ֙עוּ֙ שֹֽׁמְרֵ֣י הַבַּ֔יִת
וְהִֽתְעַוְּת֖וּ אַנְשֵׁ֣י הֶחָ֑יִל
וּבָֽטְל֤וּ הַטֹּֽחֲנוֹת֙ כִּ֣י מִעֵ֔טוּ
וְחָֽשְׁכ֥וּ הָֽרֹא֖וֹת בָּֽאֲרֻבּֽוֹת:
ד וְסֻגְּר֤וּ דְלָתַ֙יִם֙ בַּשּׁ֔וּק
בִּשְׁפַ֖ל ק֥וֹל הַֽטַּֽחֲנָ֑ה

(וּבְמַרְאֵי כְּתִיב)

morning sow your seed, and in the evening give your
hand no rest. For you do not know which will prosper,
this or that, or whether both will be good.
⁷Truly the light is sweet, and it is a pleasant thing for the
eyes to behold the sun. ⁸But if a man lives many years
and rejoices in all of them, still let him remember the
days of darkness; for they will be many. All that comes
is vanity.
⁹Rejoice in your youth, you who are young, let your
heart give you joy in the days of your youth. And walk
in the ways of your heart, and in the sight of your eyes.
But this you must know: for all these things God will
call you to account. ¹⁰Therefore, remove grief from your
heart, and put away evil from your flesh; for childhood
and youth are vanity.

12 ¹Remember now your creator in the days of your youth,
before the evil days come, and the years draw nigh
when you will say, "I have no pleasure in them," ²while
the sun, the light, the moon, and the stars are not
darkened, and the clouds return after the rain:
³On the day when the keepers of the house shall totter,
And the strong men shall bow themselves,
And the grinders cease because they are few,
And they that look through the windows are darkened;
⁴And the double doors shall be shut in the markets,
When the sound of the grinding is low;

"Of making many books there is no end." 12:12

וְיָקוּם לְקוֹל הַצִּפּוֹר

וְיִשַּׁחוּ כָּל־בְּנוֹת הַשִּׁיר:

ה גַּם מִגָּבֹהַּ יִרָאוּ וְחַתְחַתִּים בַּדֶּרֶךְ

וְיָנֵאץ הַשָּׁקֵד וְיִסְתַּבֵּל הֶחָגָב

וְתָפֵר הָאֲבִיּוֹנָה

כִּי־הֹלֵךְ הָאָדָם אֶל־בֵּית עוֹלָמוֹ

וְסָבְבוּ בַשּׁוּק הַסּוֹפְדִים:

י עַד אֲשֶׁר לֹא־יֵרָתֵק* חֶבֶל הַכֶּסֶף

וְתָרֻץ גֻּלַּת הַזָּהָב

וְתִשָּׁבֶר כַּד עַל־הַמַּבּוּעַ

וְנָרֹץ הַגַּלְגַּל אֶל־הַבּוֹר:

ז וְיָשֹׁב הֶעָפָר עַל־הָאָרֶץ כְּשֶׁהָיָה

וְהָרוּחַ תָּשׁוּב

אֶל־הָאֱלֹהִים אֲשֶׁר נְתָנָהּ:

ח הֲבֵל הֲבָלִים אָמַר הַקּוֹהֶלֶת הַכֹּל הָבֶל:

ט וְיֹתֵר שֶׁהָיָה קֹהֶלֶת חָכָם עוֹד לִמַּד־דַּעַת אֶת־

הָעָם וְאִזֵּן וְחִקֵּר תִּקֵּן מְשָׁלִים הַרְבֵּה: בִּקֵּשׁ

קֹהֶלֶת לִמְצֹא דִּבְרֵי־חֵפֶץ וְכָתוּב יֹשֶׁר דִּבְרֵי

אֱמֶת: יא דִּבְרֵי חֲכָמִים כַּדָּרְבֹנוֹת וּכְמַשְׂמְרוֹת

נְטוּעִים בַּעֲלֵי אֲסֻפּוֹת נִתְּנוּ מֵרֹעֶה אֶחָד:

יב וְיֹתֵר מֵהֵמָּה בְּנִי הִזָּהֵר

עֲשׂוֹת סְפָרִים הַרְבֵּה אֵין קֵץ

וְלַהַג הַרְבֵּה יְגִעַת בָּשָׂר:

(ירחק כתיב)

And one shall start up at the voice of a bird,
And all the daughters of song shall be brought low;
[5]And also when they shall be afraid of that which is
steep, and the street is full of terrors;
When the almond tree shall blossom, and the grass-
hopper shall lie heavy,
And the caperberry shall fail.
Because man goes to his long home,
And the mourners go about in the streets.
[6]Before the silver cord is snapped asunder,
And the golden bowl is shattered,
The pitcher broken at the fountain,
The wheel shattered at the cistern.
[7]And the dust returns to the earth as it was,
And the spirit returns
To God who gave it.
[8]Vanity of vanities, says Kohelet, all is vanity.
[9]And the more Kohelet exulted in wisdom, the more he
taught the people knowledge, gave good counsel, and
sought out and set in order many proverbs. [10]Kohelet
tried to find out words of delight, also just records—
words of truth. [11]The words of the wise are as goads, and
as nails driven deep are those composed in collections,
which are given by one shepherd.
[12]And furthermore, my son, be admonished:
Of making many books there is no end;
And much study is a weariness of the flesh.

יג סוֹף* דָּבָר הַכֹּל נִשְׁמָע אֶת־הָאֱלֹהִים יְרָא ֹ וְאֶת־
מִצְוֺתָיו שְׁמוֹר כִּי־זֶה כָּל־הָאָדָם: יד כִּי אֶת־כָּל־
מַעֲשֶׂה הָאֱלֹהִים יָבִא בְמִשְׁפָּט עַל כָּל־נֶעְלָם אִם־
טוֹב וְאִם־רָע:

(ס׳ רבתי)

[13]The conclusion of the oration sums up the whole: fear God, and keep His commandments; for this is the whole man. [14]For God shall bring every work into judgment concerning every secret thing, whether it is good or evil.

AFTER READING FROM
THE SCROLL OF ECCLESIASTES

לֹא עַל צִדְקוֹתֵינוּ אֲנַחְנוּ מַפִּילִים תַּחֲנוּנֵינוּ לְפָנֶיךָ, כִּי עַל רַחֲמֶיךָ
הָרַבִּים. מָה אֲנַחְנוּ, מַה חַיֵּינוּ, מַה חַסְדֵּנוּ, מַה צִּדְקוֹתֵינוּ, מַה
יְשׁוּעָתֵנוּ, מַה כֹּחֵנוּ, מַה גְּבוּרָתֵנוּ, מַה נֹּאמַר לְפָנֶיךָ, יְיָ אֱלֹהֵינוּ
וֵאלֹהֵי אֲבוֹתֵינוּ, אֲבָל אֲנַחְנוּ עַמְּךָ בְּנֵי בְרִיתֶךָ.

Sovereign of all worlds! Not because of our righteous acts do we
lay our supplications before Thee, but because of Thine abundant
mercies. What are we? What is our life? What is our piety?
What our righteousness? What our helpfulness? What our
strength? What our might? What shall we say before Thee, our
God and God of our ancestors? Nevertheless, we are Thy people,
the children of Thy covenant, descendants of Abraham and
Sarah, who truly loved Thee; the children of Israel ennobled by
the call to Thy service, partners in the tasks of creation.

The Torah of God is whole,
and can bring wholeness to our being.
The testimony of God is to be trusted,
making wise the open-hearted.
The precepts of God are right;
they bring joy into our lives.
The commandment of God is clear,
enlightening the mind.
Reverence for God is elemental,
enduring forever.
The ordinances of God are true,
they are righteous altogether;
more to be desired are they than gold,
yea, than much fine gold;
sweeter also than honey and the honeycomb.

תּוֹרַת יְיָ תְּמִימָה, מְשִׁיבַת נָפֶשׁ.

פִּקּוּדֵי יְיָ יְשָׁרִים, מְשַׂמְּחֵי־לֵב.

מִצְוַת יְיָ בָּרָה, מְאִירַת עֵינָיִם.

יִרְאַת יְיָ טְהוֹרָה, עוֹמֶדֶת לָעַד.

מִשְׁפְּטֵי־יְיָ אֱמֶת, צָדְקוּ יַחְדָּו;

הַנֶּחֱמָדִים מִזָּהָב וּמִפַּז רָב;

וּמְתוּקִים מִדְּבַשׁ וְנֹפֶת צוּפִים.

THE SCROLL OF ESTHER

INTRODUCTION TO
THE SCROLL OF ESTHER

After the defeat of the Nazis, more than 1600 Torah scrolls came to London's Westminster Synagogue from Prague. Many were damaged, but they had somehow survived the destruction which had overtaken their communities. When Solomon Freehof was consulted regarding their use in synagogues, he cited the tradition that "all depends on fate, even the sacred writings."

Some scrolls are fortunate, live happy lives, and partake in joyous occasions; other scrolls suffer; but all are sacred. Half a century ago, Jacob Hoschander had applied this traditional maxim to the Scroll of Esther. He felt that fate—and modern scholarship—had been unkind to this text which itself recorded a people caught in the web of fate. Fate and the scholars *were* unkind to the Megillah. Robert Pfeiffer considered the Scroll of Esther "a brilliant hoax" used to reinforce patriotism in Maccabean times; oddly enough, he echoes Spinoza here. And a UAHC text (Schauss' *Jewish Festivals*) says of the scroll that "it has no religious content and can arouse no pious thoughts." That, at least, can be challenged. Josephus, commenting on Haman's dying the death he had planned for Mordecai, cries out that he "cannot forbear to admire God, and to learn hence His wisdom and His justice" (*Antiquities* XI, vi, 11).

Today, we cannot accept Hoschander's stance that this book records actual historical events; but we will find that it leads us into history. The events described here, if not historically verifiable, are paradigms of historic events which have plagued the Jewish people in every era. "There is a certain people scattered . . . among the peoples . . . of your kingdom. . . . Their laws are different. . . . It is not in the king's interest to tolerate them" (3:8) are the words and the ranting cry we have heard in our time. Every generation has seen the events described in the Scroll of Esther: the persecution, the destruction, and the occasion-

al deliverance. Purim celebrations in Prague or in Frankfurt asserted the truth of this narrative for other times and places. But "all depends on fate." We have shared the dark fate which befell the scrolls of our time. That is why we can read the Scroll of Esther with greater understanding.

There is a strange coincidence in the Scroll of Esther which compels reflection. In this book there emerges an emphasis on Jewish identity as Jewish *national* identity—ethnic identity, if you will. The word 'Jew' emerges in a definite way. The book thus presages that secular view of Jewry which was to emerge in modern times. At the same time, in correspondence with it, the name of God does not appear—even when we would expect it. At the very moment when Mordecai says in effect to Esther: "If you do not help us, help will come to us from . . . ," and we would expect the word 'God,' the text says ". . . help will come to us from . . . *another place,*" as if this omission of the use of a divine reference is deliberate, as if a secularist were in fact writing the book!

The Scroll of Esther does not mention the name of God. There were times when our people experienced the absence of God, as if the God upon whom our people had called in ancient times had become silent, as if God were now absent; and a secular view of our identity emerges. In a time of unbelief, we are more open to a secular text which does not mention God but is still aware that "deliverance will come to the Jews from another place." In a time of silence, we can understand why prayer does not accompany fasting (4:16), why the emphasis is on the action that must arise out of the people itself. And then we are more ready to accept that this text is a cautionary tale, literature of high quality, a paradigmatic story which can have a high content of truth. Maimonides recognized this when he said that only the Torah and the Scroll of Esther would remain after the coming of the Messiah. Purim, the people's celebration, is still to be observed. That, in fact, is a basic purpose of this scroll: to explain the origin of Purim, to regulate the manner of celebration, and to enshrine it as an observance for all generations.

The existential reality of a people's self-affirmation can be taught by a tale which demands the suspension of disbelief. Would a Persian ruler permit the Jews to kill 75,000 Persians?

Can a banquet last over 180 days? Must preparations for a "Miss Persia" contest go on for twelve months? Will gallows stretch into the sky to the height of 83 feet? Why not? A tale told at night to a suffering people can combine all the old dreams and add new fancies. David Daube stresses a Moses/Mordecai identification. Without entering the scholarly argument, we can see that feelings of exodus and of deliverance inform the Purim celebration as well as the Passover Seder. And why not fill the cup to overflowing—a good Purim tradition? The embellishments and sartorial wit which imbue this book make it a classic of the storytelling art form. All the elements are here: the beautiful heroine against the wicked villain; the blood feud between Haman the Agagite and Mordecai the Jew; the drunken Ahasuerus, with a new girl for every night and a head of straw. High drama contrasts with comic relief.

Maurice Samuel, perhaps more than anyone else, has caught the satire and wit of the text in his depiction of Ahasuerus, the comic as fool:

> ... winter fool and summer fool. The winter fool enters concealed in parka, overcoat, earmuffs, galoshes, muffler and gloves, a formidable figure of a man. He removes the wraps ceremoniously one by one, and what do we behold? A fool, an authentic and unmistakable fool ... The summer fool, on the other hand, rushes in bareheaded and in shorts, without defenses or pretenses, a fool at first sight. Ahasuerus is a winter fool.
>
> (Maurice Samuel, *Certain People of the Book*, p. 5)

The king is a fool who needs a royal council and a deputation to deal with his wife, but who will surrender his authority to Haman and order the Jews killed without a moment's thought. When clowns are king, satire becomes bitter. The cruelty of the blind and mindless authority is revealed, the unstable force viewed with alarm by the minorities under its control. Some of that cruelty is transferred from the outer to the inner group, when the minority briefly comes to power. The "happy ending," revelling as it does in gore and killing, rises out of the conditions surrounding the tale, the primitive elements absorbed in it, and the need of the captive to rebel against the oppressor (cf. Psalm

137). This does not justify the cruelty; rather it reminds us not to conceal our dark traits from ourselves.

Another reading of the king's character is possible. After all, the 'fool' survives in a world of constant intrigues, a veritable Claudius whose ability to survive is cloaked in the mantle of a fool. Jonathan Magonet has outlined the arguments, ranging from rabbinic times until now, which see Ahasuerus as a 'melech pikeach' (Megillah 12a), a shrewd king who is anything but a fool. Even then, his survival as an amoral opportunist only emphasizes the bleakness of a power structure dedicated to its own survival at the expense of minorities and without loyalty to its own adherents.

The more we search, the more we find in the text. Thus, in the celebration of Purim, one can find archaic observances surviving in some forms even today. Among ancient peoples, prior to the new year or the spring new year festival, there ensued for a day the observance of Chaos before the new Creation. A deliberate upset of institutional norms was practiced prior to returning to the established order through the New Year rites. For one day, the normal course of events was overthrown. Fools or children were crowned or installed as leaders for a day and marched through the streets with great fanfare. The actual leaders—sages or rulers—were mocked in parodies, and drinking and disorder overturned normal values. Some of this survives in Purim. Purim fools were formerly enthroned as kings and queens. The *"Adlayada"* in Israel resembles Mardi Gras. Leaders are still mocked in the Purim Shpiel (satire), and it became a virtue to drink to the point where "one cannot tell the difference between Mordecai and Haman." Before the new creation hailed in Passover comes the chaos of Purim—chaos preceding the emergence of the higher messianic order.

Let us look at the text. It can be dry and wooden. It has to strive for simplicity, because the plot is all the more complex. The harem intrigue of Esther is balanced by the court intrigue of Mordecai. Perhaps the old Persian tales of their gods were utilized by the storyteller—Ishtar and Marduk against the Elamite Humman. But whatever elements are incorporated into the story, it becomes an original celebration of the Jewish experience.

The author is unknown to us, although he has a firm grasp of

life under the Persians. Ben Sirach does not mention the heroes of this book in his list of Jewish notables (but then, he also omits Ezra!). We can only be certain that the book was written before II Maccabees—and the commentaries, expansions, and reworking of this tale have not ceased since then.

For more than 2,000 years, the Scroll of Esther has been a world inhabited by the Jews wherever they lived. Even now, when we move toward fuller use of the Five Scrolls, Esther remains *the* Megillah for us. It all depends on fate, after all. And as this scroll is unrolled for us, year after year, as it takes on the form of letters sent to the far corners of the world, this tale of darkness and light speaks of the human condition as much as of the fate of the Jews. Fiction becomes fact in this description of humanity. It is not wine which befuddles us into thinking that Haman and Mordecai are the same: the mystical numerology of *gematria,* the Jewish mystical tradition, and psychology all recognize traits of both in all of us. But good *will* conquer evil; and the reading of the Megillah enters our homes and synagogues each year to renew this hope for all of us.

סֵדֶר עֲבוֹדַת פּוּרִים

SERVICE FOR THE READING OF
THE SCROLL OF ESTHER

וַיִּכְתֹּב מָרְדְּכַי אֶת־הַדְּבָרִים הָאֵלֶּה, וַיִּשְׁלַח סְפָרִים אֶל־כָּל־
הַיְּהוּדִים אֲשֶׁר בְּכָל־מְדִינוֹת הַמֶּלֶךְ אֲחַשְׁוֵרוֹשׁ, הַקְּרוֹבִים
וְהָרְחוֹקִים.

And Mordecai sent letters to all the Jews, . . . to all the Jews, near
and far, to enjoin upon them that they should keep the fourteenth
day of the month of Adar, and the fifteenth day of the month of
Adar the days of Purim.

אֲנַחְנוּ מְקַיְּמִים וּמְקַבְּלִים עָלֵינוּ וְעַל זַרְעֵנוּ לַעֲשׂוֹת אֶת הַיָּמִים
כִּכְתָבָם וְכִזְמַנָּם בְּכָל שָׁנָה וְשָׁנָה.

*We Jews ordain and take upon ourselves and upon our children and
upon all who join themselves to us that we will keep these days in the
manner prescribed and at the proper time each year.*

כַּיָּמִים אֲשֶׁר־נָחוּ בָהֶם הַיְּהוּדִים מֵאֹיְבֵיהֶם וְהַחֹדֶשׁ אֲשֶׁר נֶהְפַּךְ
לָהֶם מִיָּגוֹן לְשִׂמְחָה וּמֵאֵבֶל לְיוֹם טוֹב.

These are the days wherein the Jews had rest from their enemies
and the month which was transformed for them from sorrow to
gladness, from mourning into a festive day.

וְהַיָּמִים הָאֵלֶּה נִזְכָּרִים וְנַעֲשִׂים בְּכָל־דּוֹר וָדוֹר, מִשְׁפָּחָה
וּמִשְׁפָּחָה, מְדִינָה וּמְדִינָה, וְעִיר וָעִיר.

*Without fail we remember these days and celebrate them throughout
every generation, every family, every state, and every city.*

לַעֲשׂוֹת אוֹתָם יְמֵי מִשְׁתֶּה וְשִׂמְחָה וּמִשְׁלוֹחַ מָנוֹת אִישׁ לְרֵעֵהוּ
וּמַתָּנוֹת לָאֶבְיוֹנִים.

We will make them days of feasting and gladness and of sending gifts to one another and presents to those in need.

לַיְּהוּדִים הָיְתָה אוֹרָה וְשִׂמְחָה וְשָׂשׂוֹן וִיקָר. כֵּן תִּהְיֶה לָנוּ.

The Jews have known light and joy and gladness and honor;
so may it be for us!

§ זֶה הַיּוֹם יוֹם פּוּרִים *Zeh ha-yom yom Purim*

מַה נָּעִים וּמַה טּוֹב. *ma na-im u-ma tov.*

זְמִירוֹת נְזַמֵּרָה *Ze-mi-rot ne-za-mei-ra*

וְנִשְׂמַח עַד אֵין סוֹף. *ve-nis-mach ad ein sof.*

שְׂמַח, מָרְדְּכַי, שְׂמַח, *Se-mach, Mor-de-chai, se-mach,*

הַצָּרוֹת נָא שְׁכַח. *ha-tsa-rot na she-chach.*

לָנֶצַח לֹא נִשְׁכַּח הַנֵּס. *La-ne-tsach lo nish-kach ha-neis.*

הוֹי שִׁירוּ־נָא שִׁיר *Hoi shi-ru na shir*

כִּי בְּשׁוּשָׁן הָעִיר *ki be-Shu-shan ha-ir*

כִּי לְהָמָן הָרָשָׁע בָּא עֵת. *ki le-Ha-man ha-ra-sha ba eit.*

§ Today is Purim, children;
it comes but once a year.
Let's celebrate the story,
the happy day is here.
Be merry today,
let's dance and let's play.
Our God in glory is great:
Though Haman had might,
our Mordecai was right.
Let's always remember that day.

For Haman said to King Ahasuerus: "There is a certain people scattered abroad and dispersed among the people in all of the

provinces of thy kingdom; and their laws are different from every other people, nor do they keep the king's law; therefore it is not in the king's interest to tolerate them."

אָרוּר הָמָן אֲשֶׁר בִּקֵּשׁ לְאַבְּדִי.

Accursed are those who seek only destruction.

"Do not think," said Mordecai to Queen Esther, "do not think in your heart that you of all the rest will escape because you are in the palace of the king."

בָּרוּךְ מָרְדְּכַי הַיְּהוּדִי.

Blessed be Mordecai the Jew.

And Esther said: "I will go unto the king though it is against the law; and if I perish, I perish."

בְּרוּכָה אֶסְתֵּר מְגִנָּה בַּעֲדִי.

Blessed be Esther our shield, protector on our behalf.

For if you remain silent at this time, relief and deliverance will come to the Jews from another place.

בָּרוּךְ הַמָּקוֹם, בָּרוּךְ הוּא.

Praised be God who calls us to acts of deliverance.

All rise

בָּרְכוּ אֶת יְיָ הַמְבֹרָךְ.

בָּרוּךְ יְיָ הַמְבֹרָךְ לְעוֹלָם וָעֶד.

בָּרוּךְ אַתָּה, יְיָ אֱלֹהֵינוּ, מֶלֶךְ הָעוֹלָם, יוֹצֵר אוֹר וּבוֹרֵא חֹשֶׁךְ, עוֹשֶׂה שָׁלוֹם וּבוֹרֵא אֶת הַכֹּל.

We praise You, O God, Sovereign of existence, who forms light and creates darkness, who brings light out of darkness, and in our fear brings us hope.

Light and joy, gladness and honor!
In these too we seek our God:
in laughter, song, and dancing,
in the Teaching and the Law.
In the telling of the story,
in the acting of the tale,
do we fulfill the commandment
that God's promise be fulfilled:
to deliver us from sorrow to joy,
from mourning to festive day.

בָּרוּךְ אַתָּה, יְיָ אֱלֹהֵינוּ, מֶלֶךְ הָעוֹלָם, הַבּוֹחֵר בְּעַמּוֹ יִשְׂרָאֵל בְּאַהֲבָה.

We praise You, God, who still is calling to the people Israel in light, in love, in promise.

שְׁמַע יִשְׂרָאֵל, יְיָ אֱלֹהֵינוּ, יְיָ אֶחָד!

Hear, O Israel: Adonai is our God, Adonai is One!

בָּרוּךְ שֵׁם כְּבוֹד מַלְכוּתוֹ לְעוֹלָם וָעֶד.

Praised be God's name whose glorious kingdom is forever and ever.

All are seated

וְאָהַבְתָּ אֵת יְיָ אֱלֹהֶיךָ בְּכָל־לְבָבְךָ וּבְכָל־נַפְשְׁךָ וּבְכָל־מְאֹדֶךָ. וְהָיוּ הַדְּבָרִים הָאֵלֶּה אֲשֶׁר אָנֹכִי מְצַוְּךָ הַיּוֹם עַל־לְבָבֶךָ. וְשִׁנַּנְתָּם לְבָנֶיךָ, וְדִבַּרְתָּ בָּם בְּשִׁבְתְּךָ בְּבֵיתֶךָ, וּבְלֶכְתְּךָ בַדֶּרֶךְ וּבְשָׁכְבְּךָ וּבְקוּמֶךָ. וּקְשַׁרְתָּם לְאוֹת עַל־יָדֶךָ, וְהָיוּ לְטֹטָפֹת בֵּין עֵינֶיךָ, וּכְתַבְתָּם עַל־מְזֻזוֹת בֵּיתֶךָ וּבִשְׁעָרֶיךָ. לְמַעַן תִּזְכְּרוּ וַעֲשִׂיתֶם אֶת־כָּל־מִצְוֹתָי, וִהְיִיתֶם קְדוֹשִׁים לֵאלֹהֵיכֶם. אֲנִי יְיָ אֱלֹהֵיכֶם.

And thou shalt love Adonai, thy God, with all thy heart, with all thy soul, and with all thy might. And these words, which I command thee this day, shall be upon thy heart. Thou shalt teach them diligently unto thy children, and shalt speak of them when thou sittest in thy house, when thou walkest by the way, when thou liest down, and when thou risest up. Thou shalt bind them for a sign upon thy hand, and they shall be for frontlets between thine eyes. Thou shalt write them upon the doorposts of thy house and upon thy gates: that ye may remember and do all My commandments and be holy unto your God. I am Adonai, your God.

God redeems us from the power of despots;

God delivers us from the fist of tyrants.

God avenges oppression;

God requites the mortal enemy.

Pharaoh came to know the strong hand of God,

and every Haman, God's outstretched arm.

Despite all that befalls us,

still we live.

God's children pass through the deadly waters,

and the enemy sinks in the depth of the sea.

With Moses and Miriam still we sing,

with Esther and Mordecai and Shushan rejoicing:

מִי־כָמֹכָה בָּאֵלִים, יְיָ. מִי כָּמֹכָה נֶאְדָּר בַּקֹּדֶשׁ, נוֹרָא תְהִלֹּת,
עֹשֵׂה־פֶלֶא.

A new song the redeemed sang unto Your Name.
They proclaimed Your sovereignty and said:

יְיָ יִמְלֹךְ לְעוֹלָם וָעֶד.

God shall reign forever and ever.

צוּר יִשְׂרָאֵל, קוּמָה בְּעֶזְרַת יִשְׂרָאֵל. גּוֹאֲלֵנוּ יְיָ צְבָאוֹת שְׁמוֹ,
קְדוֹשׁ יִשְׂרָאֵל. בָּרוּךְ אַתָּה, יְיָ, גָּאַל יִשְׂרָאֵל.

O Rock of Israel, redeem those who are oppressed and deliver
those who are persecuted. Praised be God, our Redeemer, the
Holy One of Israel.

עוּצוּ עֵצָה וְתֻפָר,
דַּבְּרוּ דָבָר וְלֹא יָקוּם,
כִּי עִמָּנוּ אֵל.

Take counsel, O enemy,
it will come to nought!
Devise crafty plans,
they shall not stand.
For God is with us,
God is with us.

§   עוּצוּ עֵצָה וְתֻפָר,   *U-tsu ei-tsa ve-tu-far,*

דַּבְּרוּ דָבָר וְלֹא יָקוּם,   *da-be-ru da-var ve-lo ya-kum,*

כִּי עִמָּנוּ אֵל.   *ki i-ma-nu Eil.*

All rise

God of the Fathers, God of the Mothers,

God of Abraham, God of Sarah,

who raised up Mordecai as a shield of the people,

and called Esther to become our protection;

God of the Elders, God of little children,

who calls us to challenges harsh and demanding,

who demands of us strength and endurance and courage,

and asks of us laughter at times of redemption.

בָּרוּךְ אַתָּה, יְיָ אֱלֹהֵינוּ וֵאלֹהֵי אֲבוֹתֵינוּ, אֱלֹהֵי אַבְרָהָם, אֱלֹהֵי
יִצְחָק, וֵאלֹהֵי יַעֲקֹב. הָאֵל הַגָּדוֹל, הַגִּבּוֹר וְהַנּוֹרָא, אֵל עֶלְיוֹן, גּוֹמֵל
חֲסָדִים טוֹבִים, וְקוֹנֵה הַכֹּל, וְזוֹכֵר חַסְדֵי אָבוֹת, וּמֵבִיא גְאֻלָּה לִבְנֵי
בְנֵיהֶם, לְמַעַן שְׁמוֹ, בְּאַהֲבָה. מֶלֶךְ עוֹזֵר וּמוֹשִׁיעַ וּמָגֵן. בָּרוּךְ אַתָּה
יְיָ, מָגֵן אַבְרָהָם.

For victories and triumphs and days of deliverance,

for miracles in those days and in this season,

in days of Esther and Mordecai, in Shushan, that great city;

for victories and triumphs and days of deliverance,

when the wicked Haman rose up against us,

who sought to destroy, to slay, and make perish

Jews young and old; men, women, and children—

As in those days and in this season,

for victories and triumphs, for days of deliverance,

let us thank and praise our God!

All are seated

For the wonders and for the deliverance
and for the mighty acts and for the triumphs,
that You performed for our ancestors
in those days and in this season.

§ עַל הַנִּסִּים וְעַל הַפֻּרְקָן, וְעַל הַגְּבוּרוֹת וְעַל הַתְּשׁוּעוֹת, שֶׁעָשִׂיתָ
לַאֲבוֹתֵינוּ בַּיָּמִים הָהֵם, בַּזְּמַן הַזֶּה.

(For the wonders and for the deliverance
and for the mighty acts and for the triumphs,
that You performed for our ancestors
in those days and in this season.)

The Scroll of Esther was composed under the inspiration of the Holy Spirit—so say the sages of old.

And the decree of Esther established these matters of Purim and it was recorded in the book.

As the scroll is opened and readers come forward,
Shoshanat Ya-akov is sung:

שׁוֹשַׁנַּת יַעֲקֹב צָהֲלָה וְשָׂמֵחָה

בִּרְאוֹתָם יַחַד תְּכֵלֶת מָרְדְּכַי.

תְּשׁוּעָתָם הָיִיתָ לָנֶצַח,

וְתִקְוָתָם בְּכָל־דּוֹר וָדוֹר.

לְהוֹדִיעַ שֶׁכָּל־קוֹיֶךָ לֹא יֵבֹשׁוּ

וְלֹא יִכָּלְמוּ לָנֶצַח כָּל־הַחוֹסִים בָּךְ.

The flower of Jacob rejoices
as the Jews of Shushan shout for joy.
Each time we read the story,
and see Mordecai clad in purple;

each time we tell the tale,
we renew the hope of generations:
From darkness to light, from sorrow to joy
and, for all, a festive day.

Blessings before reading of the Scroll of Esther

בָּרוּךְ אַתָּה, יְיָ אֱלֹהֵינוּ, מֶלֶךְ הָעוֹלָם, אֲשֶׁר קִדְּשָׁנוּ בְּמִצְוֹתָיו
וְצִוָּנוּ עַל מִקְרָא מְגִלָּה.

Ba-ruch a-ta, A-do-nai E-lo-hei-nu, me-lech ha-o-lam, a-sher ki-de-sha-nu be-mits-vo-tav ve-tsi-va-nu al mik-ra me-gi-la.

We praise You, O God, Sovereign of existence, who has hallowed our lives with commandments and commanded us to read this scroll.

בָּרוּךְ אַתָּה, יְיָ אֱלֹהֵינוּ, מֶלֶךְ הָעוֹלָם, שֶׁעָשָׂה נִסִּים לַאֲבוֹתֵינוּ
בַּיָּמִים הָהֵם, בַּזְּמַן הַזֶּה.

*Ba-ruch a-ta, A-do-nai E-lo-hei-nu, me-lech ha-o-lam, she-a-sa ni-sim
la-a-vo-tei-nu ba-ya-mim ha-heim, ba-ze-man ha-zeh.*

*We praise You, O God, Sovereign of existence, who did miracles for our
ancestors in those days, as at this season.*

בָּרוּךְ אַתָּה, יְיָ אֱלֹהֵינוּ, מֶלֶךְ הָעוֹלָם, שֶׁהֶחֱיָנוּ וְקִיְּמָנוּ
וְהִגִּיעָנוּ לַזְּמַן הַזֶּה.

*Ba-ruch a-ta, A-do-nai E-lo-hei-nu, me-lech ha-o-lam, she-he-che-
ya-nu ve-ki-ye-ma-nu ve-hi-gi-a-nu la-ze-man ha-zeh.*

*We praise You, O God, Sovereign of existence, who has kept us alive,
sustained us, and enabled us to celebrate this festive day.*

READING OF THE SCROLL OF ESTHER

Blessing following the reading

בָּרוּךְ אַתָּה, יְיָ אֱלֹהֵינוּ, מֶלֶךְ הָעוֹלָם, הָרָב אֶת־רִיבֵנוּ, וְהַדָּן אֶת־
דִּינֵנוּ, וְהַנּוֹקֵם אֶת־נִקְמָתֵנוּ, וְהַמְשַׁלֵּם גְּמוּל לְכָל אוֹיְבֵי נַפְשֵׁנוּ,
וְהַנִּפְרָע לָנוּ מִצָּרֵינוּ. בָּרוּךְ אַתָּה, יְיָ, הַנִּפְרָע לְעַמּוֹ יִשְׂרָאֵל מִכָּל
צָרֵיהֶם, הָאֵל הַמּוֹשִׁיעַ.

*Ba-ruch a-ta, A-do-nai E-lo-hei-nu, me-lech ha-o-lam, ha-rav et
ri-vei-nu, ve-ha-dan et di-nei-nu, ve-ha-no-keim et nik-ma-tei-nu,
ve-ha-me-sha-leim ge-mul le-chol o-ye-vei naf-shei-nu, ve-ha-nif-ra
la-nu mi-tsa-rei-nu. Ba-ruch a-ta, A-do-nai, ha-nif-ra le-a-mo
Yis-ra-eil mi-kol tsa-rei-hem, ha-Eil ha-mo-shi-a.*

*We praise You, O God, Sovereign of existence, who pleads the
cause of our justice; God of righteous judgment, who enables us to
survive the vicious onslaught of the destroyer; God of deliverance!*

Praised are You, O God of life,
whose will it is to end all strife,
whose word still hallows Israel's soul,
who bade us read Queen Esther's scroll;
because her courage and her will
give us strength of spirit still,
strengthen us to keep Your ways,
and help us live to sing Your praise.

(Concluding prayers begin on page 371)

א א וַיְהִי בִּימֵי אֲחַשְׁוֵרוֹשׁ הוּא אֲחַשְׁוֵרוֹשׁ הַמֹּלֵךְ
מֵהֹדּוּ וְעַד־כּוּשׁ שֶׁבַע וְעֶשְׂרִים וּמֵאָה מְדִינָה:
ב בַּיָּמִים הָהֵם כְּשֶׁבֶת ׀ הַמֶּלֶךְ אֲחַשְׁוֵרוֹשׁ עַל כִּסֵּא
מַלְכוּתוֹ אֲשֶׁר בְּשׁוּשַׁן הַבִּירָה: ג בִּשְׁנַת שָׁלוֹשׁ
לְמָלְכוֹ עָשָׂה מִשְׁתֶּה לְכָל־שָׂרָיו וַעֲבָדָיו חֵיל ׀
פָּרַס וּמָדַי הַפַּרְתְּמִים וְשָׂרֵי הַמְּדִינוֹת לְפָנָיו:
ד בְּהַרְאֹתוֹ אֶת־עֹשֶׁר כְּבוֹד מַלְכוּתוֹ וְאֶת־יְקָר
תִּפְאֶרֶת גְּדוּלָתוֹ יָמִים רַבִּים שְׁמוֹנִים וּמְאַת יוֹם:
ה וּבִמְלֹאות* ׀ הַיָּמִים הָאֵלֶּה עָשָׂה הַמֶּלֶךְ לְכָל־
הָעָם הַנִּמְצְאִים בְּשׁוּשַׁן הַבִּירָה לְמִגָּדוֹל וְעַד־
קָטָן מִשְׁתֶּה שִׁבְעַת יָמִים בַּחֲצַר גִּנַּת בִּיתַן הַמֶּלֶךְ:
ו חוּר* ׀ כַּרְפַּס וּתְכֵלֶת אָחוּז בְּחַבְלֵי־בוּץ וְאַרְגָּמָן
עַל־גְּלִילֵי כֶסֶף וְעַמּוּדֵי שֵׁשׁ מִטּוֹת ׀ זָהָב וָכֶסֶף עַל
רִצְפַת בַּהַט־וָשֵׁשׁ וְדַר וְסֹחָרֶת: ז וְהַשְׁקוֹת בִּכְלֵי
זָהָב וְכֵלִים מִכֵּלִים שׁוֹנִים וְיֵין מַלְכוּת רָב כְּיַד
הַמֶּלֶךְ: ח וְהַשְּׁתִיָּה כַדָּת אֵין אֹנֵס כִּי־כֵן ׀ יִסַּד
הַמֶּלֶךְ עַל כָּל־רַב בֵּיתוֹ לַעֲשׂוֹת כִּרְצוֹן אִישׁ־
וָאִישׁ: ט גַּם וַשְׁתִּי הַמַּלְכָּה עָשְׂתָה מִשְׁתֵּה נָשִׁים
בֵּית הַמַּלְכוּת אֲשֶׁר לַמֶּלֶךְ אֲחַשְׁוֵרוֹשׁ:
י בַּיּוֹם הַשְּׁבִיעִי כְּטוֹב לֵב־הַמֶּלֶךְ בַּיָּיִן אָמַר
לִמְהוּמָן בִּזְּתָא חַרְבוֹנָא בִּגְתָא וַאֲבַגְתָא זֵתַר
וְכַרְכַּס שִׁבְעַת הַסָּרִיסִים הַמְשָׁרְתִים אֶת־פְּנֵי
הַמֶּלֶךְ אֲחַשְׁוֵרוֹשׁ: יא לְהָבִיא אֶת־וַשְׁתִּי הַמַּלְכָּה

(ח׳ רבתי)   (ובמלואת כתיב)

I ¹Now it came to pass in the days of Ahasuerus, the same Ahasuerus who reigned from India as far as Ethiopia, over a hundred and twenty-seven provinces: ²That in those days, when the King Ahasuerus sat on the throne of his kingdom, in Shushan the capital, ³in the third year of his reign, that he gave a banquet for all his officers and servants. The military force of Persia and Media, the nobles and rulers of the provinces were before him, ⁴while he showed the riches and glory of his kingdom and the precious things of his great majesty many days, even a hundred and eighty days. ⁵When these days were completed, the king gave a banquet for all the people that were present in Shushan the capital, both great and small, in the enclosure of the king's palace garden. ⁶There were hangings of white cotton and of blue, fastened with cords of fine linen and purple to silver cylinders and pillars of marble. The couches were of gold and silver, upon a pavement of alabaster, marble, mother-of-pearl and precious stone. ⁷They served wine in golden vessels, all of them different in design, and royal wine in abundance, as befits a king. ⁸And the drinking was according to the law; there was no compulsion. For the king had commanded all the officers of his house to do according to every man's pleasure. ⁹Queen Vashti also gave a banquet for the women in the royal house of King Ahasuerus.

¹⁰On the seventh day, when the heart of the king was merry with wine, he commanded Mehuman, Bizzetha, Harbona, Bigtha and Abagtha, Zethar and Carcas, the seven eunuchs who attended King Ahasuerus, ¹¹to bring

"Now it came to pass..."   1:1

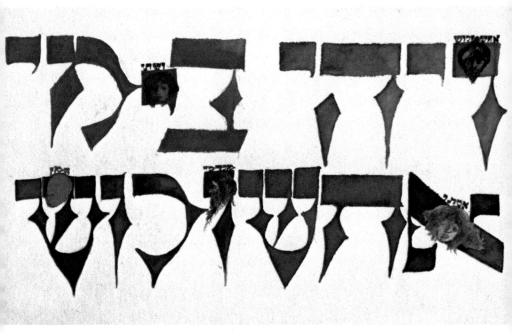

לִפְנֵי הַמֶּ֫לֶךְ בְּכֶ֫תֶר מַלְכ֑וּת לְהַרְא֣וֹת הָעַמִּ֤ים
וְהַשָּׂרִים֙ אֶת־יָפְיָ֔הּ כִּי־טוֹבַ֥ת מַרְאֶ֖ה הִֽיא׃
יג וַתְּמָאֵ֞ן הַמַּלְכָּ֣ה וַשְׁתִּ֗י לָבוֹא֙ בִּדְבַ֣ר הַמֶּ֫לֶךְ֙ אֲשֶׁ֖ר
בְּיַ֣ד הַסָּרִיסִ֑ים וַיִּקְצֹ֤ף הַמֶּ֫לֶךְ֙ מְאֹ֔ד וַחֲמָת֖וֹ בָּעֲרָ֥ה
בֽוֹ׃
יג וַיֹּ֣אמֶר הַמֶּ֫לֶךְ֙ לַחֲכָמִ֖ים יֹדְעֵ֣י הָעִתִּ֑ים כִּי־כֵן֙ דְּבַ֣ר
הַמֶּ֫לֶךְ לִפְנֵ֔י כָּל־יֹדְעֵ֖י דָּ֥ת וָדִֽין׃ יד וְהַקָּרֹ֣ב אֵלָ֗יו
כַּרְשְׁנָ֤א שֵׁתָר֙ אַדְמָ֣תָא תַרְשִׁ֔ישׁ מֶ֖רֶס מַרְסְנָ֣א
מְמוּכָ֑ן שִׁבְעַ֣ת שָׂרֵ֣י ׀ פָּרַ֣ס וּמָדַ֗י רֹאֵי֙ פְּנֵ֣י הַמֶּ֫לֶךְ
הַיֹּשְׁבִ֥ים רִאשֹׁנָ֖ה בַּמַּלְכֽוּת׃ טו כְּדָת֙ מַה־לַּעֲשׂ֔וֹת
בַּמַּלְכָּ֖ה וַשְׁתִּ֑י עַ֣ל ׀ אֲשֶׁ֣ר לֹא־עָשְׂתָ֗ה אֶֽת־מַאֲמַר֙
הַמֶּ֫לֶךְ אֲחַשְׁוֵר֔וֹשׁ בְּיַ֖ד הַסָּרִיסִֽים׃
טו וַיֹּ֣אמֶר מְמוּכָ֗ן* לִפְנֵ֤י הַמֶּ֫לֶךְ֙ וְהַשָּׂרִ֔ים לֹ֤א עַל־
הַמֶּ֫לֶךְ֙ לְבַדּ֔וֹ עָוְתָ֖ה וַשְׁתִּ֣י הַמַּלְכָּ֑ה כִּ֤י עַל־כָּל־
הַשָּׂרִים֙ וְעַל־כָּל־הָ֣עַמִּ֔ים אֲשֶׁ֖ר בְּכָל־מְדִינ֥וֹת
הַמֶּ֫לֶךְ אֲחַשְׁוֵרֽוֹשׁ׃ יו כִּֽי־יֵצֵ֤א דְבַר־הַמַּלְכָּה֙ עַל־
כָּל־הַנָּשִׁ֔ים לְהַבְז֥וֹת בַּעְלֵיהֶ֖ן בְּעֵינֵיהֶ֑ן בְּאָמְרָ֗ם
הַמֶּ֫לֶךְ אֲחַשְׁוֵר֗וֹשׁ אָמַ֞ר לְהָבִ֨יא אֶת־וַשְׁתִּ֧י
הַמַּלְכָּ֛ה לְפָנָ֖יו וְלֹא־בָֽאָה׃ יח וְֽהַיּ֨וֹם הַזֶּ֜ה
תֹּאמַ֣רְנָה ׀ שָׂר֣וֹת פָּֽרַס־וּמָדַ֗י אֲשֶׁ֤ר שָׁמְעוּ֙ אֶת־
דְּבַ֣ר הַמַּלְכָּ֔ה לְכֹ֖ל שָׂרֵ֣י הַמֶּ֑לֶךְ וּכְדַ֖י בִּזָּי֥וֹן וָקָֽצֶף׃
יט אִם־עַל־הַמֶּ֨לֶךְ ט֜וֹב יֵצֵ֤א דְבַר־מַלְכוּת֙ מִלְּפָנָ֔יו
וְיִכָּתֵ֛ב בְּדָתֵ֥י פָֽרַס־וּמָדַ֖י וְלֹ֣א יַעֲב֑וֹר אֲשֶׁ֖ר לֹא־

(מומכן כתיב)

Queen Vashti before the king wearing the royal crown, to show her beauty to the people and to the nobles, for she was beautiful. [12]But Queen Vashti refused to come at the king's command conveyed by the eunuchs. This enraged the king greatly, and his anger burned inside of him.

[13]Then the king said to the sages who knew the times (for it was his royal custom to consult all who knew law and judgment, [14]those closest to him being Carshena, Shethar, Admatha, Tarshish, Meres, Marsena, and Memucan, the seven nobles of Persia and Media who had access to the king and held first place in the kingdom): [15]"What law shall be applied to Queen Vashti, since she has not obeyed the command of King Ahasuerus conveyed by his eunuchs?"

[16]Then Memucan answered before the king and the nobles: "Queen Vashti has not only done wrong to the king, but also to all the nobles, and to all the people in all the provinces of King Ahasuerus. [17]For this deed of the queen will be reported to all women. Their husbands will appear contemptible to them when they hear the news: King Ahasuerus ordered Queen Vashti to be brought before him—and she did not come!

[18]This very day, the ladies of Persia and Media who have heard of the deed of the queen will tell it to all the king's nobles. There will be a surfeit of contempt and anger.

[19]If it please the king, let a royal command go out from him, and let it be written into the laws of the Persians

Ahasuerus   1:2

תָבוֹא וַשְׁתִּ֜י לִפְנֵי֙ הַמֶּ֣לֶךְ אֲחַשְׁוֵר֔וֹשׁ וּמַלְכוּתָהּ֙
יִתֵּ֣ן הַמֶּ֔לֶךְ לִרְעוּתָ֖הּ הַטּוֹבָ֣ה מִמֶּ֑נָּה: כ וְנִשְׁמַע֩
פִּתְגָ֨ם הַמֶּ֤לֶךְ אֲשֶֽׁר־יַעֲשֶׂה֙ בְּכָל־מַלְכוּת֔וֹ כִּ֥י רַבָּ֖ה
הִ֑יא וְכָל־הַנָּשִׁ֗ים יִתְּנ֤וּ יְקָר֙ לְבַעְלֵיהֶ֔ן לְמִגָּד֖וֹל
וְעַד־קָטָֽן:
כא וַיִּיטַב֙ הַדָּבָ֔ר בְּעֵינֵ֥י הַמֶּ֖לֶךְ וְהַשָּׂרִ֑ים וַיַּ֥עַשׂ
הַמֶּ֖לֶךְ כִּדְבַ֥ר מְמוּכָֽן: כב וַיִּשְׁלַ֤ח סְפָרִים֙ אֶל־כָּל־
מְדִינ֣וֹת הַמֶּ֔לֶךְ אֶל־מְדִינָ֤ה וּמְדִינָה֙ כִּכְתָבָ֔הּ וְאֶל־
עַ֥ם וָעָ֖ם כִּלְשׁוֹנ֑וֹ לִהְי֤וֹת כָּל־אִישׁ֙ שֹׂרֵ֣ר בְּבֵית֔וֹ
וּמְדַבֵּ֖ר כִּלְשׁ֥וֹן עַמּֽוֹ:
ב א אַחַר֙ הַדְּבָרִ֣ים הָאֵ֔לֶּה כְּשֹׁ֕ךְ חֲמַ֖ת הַמֶּ֣לֶךְ
אֲחַשְׁוֵר֑וֹשׁ זָכַ֣ר אֶת־וַשְׁתִּי֙ וְאֵ֣ת אֲשֶׁר־עָשָׂ֔תָה
וְאֵ֥ת אֲשֶׁר־נִגְזַ֖ר עָלֶֽיהָ: ב וַיֹּאמְר֥וּ נַעֲרֵי־הַמֶּ֖לֶךְ
מְשָׁרְתָ֑יו יְבַקְשׁ֥וּ לַמֶּ֖לֶךְ נְעָר֥וֹת בְּתוּל֖וֹת טוֹב֥וֹת
מַרְאֶֽה: ג וְיַפְקֵ֨ד הַמֶּ֜לֶךְ פְּקִידִים֮ בְּכָל־מְדִינ֣וֹת
מַלְכוּתוֹ֒ וְיִקְבְּצ֣וּ אֶת־כָּל־נַעֲרָֽה־בְ֠תוּלָ֤ה טוֹבַ֨ת
מַרְאֶ֜ה אֶל־שׁוּשַׁ֤ן הַבִּירָה֙ אֶל־בֵּ֣ית הַנָּשִׁ֔ים אֶל־יַ֣ד
הֵגֶ֛א סְרִ֥יס הַמֶּ֖לֶךְ שֹׁמֵ֣ר הַנָּשִׁ֑ים וְנָת֖וֹן תַּמְרֻקֵיהֶֽן:
ד וְהַֽנַּעֲרָ֗ה אֲשֶׁ֨ר תִּיטַ֤ב בְּעֵינֵ֤י הַמֶּ֙לֶךְ֙ תִּמְלֹ֣ךְ תַּ֣חַת
וַשְׁתִּ֑י וַיִּיטַ֧ב הַדָּבָ֛ר בְּעֵינֵ֥י הַמֶּ֖לֶךְ וַיַּ֥עַשׂ כֵּֽן:
ה אִ֣ישׁ יְהוּדִ֔י הָיָ֖ה בְּשׁוּשַׁ֣ן הַבִּירָ֑ה וּשְׁמ֣וֹ מָרְדֳּכַ֗י בֶּ֣ן
יָאִ֧יר בֶּן־שִׁמְעִ֛י בֶּן־קִ֖ישׁ אִ֥ישׁ יְמִינִֽי: ו אֲשֶׁ֤ר הָגְלָה֙
מִירֽוּשָׁלַ֔יִם עִם־הַגֹּלָה֙ אֲשֶׁ֣ר הָגְלְתָ֔ה עִ֖ם יְכָנְיָ֣ה

and Medes, which no one can revoke, that Vashti come no more before King Ahasuerus. And let the king give her royal position to someone who is more worthy. ²⁰And when this royal decree which he will make is heard throughout all his kingdom, which is great, all the wives shall give honor to their husbands, both high and low."

²¹And the advice pleased the king and the nobles, and the king did what Memucan had suggested: ²²He sent letters to all the king's provinces, to every province according to its form of script and to every people according to its language, that every man should be master in his own house, and speak his own language.

2 ¹After these events, when the wrath of King Ahasuerus had subsided, he remembered Vashti and what she had done and what had been decreed against her. ²The king's servants who attended him then said: "Let beautiful young virgins be sought out for the king. ³And let the king appoint officers in all the provinces of his kingdom, that they may gather together all the beautiful young virgins to Shushan the capital, to the house of the women, into the custody of Hege, the king's eunuch in charge of the women; and let their ointments be given to them. ⁴And let the maiden who pleases the king be queen instead of Vashti." And the advice pleased the king; and he did so.

⁵Now in Shushan the capital there was a certain Jew whose name was Mordecai, the son of Jair, the son of Shimai, the son of Kish, a Benjaminite. ⁶He had been carried away from Jerusalem with the captives who had been carried away with Jeconiah, king of Judah,

Vashti   1:11

מֶ֥לֶךְ־יְהוּדָ֖ה אֲשֶׁ֣ר הֶגְלָ֑ה נְבוּכַדְנֶאצַּ֖ר מֶ֥לֶךְ בָּבֶֽל׃

⁷וַיְהִ֨י אֹמֵ֜ן אֶת־הֲדַסָּ֗ה הִ֤יא אֶסְתֵּר֙ בַּת־דֹּד֔וֹ כִּ֛י אֵ֥ין
לָ֖הּ אָ֣ב וָאֵ֑ם וְהַנַּעֲרָ֤ה יְפַת־תֹּ֙אַר֙ וְטוֹבַ֣ת מַרְאֶ֔ה
וּבְמ֤וֹת אָבִ֙יהָ֙ וְאִמָּ֔הּ לְקָחָ֧הּ מָרְדֳּכַ֛י ל֖וֹ לְבַֽת׃

⁸וַיְהִ֗י בְּהִשָּׁמַ֤ע דְּבַר־הַמֶּ֙לֶךְ֙ וְדָת֔וֹ וּֽבְהִקָּבֵ֞ץ נְעָר֥וֹת
רַבּ֛וֹת אֶל־שׁוּשַׁ֥ן הַבִּירָ֖ה אֶל־יַ֣ד הֵגָ֑י וַתִּלָּקַ֤ח
אֶסְתֵּר֙ אֶל־בֵּ֣ית הַמֶּ֔לֶךְ אֶל־יַ֥ד הֵגַ֖י שֹׁמֵ֥ר הַנָּשִֽׁים׃

⁹וַתִּיטַ֨ב הַנַּעֲרָ֣ה בְעֵינָיו֮ וַתִּשָּׂ֣א חֶ֣סֶד לְפָנָיו֒ וַ֠יְבַהֵ֠ל
אֶת־תַּמְרוּקֶ֨יהָ וְאֶת־מָֽנוֹתֶ֜הָ לָתֵ֣ת לָ֗הּ וְאֵת֙ שֶׁ֣בַע
הַנְּעָר֗וֹת הָרְאֻיֹ֛ות לָֽתֶת־לָ֖הּ מִבֵּ֣ית הַמֶּ֑לֶךְ וַיְשַׁנֶּ֧הָ
וְאֶת־נַעֲרוֹתֶ֛יהָ לְט֖וֹב בֵּ֥ית הַנָּשִֽׁים׃ ¹⁰לֹֽא־הִגִּ֣ידָה
אֶסְתֵּ֔ר אֶת־עַמָּ֖הּ וְאֶת־מֽוֹלַדְתָּ֑הּ כִּ֧י מָרְדֳּכַ֛י צִוָּ֥ה
עָלֶ֖יהָ אֲשֶׁ֥ר לֹֽא־תַגִּֽיד׃ ¹¹וּבְכָל־י֣וֹם וָי֔וֹם מָרְדֳּכַי֙
מִתְהַלֵּ֔ךְ לִפְנֵ֖י חֲצַ֣ר בֵּית־הַנָּשִׁ֑ים לָדַ֙עַת֙ אֶת־
שְׁל֣וֹם אֶסְתֵּ֔ר וּמַה־יֵּעָשֶׂ֖ה בָּֽהּ׃

¹²וּבְהַגִּ֡יעַ תֹּר֩ נַעֲרָ֨ה וְנַעֲרָ֜ה לָב֣וֹא ׀ אֶל־הַמֶּ֣לֶךְ
אֲחַשְׁוֵר֗וֹשׁ מִקֵּץ֩ הֱי֨וֹת לָ֜הּ כְּדָ֤ת הַנָּשִׁים֙ שְׁנֵ֣ים
עָשָׂ֣ר חֹ֔דֶשׁ כִּ֛י כֵּ֥ן יִמְלְא֖וּ יְמֵ֣י מְרוּקֵיהֶ֑ן שִׁשָּׁ֤ה
חֳדָשִׁים֙ בְּשֶׁ֣מֶן הַמֹּ֔ר וְשִׁשָּׁ֤ה חֳדָשִׁים֙ בַּבְּשָׂמִ֔ים
וּבְתַמְרוּקֵ֖י הַנָּשִֽׁים׃ ¹³וּבָזֶ֕ה הַנַּעֲרָ֖ה בָּאָ֣ה אֶל־
הַמֶּ֑לֶךְ אֵת֩ כָּל־אֲשֶׁ֨ר תֹּאמַ֜ר יִנָּ֤תֵֽן לָהּ֙ לָב֣וֹא עִמָּ֔הּ
מִבֵּ֥ית הַנָּשִׁ֖ים עַד־בֵּ֥ית הַמֶּֽלֶךְ׃ ¹⁴בָּעֶ֣רֶב ׀ הִ֣יא בָאָ֗ה
וּ֠בַבֹּקֶר הִ֣יא שָׁבָ֞ה אֶל־בֵּ֤ית הַנָּשִׁים֙ שֵׁנִ֔י אֶל־יַ֧ד
שַֽׁעַשְׁגַ֛ז סְרִ֥יס הַמֶּ֖לֶךְ שֹׁמֵ֣ר הַפִּֽילַגְשִׁ֑ים לֹא־תָב֣וֹא

whom King Nebuchadnezzar of Babylon had carried away. [7]And he brought up Hadassah, that is, Esther, his uncle's daughter: for she had neither father nor mother. The maid was fair and beautiful. When her father and mother died, Mordecai adopted her as his own daughter.

[8]It came to pass, when the king's command and his decree was heard, and when many maidens were brought together to Shushan the capital, into the custody of Hegai, that Esther was also brought to the king's house, into the custody of Hegai, keeper of the women. [9]The girl pleased him, and she received kindness from him. He speedily gave her ointments, and her portions, and the seven maidens chosen to be given to her from the king's house. And he moved her and her maidens into the best place of the house of the women. [10]Esther had not revealed her people or her kindred, for Mordecai had told her not to reveal it.

[11]And Mordecai walked every day in front of the court of the women's house, to inquire after Esther's welfare and how she was faring.

[12]Now when the turn of each maiden came to visit King Ahasuerus, after a prescribed twelve month period of preparation (the days of their purification were accomplished through six months with oil of myrrh, and six months with spices and other ointments for the women), [13]then every maiden came to the king in this fashion: she was allowed to take with her whatever she requested, when she went from the house of the women into the king's house. [14]In the evening she went in, and in the morning she returned

"...beautiful young virgins...for the king..." 2:2

עוֹד֙ אֶל־הַמֶּ֔לֶךְ כִּ֣י אִם־חָפֵ֥ץ בָּ֖הּ הַמֶּ֑לֶךְ וְנִקְרְאָ֥ה
בְשֵֽׁם: ^{טו} וּבְהַגִּ֣יעַ תֹּר־אֶסְתֵּ֣ר בַּת־אֲבִיחַ֣יִל ׀ דֹּ֣ד
מׇרְדֳּכַ֡י אֲשֶׁר֩ לָֽקַח־ל֨וֹ לְבַ֜ת לָב֣וֹא אֶל־הַמֶּ֗לֶךְ לֹ֤א
בִקְשָׁה֙ דָּבָ֔ר כִּ֣י אִ֔ם אֶת־אֲשֶׁ֥ר יֹאמַ֛ר הֵגַ֥י סְרִיס־
הַמֶּ֖לֶךְ שֹׁמֵ֣ר הַנָּשִׁ֑ים וַתְּהִ֤י אֶסְתֵּר֙ נֹשֵׂ֣את חֵ֔ן בְּעֵינֵ֖י
כׇּל־רֹאֶֽיהָ:
^{טז} וַתִּלָּקַ֨ח אֶסְתֵּ֜ר אֶל־הַמֶּ֤לֶךְ אֲחַשְׁוֵרוֹשׁ֙ אֶל־בֵּ֣ית
מַלְכוּת֔וֹ בַּחֹ֧דֶשׁ הָעֲשִׂירִ֛י הוּא־חֹ֥דֶשׁ טֵבֵ֖ת בִּשְׁנַת־
שֶׁ֥בַע לְמַלְכוּתֽוֹ: ^{יז} וַיֶּאֱהַ֨ב הַמֶּ֤לֶךְ אֶת־אֶסְתֵּר֙ מִכׇּל־
הַנָּשִׁ֔ים וַתִּשָּׂא־חֵ֥ן וָחֶ֛סֶד לְפָנָ֖יו מִכׇּל־הַבְּתוּלֹ֑ת
וַיָּ֤שֶׂם כֶּֽתֶר־מַלְכוּת֙ בְּרֹאשָׁ֔הּ וַיַּמְלִיכֶ֖הָ תַּ֥חַת
וַשְׁתִּֽי: ^{יח} וַיַּ֨עַשׂ הַמֶּ֜לֶךְ מִשְׁתֶּ֣ה גָד֗וֹל לְכׇל־שָׂרָיו֙
וַעֲבָדָ֔יו אֵ֖ת מִשְׁתֵּ֣ה אֶסְתֵּ֑ר וַהֲנָחָ֤ה לַמְּדִינוֹת֙ עָשָׂ֔ה
וַיִּתֵּ֥ן מַשְׂאֵ֖ת כְּיַ֥ד הַמֶּֽלֶךְ:
^{יט} וּבְהִקָּבֵ֥ץ בְּתוּל֖וֹת שֵׁנִ֑ית וּמׇרְדֳּכַ֖י יֹשֵׁ֥ב בְּשַֽׁעַר־
הַמֶּֽלֶךְ: ^כ אֵ֣ין אֶסְתֵּ֗ר מַגֶּ֤דֶת מֽוֹלַדְתָּהּ֙ וְאֶת־עַמָּ֔הּ
כַּאֲשֶׁ֛ר צִוָּ֥ה עָלֶ֖יהָ מׇרְדֳּכָ֑י וְאֶת־מַאֲמַ֤ר מׇרְדֳּכַי֙
אֶסְתֵּ֣ר עֹשָׂ֔ה כַּאֲשֶׁ֛ר הָיְתָ֥ה בְאׇמְנָ֖ה אִתּֽוֹ:
^{כא} בַּיָּמִ֣ים הָהֵ֔ם וּמׇרְדֳּכַ֖י יוֹשֵׁ֣ב בְּשַֽׁעַר־הַמֶּ֑לֶךְ קָצַ֩ף֩
בִּגְתָ֨ן וָתֶ֜רֶשׁ שְׁנֵֽי־סָרִיסֵ֤י הַמֶּ֙לֶךְ֙ מִשֹּׁמְרֵ֣י הַסַּ֔ף
וַיְבַקְשׁוּ֙ לִשְׁלֹ֣חַ יָ֔ד בַּמֶּ֖לֶךְ אֲחַשְׁוֵרֹֽשׁ: ^{כב} וַיִּוָּדַ֤ע

to the second home of the women, to the custody of
Shaasgaz, the king's eunuch, who kept the concubines.
She did not again visit the king, unless the king
delighted in her, and she was summoned by name.
¹⁵When the turn came for Esther, the daughter of
Abihail the uncle of Mordecai, who had adopted her
as his daughter, to go to the king, she asked for
nothing but what Hegai, the king's eunuch, the keeper
of women, advised. And Esther obtained favor in the
eyes of all who looked upon her.
¹⁶Esther was taken to King Ahasuerus into his royal
house in the tenth month, which is the month of
Tebeth, in the seventh year of his reign. ¹⁷And the king
loved Esther above all other women, and she won
more grace and favor with him than all the virgins, so
that he set the royal crown upon her head and made
her queen instead of Vashti. ¹⁸Then the king gave a
great banquet for all his nobles and his servants,
"Esther's banquet." And he granted a remission of
taxes to the provinces, and he gave gifts as befits a
king.
¹⁹Now when the virgins were gathered together a
second time, Mordecai was sitting in the gate of the
king. ²⁰Esther had not yet made known her kindred and
her people, as Mordecai had instructed her. For Esther
carried out Mordecai's command just as when she was
raised by him.
²¹In those days, while Mordecai sat in the king's gate,
two of the king's eunuchs, Bigthan and Teresh who
guarded the door, became disaffected and tried to lay
hands on King Ahasuerus. ²²But the plot became known

Mordecai   2:5

הַדָּבָר֙ לְמָרְדֳּכַ֔י וַיַּגֵּ֖ד לְאֶסְתֵּ֣ר הַמַּלְכָּ֑ה וַתֹּ֧אמֶר
אֶסְתֵּ֛ר לַמֶּ֖לֶךְ בְּשֵׁ֥ם מָרְדֳּכָֽי: כ֩ וַיְבֻקַּ֨שׁ הַדָּבָ֜ר
וַיִּמָּצֵ֗א וַיִּתָּל֤וּ שְׁנֵיהֶם֙ עַל־עֵ֔ץ וַיִּכָּתֵ֗ב בְּסֵ֛פֶר דִּבְרֵ֥י
הַיָּמִ֖ים לִפְנֵ֥י הַמֶּֽלֶךְ:

ג ×א אַחַ֣ר ׀ הַדְּבָרִ֣ים הָאֵ֗לֶּה גִּדַּל֩ הַמֶּ֨לֶךְ אֲחַשְׁוֵר֜וֹשׁ
אֶת־הָמָ֧ן בֶּֽן־הַמְּדָ֛תָא הָאֲגָגִ֖י וַֽיְנַשְּׂאֵ֑הוּ וַיָּ֙שֶׂם֙ אֶת־
כִּסְא֔וֹ מֵעַ֕ל כָּל־הַשָּׂרִ֖ים אֲשֶׁ֥ר אִתּֽוֹ: ב וְכָל־עַבְדֵ֨י
הַמֶּ֜לֶךְ אֲשֶׁר־בְּשַׁ֣עַר הַמֶּ֗לֶךְ כֹּֽרְעִ֤ים וּמִֽשְׁתַּחֲוִים֙
לְהָמָ֔ן כִּי־כֵ֖ן צִוָּה־ל֣וֹ הַמֶּ֑לֶךְ וּמָ֨רְדֳּכַ֔י לֹ֥א יִכְרַ֖ע
וְלֹ֥א יִֽשְׁתַּחֲוֶֽה: ג וַיֹּ֨אמְר֜וּ עַבְדֵ֤י הַמֶּ֙לֶךְ֙ אֲשֶׁר־
בְּשַׁ֣עַר הַמֶּ֔לֶךְ לְמָרְדֳּכָ֑י מַדּ֙וּעַ֙ אַתָּ֣ה עוֹבֵ֔ר אֵ֖ת
מִצְוַ֥ת הַמֶּֽלֶךְ: ד וַיְהִ֗י כְּאָמְרָ֤ם* אֵלָיו֙ י֣וֹם וָי֔וֹם וְלֹ֥א
שָׁמַ֖ע אֲלֵיהֶ֑ם וַיַּגִּ֣ידוּ לְהָמָ֗ן לִרְאוֹת֙ הֲיַֽעַמְדוּ֙ דִּבְרֵ֣י
מָרְדֳּכַ֔י כִּֽי־הִגִּ֥יד לָהֶ֖ם אֲשֶׁר־ה֥וּא יְהוּדִֽי: ה וַיַּ֣רְא
הָמָ֗ן כִּי־אֵ֤ין מָרְדֳּכַי֙ כֹּרֵ֣עַ וּמִֽשְׁתַּחֲוֶ֣ה ל֔וֹ וַיִּמָּלֵ֥א
הָמָ֖ן חֵמָֽה: ו וַיִּ֣בֶז בְּעֵינָ֗יו לִשְׁלֹ֤חַ יָד֙ בְּמָרְדֳּכַ֣י לְבַדּ֔וֹ
כִּֽי־הִגִּ֥ידוּ ל֖וֹ אֶת־עַ֣ם מָרְדֳּכָ֑י וַיְבַקֵּ֣שׁ הָמָ֗ן
לְהַשְׁמִ֧יד אֶת־כָּל־הַיְּהוּדִ֛ים אֲשֶׁ֛ר בְּכָל־מַלְכ֥וּת
אֲחַשְׁוֵר֖וֹשׁ עַ֥ם מָרְדֳּכָֽי:
ז בַּחֹ֤דֶשׁ הָֽרִאשׁוֹן֙ הוּא־חֹ֣דֶשׁ נִיסָ֔ן בִּשְׁנַת֙ שְׁתֵּ֣ים
עֶשְׂרֵ֔ה לַמֶּ֖לֶךְ אֲחַשְׁוֵר֑וֹשׁ הִפִּ֣יל פּוּר֩ ה֨וּא הַגּוֹרָ֜ל
לִפְנֵ֣י הָמָ֗ן מִיּ֧וֹם ׀ לְי֛וֹם וּמֵחֹ֛דֶשׁ לְחֹ֥דֶשׁ שְׁנֵים־
עָשָׂ֖ר הוּא־חֹ֥דֶשׁ אֲדָֽר: ח וַיֹּ֤אמֶר הָמָן֙ לַמֶּ֣לֶךְ

(באמרם כתיב)

to Mordecai, who revealed it to Queen Esther; and Esther told the king in Mordecai's name. [23]The matter was investigated, and it was found to be true. They were both hanged on a tree; and it was written in the book of the chronicles in the presence of the king.

3 [1]After these things, Ahasuerus promoted Haman the son of Hammedatha the Agagite, and elevated him, and set his seat above all the nobles that were with him. [2]And all the king's servants in the king's gate bowed and prostrated themselves before Haman; for the king had so commanded concerning him. [3]But Mordecai would not bow down nor prostrate himself. Then the king's servants in the king's gate said to Mordecai: "Why do you transgress the king's command?" [4]Now, when they spoke to him daily and he did not listen to them, they told Haman, to see whether Mordecai's conduct would prevail; for he had told them that he was a Jew. [5]When Haman saw that Mordecai would not bow down or prostrate himself, Haman was filled with rage. [6]But he disdained to lay hands on Mordecai alone, for they had told him of Mordecai's people. So Haman sought to exterminate all the Jews throughout the whole kingdom of Ahasuerus, Mordecai and all his people.

[7]In the first month, that is, the month of Nisan, in the twelfth year of King Ahasuerus, they cast *pur*—which means 'the lot'—before Haman from day to day and from month to month, to the twelfth month, the month Adar. [8]Then Haman said to King Ahasuerus:

Haman   3:1

אֲחַשְׁוֵרוֹשׁ יֶשְׁנוֹ עַם־אֶחָד מְפֻזָּר וּמְפֹרָד בֵּין
הָעַמִּים בְּכֹל מְדִינוֹת מַלְכוּתֶךָ וְדָתֵיהֶם שֹׁנוֹת
מִכָּל־עָם וְאֶת־דָּתֵי הַמֶּלֶךְ אֵינָם עֹשִׂים וְלַמֶּלֶךְ
אֵין־שׁוֶֹה לְהַנִּיחָם: ט אִם־עַל־הַמֶּלֶךְ טוֹב יִכָּתֵב
לְאַבְּדָם וַעֲשֶׂרֶת אֲלָפִים כִּכַּר־כֶּסֶף אֶשְׁקוֹל עַל־
יְדֵי עֹשֵׂי הַמְּלָאכָה לְהָבִיא אֶל־גִּנְזֵי הַמֶּלֶךְ: י וַיָּסַר
הַמֶּלֶךְ אֶת־טַבַּעְתּוֹ מֵעַל יָדוֹ וַיִּתְּנָהּ לְהָמָן בֶּן־
הַמְּדָתָא הָאֲגָגִי צֹרֵר הַיְּהוּדִים: יא וַיֹּאמֶר הַמֶּלֶךְ
לְהָמָן הַכֶּסֶף נָתוּן לָךְ וְהָעָם לַעֲשׂוֹת בּוֹ כַּטּוֹב
בְּעֵינֶיךָ:
יב וַיִּקָּרְאוּ סֹפְרֵי הַמֶּלֶךְ בַּחֹדֶשׁ הָרִאשׁוֹן בִּשְׁלוֹשָׁה
עָשָׂר יוֹם בּוֹ וַיִּכָּתֵב כְּכָל־אֲשֶׁר־צִוָּה הָמָן אֶל
אֲחַשְׁדַּרְפְּנֵי־הַמֶּלֶךְ וְאֶל־הַפַּחוֹת אֲשֶׁר | עַל־
מְדִינָה וּמְדִינָה וְאֶל־שָׂרֵי עַם וָעָם מְדִינָה וּמְדִינָה
כִּכְתָבָהּ וְעַם וָעָם כִּלְשׁוֹנוֹ בְּשֵׁם הַמֶּלֶךְ אֲחַשְׁוֵרֹשׁ
נִכְתָּב וְנֶחְתָּם בְּטַבַּעַת הַמֶּלֶךְ: יג וְנִשְׁלוֹחַ סְפָרִים
בְּיַד הָרָצִים אֶל־כָּל־מְדִינוֹת הַמֶּלֶךְ לְהַשְׁמִיד
לַהֲרֹג וּלְאַבֵּד אֶת־כָּל־הַיְּהוּדִים מִנַּעַר וְעַד־זָקֵן
טַף וְנָשִׁים בְּיוֹם אֶחָד בִּשְׁלוֹשָׁה עָשָׂר לְחֹדֶשׁ
שְׁנֵים־עָשָׂר הוּא־חֹדֶשׁ אֲדָר וּשְׁלָלָם לָבוֹז:
יד פַּתְשֶׁגֶן הַכְּתָב לְהִנָּתֵן דָּת בְּכָל־מְדִינָה וּמְדִינָה
גָּלוּי לְכָל־הָעַמִּים לִהְיוֹת עֲתִדִים לַיּוֹם הַזֶּה:
טו הָרָצִים יָצְאוּ דְחוּפִים בִּדְבַר הַמֶּלֶךְ וְהַדָּת נִתְּנָה

"There is a certain people scattered abroad and dispersed among the people in all the provinces of your kingdom; and their laws are different from every other people, nor do they keep the king's law: therefore, it is not in the king's interest to tolerate them. [9]If it please the king, let it be written that they may be destroyed; and I will pay ten thousand talents of silver into the hands of those in charge of the business, to bring it into the king's treasuries." [10]Then the king took the ring from his hand, and gave it to Haman the son of Hammedatha the Agagite, the Jews' enemy. [11]The king then said to Haman: "The silver is yours, and the people as well, to do with them as it pleases you."

[12]Then the king's scribes were called, on the thirteenth day of the first month, and a decree was written, just as Haman had commanded, to the king's satraps, and to the governors who were over every province, and to the nobles of every people of every province according to its writing, and to every people according to their language. It was written in the name of King Ahasuerus, and was sealed with the king's ring. [13]The letters were sent by couriers to all the king's provinces to destroy, to kill, and to exterminate all the Jews, both young and old, little children and women, in one day—the thirteenth day of the twelfth month, the month Adar—and to plunder their possessions. [14]A copy of the writings to be given out as a decree in every province was published to all the people, so that they should be ready for that day. [15]The couriers went out in haste at the king's command,

"Mordecai...put on sackcloth and ashes." 4:1

בְּשׁוּשַׁן הַבִּירָה וְהַמֶּלֶךְ וְהָמָן יָשְׁבוּ לִשְׁתּוֹת
וְהָעִיר שׁוּשָׁן נָבוֹכָה:
ד א וּמָרְדֳּכַי יָדַע אֶת־כָּל־אֲשֶׁר נַעֲשָׂה וַיִּקְרַע מָרְדֳּכַי
אֶת־בְּגָדָיו וַיִּלְבַּשׁ שַׂק וָאֵפֶר וַיֵּצֵא בְּתוֹךְ הָעִיר
וַיִּזְעַק זְעָקָה גְדוֹלָה וּמָרָה: ב וַיָּבוֹא עַד לִפְנֵי שַׁעַר־
הַמֶּלֶךְ כִּי אֵין לָבוֹא אֶל־שַׁעַר הַמֶּלֶךְ בִּלְבוּשׁ שָׂק:
ג וּבְכָל־מְדִינָה וּמְדִינָה מְקוֹם אֲשֶׁר דְּבַר־הַמֶּלֶךְ
וְדָתוֹ מַגִּיעַ אֵבֶל גָּדוֹל לַיְּהוּדִים וְצוֹם וּבְכִי
וּמִסְפֵּד שַׂק וָאֵפֶר יֻצַּע לָרַבִּים: ד וַתָּבוֹאנָה*
נַעֲרוֹת אֶסְתֵּר וְסָרִיסֶיהָ וַיַּגִּידוּ לָהּ וַתִּתְחַלְחַל
הַמַּלְכָּה מְאֹד וַתִּשְׁלַח בְּגָדִים לְהַלְבִּישׁ אֶת־
מָרְדֳּכַי וּלְהָסִיר שַׂקּוֹ מֵעָלָיו וְלֹא קִבֵּל:
ה וַתִּקְרָא אֶסְתֵּר לַהֲתָךְ מִסָּרִיסֵי הַמֶּלֶךְ אֲשֶׁר
הֶעֱמִיד לְפָנֶיהָ וַתְּצַוֵּהוּ עַל־מָרְדֳּכָי לָדַעַת מַה־זֶּה
וְעַל־מַה־זֶּה: ו וַיֵּצֵא הֲתָךְ אֶל־מָרְדֳּכָי אֶל־רְחוֹב
הָעִיר אֲשֶׁר לִפְנֵי שַׁעַר־הַמֶּלֶךְ: ז וַיַּגֶּד־לוֹ מָרְדֳּכַי
אֵת כָּל־אֲשֶׁר קָרָהוּ וְאֵת ׀ פָּרָשַׁת הַכֶּסֶף אֲשֶׁר
אָמַר הָמָן לִשְׁקוֹל עַל־גִּנְזֵי הַמֶּלֶךְ בַּיְּהוּדִים*
לְאַבְּדָם: ח וְאֶת־פַּתְשֶׁגֶן כְּתָב־הַדָּת אֲשֶׁר־נִתַּן
בְּשׁוּשָׁן לְהַשְׁמִידָם נָתַן לוֹ לְהַרְאוֹת אֶת־אֶסְתֵּר
וּלְהַגִּיד לָהּ וּלְצַוּוֹת עָלֶיהָ לָבוֹא אֶל־הַמֶּלֶךְ
לְהִתְחַנֶּן־לוֹ וּלְבַקֵּשׁ מִלְּפָנָיו עַל־עַמָּהּ: ט וַיָּבוֹא
הֲתָךְ וַיַּגֵּד לְאֶסְתֵּר אֵת דִּבְרֵי מָרְדֳּכָי: י וַתֹּאמֶר

(וַתְּבוֹאֶינָה כְּתִיב)   (בַּיְּהוּדִיִּים כְּתִיב)

and the decree was given in Shushan the capital. Then
the king and Haman sat down to drink; but the city of
Shushan was perplexed.

4 ¹When Mordecai learned all that had happened,
Mordecai rent his clothes and put on sackcloth and
ashes. He went out into the midst of the city, and
cried out with a loud and bitter cry. ²He came within
sight of the king's gate; for no one could enter the
king's gate clothed with sackcloth. ³And in every
province, wherever the king's command and decree
came, there was great mourning among the Jews, and
fasting, and weeping, and wailing; and many lay in
sackcloth and ashes. ⁴When Esther's maidens and
eunuchs came and told her, the queen was exceedingly
distressed. And she sent garments to clothe Mordecai
so that he could take off his sackcloth; but he would
not accept them.

⁵Then Esther called for Hatach, one of the eunuchs
whom the king had appointed to serve her, and gave
him a message for Mordecai, to learn what this was,
and why it was. ⁶Hatach went out to Mordecai, to the
city square in front of the king's gate; ⁷And Mordecai
told him of all that happened to him, and of the sum
of money that Haman had promised to pay to the
king's treasuries for the destruction of the Jews. ⁸Also,
he gave him a copy of the writing of the decree that
was given at Shushan to destroy them to show to
Esther and to let her know, and to charge her to go in
to the king, to make supplication to him and to entreat
him for her people. ⁹And Hatach came and told Esther
Mordecai's words. ¹⁰Esther spoke to Hatach again, and

אֶסְתֵּר לַהֲתָךְ וַתְּצַוֵּהוּ אֶל־מָרְדֳּכָי: יֹא כָּל־עַבְדֵי
הַמֶּלֶךְ וְעַם מְדִינוֹת הַמֶּלֶךְ יֹדְעִים אֲשֶׁר כָּל־אִישׁ
וְאִשָּׁה אֲשֶׁר־יָבוֹא אֶל־הַמֶּלֶךְ אֶל־הֶחָצֵר
הַפְּנִימִית אֲשֶׁר לֹא־יִקָּרֵא אַחַת דָּתוֹ לְהָמִית לְבַד
מֵאֲשֶׁר יוֹשִׁיט־לוֹ הַמֶּלֶךְ אֶת־שַׁרְבִיט הַזָּהָב וְחָיָה
וַאֲנִי לֹא נִקְרֵאתִי לָבוֹא אֶל־הַמֶּלֶךְ זֶה שְׁלוֹשִׁים
יוֹם:
יֹב וַיַּגִּידוּ לְמָרְדֳּכָי אֵת דִּבְרֵי אֶסְתֵּר: יֹג וַיֹּאמֶר
מָרְדֳּכַי לְהָשִׁיב אֶל־אֶסְתֵּר אַל־תְּדַמִּי בְנַפְשֵׁךְ
לְהִמָּלֵט בֵּית־הַמֶּלֶךְ מִכָּל־הַיְּהוּדִים: יֹד כִּי אִם־
הַחֲרֵשׁ תַּחֲרִישִׁי בָּעֵת הַזֹּאת רֶוַח וְהַצָּלָה יַעֲמוֹד
לַיְּהוּדִים מִמָּקוֹם אַחֵר וְאַתְּ וּבֵית־אָבִיךְ תֹּאבֵדוּ
וּמִי יוֹדֵעַ אִם־לְעֵת כָּזֹאת הִגַּעַתְּ לַמַּלְכוּת:
יֹה וַתֹּאמֶר אֶסְתֵּר לְהָשִׁיב אֶל־מָרְדֳּכָי: יֹו לֵךְ כְּנוֹס
אֶת־כָּל־הַיְּהוּדִים הַנִּמְצְאִים בְּשׁוּשָׁן וְצוּמוּ עָלַי
וְאַל־תֹּאכְלוּ וְאַל־תִּשְׁתּוּ שְׁלֹשֶׁת יָמִים לַיְלָה וָיוֹם
גַּם־אֲנִי וְנַעֲרֹתַי אָצוּם כֵּן וּבְכֵן אָבוֹא אֶל־הַמֶּלֶךְ
אֲשֶׁר לֹא־כַדָּת וְכַאֲשֶׁר אָבַדְתִּי אָבָדְתִּי: יֹז וַיַּעֲבֹר
מָרְדֳּכָי וַיַּעַשׂ כְּכֹל אֲשֶׁר־צִוְּתָה עָלָיו אֶסְתֵּר:
ה א וַיְהִי | בַּיּוֹם הַשְּׁלִישִׁי וַתִּלְבַּשׁ אֶסְתֵּר מַלְכוּת
וַתַּעֲמֹד בַּחֲצַר בֵּית־הַמֶּלֶךְ הַפְּנִימִית נֹכַח בֵּית
הַמֶּלֶךְ וְהַמֶּלֶךְ יוֹשֵׁב עַל־כִּסֵּא מַלְכוּתוֹ בְּבֵית
הַמַּלְכוּת נֹכַח פֶּתַח הַבָּיִת: ב וַיְהִי כִרְאוֹת הַמֶּלֶךְ
אֶת־אֶסְתֵּר הַמַּלְכָּה עֹמֶדֶת בֶּחָצֵר נָשְׂאָה חֵן

gave him a message for Mordecai: [11]"All the king's
servants and the people of the king's provinces know
that whoever, man or woman, comes to the king into
the inner court and is not summoned, there is one law
for him, namely to put him to death, except those to
whom the king shall hold out the golden sceptre that
he may live; but I have not been called to come in to
the king these thirty days."

[12]And they told Esther's words to Mordecai. [13]Then
Mordecai commanded them to answer Esther: "Do
not think in your heart that you, of all the Jews, will
escape because you are in the king's house. [14]For if you
remain completely silent at this time, relief and
deliverance will come to the Jews from another place;
but you and your father's house will be destroyed—
and who knows whether you have not come into
royal estate for such a time as this?" [15]Then Esther bade
them return this answer to Mordecai: [16]"Go, and gather
together all the Jews that are in Shushan, and fast for
me. Do not eat or drink for three days, night or day. I
and my maidens will also fast. Then I will go in to the
king, though it is against the law. And if I perish, I
perish." [17]So Mordecai went his way, and did just as
Esther had commanded him.

5   [1]And it came to pass on the third day that Esther put
on her royal apparel, and stood in the inner court of
the king's house facing the king's house, while the
king sat upon his royal throne in the royal house,
facing the entrance of the king's house. [2]And when the
king saw Esther the queen standing in the court, she
obtained favor in his sight; and the king held out to

"So the king and Haman came to the banquet..." 5:5

בְּעֵינָיו וַיּוֹשֶׁט הַמֶּלֶךְ לְאֶסְתֵּר אֶת־שַׁרְבִיט הַזָּהָב
אֲשֶׁר בְּיָדוֹ וַתִּקְרַב אֶסְתֵּר וַתִּגַּע בְּרֹאשׁ הַשַּׁרְבִיט:
ג וַיֹּאמֶר לָהּ הַמֶּלֶךְ מַה־לָּךְ אֶסְתֵּר הַמַּלְכָּה וּמַה־
בַּקָּשָׁתֵךְ עַד־חֲצִי הַמַּלְכוּת וְיִנָּתֵן לָךְ: ד וַתֹּאמֶר
אֶסְתֵּר אִם־עַל־הַמֶּלֶךְ טוֹב יָבוֹא הַמֶּלֶךְ וְהָמָן
הַיּוֹם אֶל־הַמִּשְׁתֶּה אֲשֶׁר־עָשִׂיתִי לוֹ: ה וַיֹּאמֶר
הַמֶּלֶךְ מַהֲרוּ אֶת־הָמָן לַעֲשׂוֹת אֶת־דְּבַר אֶסְתֵּר
וַיָּבֹא הַמֶּלֶךְ וְהָמָן אֶל־הַמִּשְׁתֶּה אֲשֶׁר־עָשְׂתָה
אֶסְתֵּר:
ו וַיֹּאמֶר הַמֶּלֶךְ לְאֶסְתֵּר בְּמִשְׁתֵּה הַיַּיִן מַה־
שְּׁאֵלָתֵךְ וְיִנָּתֵן לָךְ וּמַה־בַּקָּשָׁתֵךְ עַד־חֲצִי
הַמַּלְכוּת וְתֵעָשׂ: ז וַתַּעַן אֶסְתֵּר וַתֹּאמַר שְׁאֵלָתִי
וּבַקָּשָׁתִי: ח אִם־מָצָאתִי חֵן בְּעֵינֵי הַמֶּלֶךְ וְאִם־עַל־
הַמֶּלֶךְ טוֹב לָתֵת אֶת־שְׁאֵלָתִי וְלַעֲשׂוֹת אֶת־
בַּקָּשָׁתִי יָבוֹא הַמֶּלֶךְ וְהָמָן אֶל־הַמִּשְׁתֶּה אֲשֶׁר
אֶעֱשֶׂה לָהֶם וּמָחָר אֶעֱשֶׂה כִּדְבַר הַמֶּלֶךְ:
ט וַיֵּצֵא הָמָן בַּיּוֹם הַהוּא שָׂמֵחַ וְטוֹב לֵב וְכִרְאוֹת
הָמָן אֶת־מָרְדֳּכַי בְּשַׁעַר הַמֶּלֶךְ וְלֹא־קָם וְלֹא־זָע
מִמֶּנּוּ וַיִּמָּלֵא הָמָן עַל־מָרְדֳּכַי חֵמָה: י וַיִּתְאַפַּק
הָמָן וַיָּבוֹא אֶל־בֵּיתוֹ וַיִּשְׁלַח וַיָּבֵא אֶת־אֹהֲבָיו
וְאֶת־זֶרֶשׁ אִשְׁתּוֹ: יא וַיְסַפֵּר לָהֶם הָמָן אֶת־כְּבוֹד
עָשְׁרוֹ וְרֹב בָּנָיו וְאֵת כָּל־אֲשֶׁר גִּדְּלוֹ הַמֶּלֶךְ וְאֵת
אֲשֶׁר נִשְּׂאוֹ עַל־הַשָּׂרִים וְעַבְדֵי הַמֶּלֶךְ: יב וַיֹּאמֶר

Esther the golden sceptre that was in his hand. So
Esther drew near and touched the top of the sceptre.
³Then the king said to her, "What is your petition
Queen Esther, and what is your request? Even if it is
half the kingdom, it will be given to you." ⁴And
Esther answered: "If it please the king, let the king
and Haman come today to the banquet which I have
prepared for him." ⁵Then the king said: "Tell Haman
to hurry to do as Esther has said." So the king and
Haman came to the banquet which Esther had
prepared.

⁶And the king said to Esther during the banquet of
wine: "What is your petition, Queen Esther? What is
your request? Even if it is half the kingdom, it will be
done." ⁷Then Esther answered and said: "My petition
and my request is: ⁸If I have obtained favor in the sight
of the king, and if it please the king to grant my
petition, and to fulfill my request, let the king and
Haman come to the banquet which I shall prepare for
them, and I will do tomorrow as the king has said."
⁹Haman went out that day joyful and with a glad
heart. But when Haman saw Mordecai in the king's
gate, and he did not stand up or even move for him,
he was filled with rage against Mordecai. ¹⁰Never-
theless, Haman restrained himself. And when he came
home he sent and called for his friends, and for Zeresh
his wife. ¹¹And Haman told them about the splendor of
his wealth and about his many children, and all about
how the king had promoted him, and how he had
advanced him above the nobles and servants of the
king. ¹²And Haman said: "Even Esther the Queen let

הָמָן אַף לֹא־הֵבִיאָה אֶסְתֵּר הַמַּלְכָּה עִם־הַמֶּלֶךְ
אֶל־הַמִּשְׁתֶּה אֲשֶׁר־עָשָׂתָה כִּי אִם־אוֹתִי וְגַם־
לְמָחָר אֲנִי קָרוּא־לָהּ עִם־הַמֶּלֶךְ: "וְכָל־זֶה אֵינֶנּוּ
שֹׁוֶה לִי בְּכָל־עֵת אֲשֶׁר אֲנִי רֹאֶה אֶת־מָרְדֳּכַי
הַיְּהוּדִי יוֹשֵׁב בְּשַׁעַר הַמֶּלֶךְ: "וַתֹּאמֶר לוֹ זֶרֶשׁ
אִשְׁתּוֹ וְכָל־אֹהֲבָיו יַעֲשׂוּ־עֵץ גָּבֹהַּ חֲמִשִּׁים אַמָּה
וּבַבֹּקֶר ׀ אֱמֹר לַמֶּלֶךְ וְיִתְלוּ אֶת־מָרְדֳּכַי עָלָיו וּבֹא
עִם־הַמֶּלֶךְ אֶל־הַמִּשְׁתֶּה שָׂמֵחַ וַיִּיטַב הַדָּבָר לִפְנֵי
הָמָן וַיַּעַשׂ הָעֵץ:

ו א בַּלַּיְלָה הַהוּא נָדְדָה שְׁנַת הַמֶּלֶךְ וַיֹּאמֶר לְהָבִיא
אֶת־סֵפֶר הַזִּכְרֹנוֹת דִּבְרֵי הַיָּמִים וַיִּהְיוּ נִקְרָאִים
לִפְנֵי הַמֶּלֶךְ: "וַיִּמָּצֵא כָתוּב אֲשֶׁר הִגִּיד מָרְדֳּכַי
עַל־בִּגְתָנָא וָתֶרֶשׁ שְׁנֵי סָרִיסֵי הַמֶּלֶךְ מִשֹּׁמְרֵי
הַסַּף אֲשֶׁר בִּקְשׁוּ לִשְׁלֹחַ יָד בַּמֶּלֶךְ אֲחַשְׁוֵרוֹשׁ:
"וַיֹּאמֶר הַמֶּלֶךְ מַה־נַּעֲשָׂה יְקָר וּגְדוּלָּה לְמָרְדֳּכַי
עַל־זֶה וַיֹּאמְרוּ נַעֲרֵי הַמֶּלֶךְ מְשָׁרְתָיו לֹא־נַעֲשָׂה
עִמּוֹ דָּבָר: "וַיֹּאמֶר הַמֶּלֶךְ מִי בֶחָצֵר וְהָמָן בָּא
לַחֲצַר בֵּית־הַמֶּלֶךְ הַחִיצוֹנָה לֵאמֹר לַמֶּלֶךְ
לִתְלוֹת אֶת־מָרְדֳּכַי עַל־הָעֵץ אֲשֶׁר־הֵכִין לוֹ:
"וַיֹּאמְרוּ נַעֲרֵי הַמֶּלֶךְ אֵלָיו הִנֵּה הָמָן עֹמֵד בֶּחָצֵר
וַיֹּאמֶר הַמֶּלֶךְ יָבוֹא: "וַיָּבוֹא הָמָן וַיֹּאמֶר לוֹ הַמֶּלֶךְ
מַה־לַעֲשׂוֹת בָּאִישׁ אֲשֶׁר הַמֶּלֶךְ חָפֵץ בִּיקָרוֹ
וַיֹּאמֶר הָמָן בְּלִבּוֹ לְמִי יַחְפֹּץ הַמֶּלֶךְ לַעֲשׂוֹת יְקָר
יוֹתֵר מִמֶּנִּי: "וַיֹּאמֶר הָמָן אֶל־הַמֶּלֶךְ אִישׁ אֲשֶׁר
הַמֶּלֶךְ חָפֵץ בִּיקָרוֹ: "יָבִיאוּ לְבוּשׁ מַלְכוּת אֲשֶׁר

no one come in with the king to the banquet that she had prepared except me. And tomorrow I am again invited by her together with the king. ¹³But all this means nothing to me as long as I see Mordecai the Jew sitting at the king's gate." ¹⁴Then Zeresh his wife and all his friends said to him: "Let a gallows be made, fifty cubits high, and speak to the king tomorrow that Mordecai can be hanged. Then go merrily with the king to the banquet." The proposal pleased Haman; and he caused the gallows to be made.

6 ¹That night, sleep fled from the king, and he commanded to bring the book of records of the chronicles; and they were read before the king. ²And it was found written that Mordecai had told of Bigthana and Teresh, two of the king's eunuchs, keepers of the door, who had tried to lay hands on King Ahasuerus. ³And the king said: "What honor and dignity has been bestowed upon Mordecai for this?" Then said the king's servants who ministered to him: "Nothing has been done for him." ⁴And the king said: "Who is in the court?" Now Haman had entered the outer court of the king's house, to speak to the king to hang Mordecai on the gallows which he had prepared for him. ⁵So the king's servants said to him: "Behold, Haman is standing in the court." "Let him enter," said the king. ⁶So Haman came in. And the king said to him: "What shall be done to the man whom the king delights to honor?" Now Haman thought in his heart: "Whom would the king delight to honor more than myself?" ⁷And Haman answered the king: "For the man whom the king delights to honor— ⁸let royal

"If Mordecai...is of Jewish seed..."   6:13

לָבַשׁ־בּוֹ הַמֶּלֶךְ וְסוּס אֲשֶׁר רָכַב עָלָיו הַמֶּלֶךְ
וַאֲשֶׁר נִתַּן כֶּתֶר מַלְכוּת בְּרֹאשׁוֹ: ט וְנָתוֹן הַלְּבוּשׁ
וְהַסּוּס עַל־יַד־אִישׁ מִשָּׂרֵי הַמֶּלֶךְ הַפַּרְתְּמִים
וְהִלְבִּשׁוּ אֶת־הָאִישׁ אֲשֶׁר הַמֶּלֶךְ חָפֵץ בִּיקָרְוֹ
וְהִרְכִּיבֻהוּ עַל־הַסּוּס בִּרְחוֹב הָעִיר וְקָרְאוּ לְפָנָיו
כָּכָה יֵעָשֶׂה לָאִישׁ אֲשֶׁר הַמֶּלֶךְ חָפֵץ בִּיקָרוֹ:
י וַיֹּאמֶר הַמֶּלֶךְ לְהָמָן מַהֵר קַח אֶת־הַלְּבוּשׁ וְאֶת־
הַסּוּס כַּאֲשֶׁר דִּבַּרְתָּ וַעֲשֵׂה־כֵן לְמָרְדֳּכַי הַיְּהוּדִי
הַיּוֹשֵׁב בְּשַׁעַר הַמֶּלֶךְ אַל־תַּפֵּל דָּבָר מִכֹּל אֲשֶׁר
דִּבַּרְתָּ: יא וַיִּקַּח הָמָן אֶת־הַלְּבוּשׁ וְאֶת־הַסּוּס
וַיַּלְבֵּשׁ אֶת־מָרְדֳּכָי וַיַּרְכִּיבֵהוּ בִּרְחוֹב הָעִיר
וַיִּקְרָא לְפָנָיו כָּכָה יֵעָשֶׂה לָאִישׁ אֲשֶׁר הַמֶּלֶךְ חָפֵץ
בִּיקָרוֹ:
יב וַיָּשָׁב מָרְדֳּכַי אֶל־שַׁעַר הַמֶּלֶךְ וְהָמָן נִדְחַף אֶל־
בֵּיתוֹ אָבֵל וַחֲפוּי רֹאשׁ: יג וַיְסַפֵּר הָמָן לְזֶרֶשׁ
אִשְׁתּוֹ וּלְכָל־אֹהֲבָיו אֵת כָּל־אֲשֶׁר קָרָהוּ וַיֹּאמְרוּ
לוֹ חֲכָמָיו וְזֶרֶשׁ אִשְׁתּוֹ אִם מִזֶּרַע הַיְּהוּדִים
מָרְדֳּכַי אֲשֶׁר הַחִלּוֹתָ לִנְפֹּל לְפָנָיו לֹא־תוּכַל לוֹ
כִּי־נָפוֹל תִּפּוֹל לְפָנָיו:
יד עוֹדָם מְדַבְּרִים עִמּוֹ וְסָרִיסֵי הַמֶּלֶךְ הִגִּיעוּ
וַיַּבְהִלוּ לְהָבִיא אֶת־הָמָן אֶל־הַמִּשְׁתֶּה אֲשֶׁר־
עָשְׂתָה אֶסְתֵּר:
ז א וַיָּבֹא הַמֶּלֶךְ וְהָמָן לִשְׁתּוֹת עִם־אֶסְתֵּר הַמַּלְכָּה:
ב וַיֹּאמֶר הַמֶּלֶךְ לְאֶסְתֵּר גַּם בַּיּוֹם הַשֵּׁנִי בְּמִשְׁתֵּה
הַיַּיִן מַה־שְּׁאֵלָתֵךְ אֶסְתֵּר הַמַּלְכָּה וְתִנָּתֵן לָךְ

apparel be brought which the king has worn, and a horse which the king has ridden, with a royal crown set upon its head. ⁹And let this garment and horse be delivered to the hand of one of the king's most exalted nobles; and let them clothe the man whom the king delights to honor and bring him on horseback through the square of the city, and proclaim before him: 'Thus shall be done to the man whom the king delights to honor!'" ¹⁰Then the king said to Haman: "Make haste, and take the apparel and the horse, as you have said, and do this to Mordecai the Jew who sits at the king's gate; let nothing fail of all that you have spoken."

¹¹Haman then took the apparel and the horse, and clothed Mordecai, and brought him on horseback through the square of the city, and proclaimed before him: "Thus shall be done to the man whom the king delights to honor!"

¹²Then Mordecai returned to the king's gate, but Haman hastened home, mourning, with his head covered. ¹³When Haman told his wife Zeresh and all his friends everything that had happened to him, his advisers and his wife Zeresh said to him: "If Mordecai, before whom you have begun to fall, is of Jewish seed, you will not prevail against him, but you will surely fall before him."

¹⁴While they were still talking with him, the king's eunuchs came, and hastened to bring Haman to the banquet which Esther had prepared.

7 ¹So the king and Haman came to feast with Queen Esther. ²Again, the king said to Esther on the second day of the banquet of wine: "What is your petition,

Esther 7:3

אמנון

וּמַה־בַּקָּשָׁתֵ֖ךְ עַד־חֲצִ֥י הַמַּלְכ֖וּת וְתֵעָֽשׂ: ³ וַתַּ֨עַן
אֶסְתֵּ֤ר הַמַּלְכָּה֙ וַתֹּאמַ֔ר אִם־מָצָ֨אתִי חֵ֤ן בְּעֵינֶ֨יךָ֙
הַמֶּ֔לֶךְ וְאִם־עַל־הַמֶּ֖לֶךְ ט֑וֹב תִּנָּֽתֶן־לִ֤י נַפְשִׁי֙
בִּשְׁאֵ֣לָתִ֔י וְעַמִּ֖י בְּבַקָּשָׁתִֽי: ⁴ כִּ֤י נִמְכַּ֨רְנוּ֙ אֲנִ֣י וְעַמִּ֔י
לְהַשְׁמִ֖יד לַהֲר֣וֹג וּלְאַבֵּ֑ד וְ֠אִלּוּ לַעֲבָדִ֨ים
וְלִשְׁפָח֤וֹת נִמְכַּ֨רְנוּ֙ הֶחֱרַ֔שְׁתִּי כִּ֣י אֵ֥ין הַצָּ֛ר שֹׁוֶ֖ה
בְּנֵ֥זֶק הַמֶּֽלֶךְ:
⁵ וַיֹּ֨אמֶר֙ הַמֶּ֣לֶךְ אֲחַשְׁוֵר֔וֹשׁ וַיֹּ֖אמֶר לְאֶסְתֵּ֣ר
הַמַּלְכָּ֑ה מִ֣י ה֥וּא זֶה֙ וְאֵֽי־זֶ֣ה ה֔וּא אֲשֶׁר־מְלָא֥וֹ לִבּ֖וֹ
לַעֲשׂ֥וֹת כֵּֽן: ⁶ וַתֹּ֣אמֶר אֶסְתֵּ֔ר אִ֥ישׁ צַ֖ר וְאוֹיֵ֑ב הָמָ֤ן
הָרָ֣ע הַזֶּ֔ה וְהָמָ֣ן נִבְעַ֔ת מִלִּפְנֵ֥י הַמֶּ֖לֶךְ וְהַמַּלְכָּֽה:
⁷ וְהַמֶּ֜לֶךְ קָ֤ם בַּחֲמָתוֹ֙ מִמִּשְׁתֵּ֣ה הַיַּ֔יִן אֶל־גִּנַּ֖ת
הַבִּיתָ֑ן וְהָמָ֣ן עָמַ֗ד לְבַקֵּ֤שׁ עַל־נַפְשׁוֹ֙ מֵֽאֶסְתֵּ֣ר
הַמַּלְכָּ֔ה כִּ֣י רָאָ֔ה כִּֽי־כָלְתָ֥ה אֵלָ֛יו הָרָעָ֖ה מֵאֵ֥ת
הַמֶּֽלֶךְ: ⁸ וְהַמֶּ֣לֶךְ שָׁב֩ מִגִּנַּ֨ת הַבִּיתָ֜ן אֶל־בֵּ֣ית ׀
מִשְׁתֵּ֣ה הַיַּ֗יִן וְהָמָן֙ נֹפֵ֔ל עַל־הַמִּטָּה֙ אֲשֶׁ֣ר אֶסְתֵּ֣ר
עָלֶ֔יהָ וַיֹּ֣אמֶר הַמֶּ֔לֶךְ הֲ֠גַם לִכְבּ֧וֹשׁ אֶת־הַמַּלְכָּ֛ה
עִמִּ֖י בַּבָּ֑יִת הַדָּבָ֗ר יָצָא֙ מִפִּ֣י הַמֶּ֔לֶךְ וּפְנֵ֥י הָמָ֖ן חָפֽוּ:
⁹ וַיֹּ֣אמֶר חַ֠רְבוֹנָ֞ה אֶחָ֨ד מִן־הַסָּרִיסִ֜ים לִפְנֵ֣י הַמֶּ֗לֶךְ
גַּ֣ם הִנֵּה־הָעֵ֣ץ אֲשֶׁר־עָשָׂ֣ה הָמָ֣ן לְֽמָרְדֳּכַ֞י אֲשֶׁ֣ר
דִּבֶּר־ט֣וֹב עַל־הַמֶּ֗לֶךְ עֹמֵד֙ בְּבֵ֣ית הָמָ֔ן גָּבֹ֖הַּ
חֲמִשִּׁ֣ים אַמָּ֑ה וַיֹּ֥אמֶר הַמֶּ֖לֶךְ תְּלֻ֥הוּ עָלָֽיו: ¹⁰ וַיִּתְלוּ֙
אֶת־הָמָ֔ן עַל־הָעֵ֖ץ אֲשֶׁר־הֵכִ֣ין לְמָרְדֳּכָ֑י וַחֲמַ֥ת
הַמֶּ֖לֶךְ שָׁכָֽכָה:

Queen Esther? It will be granted to you. What is your request? Even if it is half the kingdom, it will be done." ³Then Queen Esther answered and said: "If I have found favor in your sight, O King, and if it please the king, let my life be given to me at my petition, and my people at my request. ⁴For we are sold, I and my people, to be exterminated, to be slain, and to perish. Yet, had we only been sold for bondsmen and bondswomen, I would have remained silent, for the adversary would not have been worth disturbing the king."

⁵Then King Ahasuerus answered and said to Queen Esther: "Who is he, and where is he who does presume in his heart to do so?" ⁶And Esther said: "The adversary and enemy is this wicked Haman"; then Haman was afraid before the king and the queen. ⁷And the king arose in his wrath from the banquet of wine and went into the palace garden. Haman stood up to plead for his life from Queen Esther, for he saw that evil was determined against him by the king. ⁸Then the king returned from the palace garden to the house of the wine banquet; and Haman had fallen upon the bed upon which Esther was. The king then said: "Will he violate the queen in my presence here in the house?" As the words left the mouth of the king, they covered Haman's face. ⁹Harbonah, one of the eunuchs, said before the king: "See also, in Haman's house, the gallows fifty feet high which Haman had made for Mordecai who spoke for the good of the king." "Hang him on it," said the king. ¹⁰So they hanged Haman on the gallows which he had prepared for

ח אבַּיּוֹם הַהוּא נָתַן הַמֶּלֶךְ אֲחַשְׁוֵרוֹשׁ לְאֶסְתֵּר
הַמַּלְכָּה אֶת־בֵּית הָמָן צֹרֵר הַיְּהוּדִים* וּמָרְדֳּכַי
בָּא לִפְנֵי הַמֶּלֶךְ כִּי־הִגִּידָה אֶסְתֵּר מָה הוּא־לָהּ:
בוַיָּסַר הַמֶּלֶךְ אֶת־טַבַּעְתּוֹ אֲשֶׁר הֶעֱבִיר מֵהָמָן
וַיִּתְּנָהּ לְמָרְדֳּכָי וַתָּשֶׂם אֶסְתֵּר אֶת־מָרְדֳּכַי עַל־
בֵּית הָמָן: גוַתּוֹסֶף אֶסְתֵּר וַתְּדַבֵּר לִפְנֵי הַמֶּלֶךְ
וַתִּפֹּל לִפְנֵי רַגְלָיו וַתֵּבְךְּ וַתִּתְחַנֶּן־לוֹ לְהַעֲבִיר
אֶת־רָעַת הָמָן הָאֲגָגִי וְאֵת מַחֲשַׁבְתּוֹ אֲשֶׁר חָשַׁב
עַל־הַיְּהוּדִים: דוַיּוֹשֶׁט הַמֶּלֶךְ לְאֶסְתֵּר אֵת שַׁרְבִט
הַזָּהָב וַתָּקָם אֶסְתֵּר וַתַּעֲמֹד לִפְנֵי הַמֶּלֶךְ:
הוַתֹּאמֶר אִם־עַל־הַמֶּלֶךְ טוֹב וְאִם־מָצָאתִי חֵן
לְפָנָיו וְכָשֵׁר הַדָּבָר לִפְנֵי הַמֶּלֶךְ וְטוֹבָה אֲנִי
בְּעֵינָיו יִכָּתֵב לְהָשִׁיב אֶת־הַסְּפָרִים מַחֲשֶׁבֶת הָמָן
בֶּן־הַמְּדָתָא הָאֲגָגִי אֲשֶׁר כָּתַב לְאַבֵּד אֶת־
הַיְּהוּדִים אֲשֶׁר בְּכָל־מְדִינוֹת הַמֶּלֶךְ: ווכִּי אֵיכָכָה
אוּכַל וְרָאִיתִי בָּרָעָה אֲשֶׁר־יִמְצָא אֶת־עַמִּי
וְאֵיכָכָה אוּכַל וְרָאִיתִי בְּאָבְדַן מוֹלַדְתִּי:
זוַיֹּאמֶר הַמֶּלֶךְ אֲחַשְׁוֵרֹשׁ לְאֶסְתֵּר הַמַּלְכָּה
וּלְמָרְדֳּכַי הַיְּהוּדִי הִנֵּה בֵית־הָמָן נָתַתִּי לְאֶסְתֵּר
וְאֹתוֹ תָּלוּ עַל־הָעֵץ עַל אֲשֶׁר־שָׁלַח יָדוֹ
בַּיְּהוּדִים*: חוְאַתֶּם כִּתְבוּ עַל־הַיְּהוּדִים כַּטּוֹב
בְּעֵינֵיכֶם בְּשֵׁם הַמֶּלֶךְ וְחִתְמוּ בְּטַבַּעַת הַמֶּלֶךְ כִּי־
כְתָב אֲשֶׁר־נִכְתָּב בְּשֵׁם־הַמֶּלֶךְ וְנַחְתּוֹם בְּטַבַּעַת

(הַיְּהוּדִיִּים כתיב)   (בַּיְּהוּדִיִּים כתיב)

Mordecai; and the king's wrath abated.

8 ¹On that day, King Ahasuerus gave the house of Haman, the Jews' adversary, to Queen Esther; and Mordecai came before the king, for Esther had revealed what he was to her. ²And the king took off his ring, which he had taken from Haman, and gave it to Mordecai. And Esther set Mordecai over the house of Haman. ³And Esther spoke again before the king, and fell down at his feet. She wept, and implored him to avert the evil plan of Haman the Agagite and the device which he had planned against the Jews. ⁴Then the king held out the golden sceptre to Esther. So Esther arose, and stood before the king. ⁵And she said: "If it please the king, and if I have found favor in his sight, and the proposal seems right to the king, and I am pleasing in his sight, let it be written to recall the letters devised by Haman the son of Hammedatha the Agagite which he wrote to destroy the Jews who are in all the king's provinces. ⁶For how can I endure to see the evil which will come upon my people? And how can I endure to see the destruction of my kindred?" ⁷Then King Ahasuerus said to Queen Esther and to Mordecai the Jew: "I have given Haman's house to Esther, and he has been hanged on the gallows, because he laid his hands upon the Jews. ⁸You may further write with regard to the Jews as you like, in the king's name, and seal it with the king's ring; for an edict which is written in the king's name and sealed with the king's ring may not be recalled."

הַמֶּ֫לֶךְ אֵ֥ין לְהָשִׁ֖יב:

י וַיִּקָּרְא֣וּ סֹפְרֵֽי־הַמֶּ֡לֶךְ בָּֽעֵת־הַהִ֣יא בַּחֹ֣דֶשׁ
הַשְּׁלִישִׁ֡י הוּא־חֹ֣דֶשׁ סִיוָן֩ בִּשְׁלוֹשָׁ֨ה וְעֶשְׂרִים֮ בּוֹ֒
וַיִּכָּתֵ֣ב כְּכָל־אֲשֶׁר־צִוָּ֣ה מָרְדֳּכַ֣י אֶל־הַיְּהוּדִ֗ים וְאֶ֣ל
הָאֲחַשְׁדַּרְפְּנִים֩ וְהַפַּחוֹת֙ וְשָׂרֵ֣י הַמְּדִינ֔וֹת אֲשֶׁ֣ר ׀
מֵהֹ֣דּוּ וְעַד־כּ֗וּשׁ שֶׁ֤בַע וְעֶשְׂרִים֙ וּמֵאָ֣ה מְדִינָ֔ה
מְדִינָ֤ה וּמְדִינָה֙ כִּכְתָבָ֔הּ וְעַ֥ם וָעָ֖ם כִּלְשֹׁנ֑וֹ וְאֶ֨ל־
הַיְּהוּדִ֔ים כִּכְתָבָ֖ם וְכִלְשׁוֹנָֽם: יא וַיִּכְתֹּ֞ב בְּשֵׁם֙ הַמֶּ֣לֶךְ
אֲחַשְׁוֵרֹ֗שׁ וַיַּחְתֹּ֖ם בְּטַבַּ֣עַת הַמֶּ֑לֶךְ וַיִּשְׁלַ֣ח סְפָרִ֡ים
בְּיַד֩ הָרָצִ֨ים בַּסּוּסִ֜ים רֹֽכְבֵ֤י הָרֶ֙כֶשׁ֙ הָֽאֲחַשְׁתְּרָנִ֔ים
בְּנֵ֖י הָֽרַמָּכִֽים: יב אֲשֶׁר֩ נָתַ֨ן הַמֶּ֜לֶךְ לַיְּהוּדִ֣ים ׀ אֲשֶׁ֣ר ׀
בְּכָל־עִיר־וָעִ֗יר לְהִקָּהֵל֮ וְלַעֲמֹ֣ד עַל־נַפְשָׁם֒
לְהַשְׁמִיד֩ לַהֲרֹ֨ג וּלְאַבֵּ֜ד אֶת־כָּל־חֵ֨יל עַ֤ם וּמְדִינָה֙
הַצָּרִ֣ים אֹתָ֔ם טַ֖ף וְנָשִׁ֑ים וּשְׁלָלָ֖ם לָבֽוֹז: יג בְּי֣וֹם
אֶחָ֔ד בְּכָל־מְדִינ֖וֹת הַמֶּ֣לֶךְ אֲחַשְׁוֵר֑וֹשׁ בִּשְׁלוֹשָׁ֥ה
עָשָׂ֛ר לְחֹ֥דֶשׁ שְׁנֵים־עָשָׂ֖ר הוּא־חֹ֥דֶשׁ אֲדָֽר:
יד פַּתְשֶׁ֣גֶן הַכְּתָ֗ב לְהִנָּ֤תֵֽן דָּת֙ בְּכָל־מְדִינָ֣ה וּמְדִינָ֔ה
גָּל֖וּי לְכָל־הָעַמִּ֑ים וְלִהְי֨וֹת הַיְּהוּדִ֤ים עֲתִידִים֙*
לַיּ֣וֹם הַזֶּ֔ה לְהִנָּקֵ֖ם מֵאֹֽיְבֵיהֶֽם: טו הָרָצִ֞ים רֹכְבֵ֤י
הָרֶ֙כֶשׁ֙ הָֽאֲחַשְׁתְּרָנִ֔ים יָ֥צְא֛וּ מְבֹהָלִ֥ים וּדְחוּפִ֖ים
בִּדְבַ֣ר הַמֶּ֑לֶךְ וְהַדָּ֥ת נִתְּנָ֖ה בְּשׁוּשַׁ֥ן הַבִּירָֽה:
טז וּמָרְדֳּכַ֞י יָצָ֣א ׀ מִלִּפְנֵ֣י הַמֶּ֗לֶךְ בִּלְב֤וּשׁ מַלְכוּת֙
תְּכֵ֣לֶת וָח֔וּר וַעֲטֶ֤רֶת זָהָב֙ גְּדוֹלָ֔ה וְתַכְרִ֥יךְ בּ֖וּץ

(הַיְּהוּדִיִּים עֲתוּדִים כְּתִיב)

⁹The king's scribes were called at that time, in the third month which is the month Sivan, on the twenty-third day. And it was written, according to all that Mordecai commanded the Jews, the satraps, governors and nobles of the provinces from India to Ethiopia, a hundred and twenty-seven provinces, to every province according to its script, to every people according to its language, and to the Jews according to their script and language. ¹⁰And he wrote in the name of King Ahasuerus and sealed it with the king's ring, and sent letters by night couriers on horses, and riders on racers, mules and young mares. ¹¹In these letters, the king allowed the Jews who were in every city to assemble and fight for their lives, to exterminate, to slay and cause to perish all the forces of the people and the provinces that might "attack them, their little ones, and their women"; and to plunder their possessions— ¹²upon one day in all the provinces of King Ahasuerus, that is, on the thirteenth day of the twelfth month, the month Adar. ¹³A copy of the writing, as a decree to be given in every province, was published for all the people, that the Jews should be ready on that day to avenge themselves on their enemies. ¹⁴So the couriers that rode upon the racers and mules went out, hastened and pressed on by the king's command. And the decree was issued in Shushan the capital.

¹⁵And Mordecai went out from the presence of the king in royal apparel of purple, blue and white, and with a great crown of gold, and with a robe of fine linen and purple wool. And the city of Shushan shouted and was

The Hanging of Haman's Sons from their Names.   9:7

וְאַרְגָּמֶן וְהָעִיר שׁוּשָׁן צָהֲלָה וְשָׂמֵחָה: ט לַיְּהוּדִים
הָיְתָה אוֹרָה וְשִׂמְחָה וְשָׂשֹׂן וִיקָר: יּ וּבְכָל־מְדִינָה
וּמְדִינָה וּבְכָל־עִיר וָעִיר מְקוֹם אֲשֶׁר דְּבַר־הַמֶּלֶךְ
וְדָתוֹ מַגִּיעַ שִׂמְחָה וְשָׂשׂוֹן לַיְּהוּדִים מִשְׁתֶּה וְיוֹם
טוֹב וְרַבִּים מֵעַמֵּי הָאָרֶץ מִתְיַהֲדִים כִּי־נָפַל פַּחַד־
הַיְּהוּדִים עֲלֵיהֶם:
ט א וּבִשְׁנֵים עָשָׂר חֹדֶשׁ הוּא־חֹדֶשׁ אֲדָר בִּשְׁלוֹשָׁה
עָשָׂר יוֹם בּוֹ אֲשֶׁר הִגִּיעַ דְּבַר־הַמֶּלֶךְ וְדָתוֹ
לְהֵעָשׂוֹת בַּיּוֹם אֲשֶׁר שִׂבְּרוּ אֹיְבֵי הַיְּהוּדִים
לִשְׁלוֹט בָּהֶם וְנַהֲפוֹךְ הוּא אֲשֶׁר יִשְׁלְטוּ הַיְּהוּדִים
הֵמָּה בְּשֹׂנְאֵיהֶם: בּ נִקְהֲלוּ הַיְּהוּדִים בְּעָרֵיהֶם
בְּכָל־מְדִינוֹת הַמֶּלֶךְ אֲחַשְׁוֵרוֹשׁ לִשְׁלֹחַ יָד
בִּמְבַקְשֵׁי רָעָתָם וְאִישׁ לֹא־עָמַד בִּפְנֵיהֶם כִּי־נָפַל
פַּחְדָּם עַל־כָּל־הָעַמִּים: גּ וְכָל־שָׂרֵי הַמְּדִינוֹת
וְהָאֲחַשְׁדַּרְפְּנִים וְהַפַּחוֹת וְעֹשֵׂי הַמְּלָאכָה אֲשֶׁר
לַמֶּלֶךְ מְנַשְּׂאִים אֶת־הַיְּהוּדִים כִּי־נָפַל פַּחַד־
מָרְדֳּכַי עֲלֵיהֶם: דּ כִּי־גָדוֹל מָרְדֳּכַי בְּבֵית הַמֶּלֶךְ
וְשָׁמְעוֹ הוֹלֵךְ בְּכָל־הַמְּדִינוֹת כִּי־הָאִישׁ מָרְדֳּכַי
הוֹלֵךְ וְגָדוֹל: הּ וַיַּכּוּ הַיְּהוּדִים בְּכָל־אֹיְבֵיהֶם מַכַּת־
חֶרֶב וְהֶרֶג וְאַבְדָן וַיַּעֲשׂוּ בְשֹׂנְאֵיהֶם כִּרְצוֹנָם:
וּ וּבְשׁוּשַׁן הַבִּירָה הָרְגוּ הַיְּהוּדִים וְאַבֵּד חֲמֵשׁ
מֵאוֹת אִישׁ: ז וְאֵת ׀

פַּרְשַׁנְדָּתָא*   וְאֵת ׀

(ת' זעירא)

glad. [16]The Jews had light and gladness, joy and honor. [17]And in every province and in every city, wherever the king's command and decree came, there was joy and gladness for the Jews, a feast and a good day. And many of the people of the land became Jews; for the fear of the Jews fell upon them.

9 [1]Now in the twelfth month, the month Adar, on the thirteenth day of the same, when the king's command and decree drew near to be executed, on the day when the enemies of the Jews had hoped to have power over them—whereas the opposite happened so that the Jews themselves gained power on those who hated them— [2]the Jews gathered together in their cities throughout all the provinces of King Ahasuerus to lay hands on those who had planned to hurt them. No one could stand before them, for fear of them had fallen over all people. [3]And all the nobles of the provinces, and the satraps and the governors, and the administrators of the king, aided the Jews; for the fear of Mordecai had fallen upon them. [4]For Mordecai was now great in the king's house, and his fame spread throughout all the provinces; for the man Mordecai grew ever more powerful. [5]So the Jews smote all their enemies with the drawn sword and with slaughter and destruction, and did what they could to those who hated them. [6]In Shushan the capital the Jews slew and destroyed five hundred men. [7]They also slew Parshandatha, and

וְאֵת ׀	דַּלְפּוֹן
וְאֵת ׀ ח	אַסְפָּתָא:
וְאֵת ׀	פּוֹרָתָא
וְאֵת ׀	אֲדַלְיָא
וְאֵת ׀ ט	אֲרִידָתָא:
וְאֵת ׀	פַּרְמַשְׁתָּא*
וְאֵת ׀	אֲרִיסַי
וְאֵת ׀	אֲרִידַי
עֲשֶׂרֶת י	וַיְזָתָא*:

בְּנֵי הָמָן בֶּן־הַמְּדָתָא צֹרֵר הַיְּהוּדִים הָרָגוּ וּבַבִּזָּה
לֹא שָׁלְחוּ אֶת־יָדָם: יא בַּיּוֹם הַהוּא בָּא מִסְפַּר
הַהֲרוּגִים בְּשׁוּשַׁן הַבִּירָה לִפְנֵי הַמֶּלֶךְ: יב וַיֹּאמֶר
הַמֶּלֶךְ לְאֶסְתֵּר הַמַּלְכָּה בְּשׁוּשַׁן הַבִּירָה הָרְגוּ
הַיְּהוּדִים וְאַבֵּד חֲמֵשׁ מֵאוֹת אִישׁ וְאֵת עֲשֶׂרֶת
בְּנֵי־הָמָן בִּשְׁאָר מְדִינוֹת הַמֶּלֶךְ מֶה עָשׂוּ וּמַה־
שְּׁאֵלָתֵךְ וְיִנָּתֵן לָךְ וּמַה־בַּקָּשָׁתֵךְ עוֹד וְתֵעָשׂ:
יג וַתֹּאמֶר אֶסְתֵּר אִם־עַל־הַמֶּלֶךְ טוֹב יִנָּתֵן גַּם־
מָחָר לַיְּהוּדִים אֲשֶׁר בְּשׁוּשָׁן לַעֲשׂוֹת כְּדָת הַיּוֹם
וְאֵת עֲשֶׂרֶת בְּנֵי־הָמָן יִתְלוּ עַל־הָעֵץ: יד וַיֹּאמֶר
הַמֶּלֶךְ לְהֵעָשׂוֹת כֵּן וַתִּנָּתֵן דָּת בְּשׁוּשָׁן וְאֵת
עֲשֶׂרֶת בְּנֵי־הָמָן תָּלוּ: טו וַיִּקָּהֲלוּ הַיְּהוּדִים* אֲשֶׁר־
בְּשׁוּשָׁן גַּם בְּיוֹם אַרְבָּעָה עָשָׂר לְחֹדֶשׁ אֲדָר
וַיַּהַרְגוּ בְשׁוּשָׁן שְׁלֹשׁ מֵאוֹת אִישׁ וּבַבִּזָּה לֹא

(הַיְּהוּדִיִּים כְּתִיב)	(ו' רַבָּתִי, ז' זְעִירָא)	(ש' זְעִירָא)

Dalphon, and [8]Aspatha, and Poratha, and Adalia, and Aridatha; [9]and Parmashta, and Arisai, and Aridai, and Vaizatha, [10]the ten sons of Haman the son of Hammedatha, the enemy of the Jews; but on the spoil they did not lay hands. [11]On that day, the number of those who were slain in Shushan the capital was reported to the king. [12]And the king said to Queen Esther: "The Jews have slain and destroyed in Shushan the capital five hundred men and the ten sons of Haman. What must they not have done in the rest of the king's provinces! And now, what is your petition? It will be granted to you. And what do you request further? It will be done!" [13]Then Esther said: "If it please the king, let it be granted to the Jews who are in Shushan to do tomorrow as they did today; and let Haman's ten sons be hanged upon the gallows." [14]The king commanded it to be done; and a decree was given at Shushan; and they hanged Haman's ten sons. [15]And the Jews in Shushan gathered again on the fourteenth day of Adar and slew three hundred men in Shushan; but they did not lay their hands on the spoil.

שָׁלְח֖וּ אֶת־יָדָֽם:

ט֠ וּשְׁאָ֨ר הַיְּהוּדִ֜ים אֲשֶׁ֣ר בִּמְדִינ֣וֹת הַמֶּ֗לֶךְ נִקְהֲל֣וּ ׀
וְעָמֹ֤ד עַל־נַפְשָׁם֙ וְנ֣וֹחַ מֵאֹ֣יְבֵיהֶ֔ם וְהָרֹג֙
בְּשֹֽׂנְאֵיהֶ֔ם חֲמִשָּׁ֥ה וְשִׁבְעִ֖ים אָ֑לֶף וּבַ֨בִּזָּ֔ה לֹ֥א
שָֽׁלְח֖וּ אֶת־יָדָֽם: י בְּיוֹם־שְׁלוֹשָׁ֥ה עָשָׂ֖ר לְחֹ֣דֶשׁ
אֲדָ֑ר וְנ֗וֹחַ בְּאַרְבָּעָ֤ה עָשָׂר֙ בּ֔וֹ וְעָשֹׂ֣ה אֹת֔וֹ י֖וֹם
מִשְׁתֶּ֥ה וְשִׂמְחָֽה: יא וְהַיְּהוּדִ֣ים* אֲשֶׁר־בְּשׁוּשָׁ֗ן
נִקְהֲלוּ֙ בִּשְׁלוֹשָׁ֤ה עָשָׂר֙ בּ֔וֹ וּבְאַרְבָּעָ֥ה עָשָׂ֖ר בּ֑וֹ
וְנ֗וֹחַ בַּחֲמִשָּׁ֤ה עָשָׂר֙ בּ֔וֹ וְעָשֹׂ֣ה אֹת֔וֹ י֖וֹם מִשְׁתֶּ֥ה
וְשִׂמְחָֽה: יב עַל־כֵּ֞ן הַיְּהוּדִ֣ים הַפְּרָזִ֗ים* הַיֹּשְׁבִים֮
בְּעָרֵ֣י הַפְּרָזוֹת֒ עֹשִׂ֗ים אֵ֠ת י֣וֹם אַרְבָּעָ֤ה עָשָׂר֙
לְחֹ֣דֶשׁ אֲדָ֔ר שִׂמְחָ֥ה וּמִשְׁתֶּ֖ה וְי֣וֹם ט֑וֹב וּמִשְׁלֹ֥חַ
מָנ֖וֹת אִ֥ישׁ לְרֵעֵֽהוּ:

כ וַיִּכְתֹּ֣ב מָרְדֳּכַ֔י אֶת־הַדְּבָרִ֖ים הָאֵ֑לֶּה וַיִּשְׁלַ֣ח
סְפָרִ֗ים אֶל־כָּל־הַיְּהוּדִים֙ אֲשֶׁר֙ בְּכָל־מְדִינ֣וֹת
הַמֶּ֣לֶךְ אֲחַשְׁוֵר֔וֹשׁ הַקְּרוֹבִ֖ים וְהָרְחוֹקִֽים: כא לְקַיֵּם֙
עֲלֵיהֶ֔ם לִהְי֣וֹת עֹשִׂ֗ים אֵ֠ת י֣וֹם אַרְבָּעָ֤ה עָשָׂר֙
לְחֹ֣דֶשׁ אֲדָ֔ר וְאֵ֛ת יוֹם־חֲמִשָּׁ֥ה עָשָׂ֖ר בּ֑וֹ בְּכָל־שָׁנָ֖ה
וְשָׁנָֽה: כב כַּיָּמִ֗ים אֲשֶׁר־נָ֨חוּ בָהֶ֤ם הַיְּהוּדִים֙
מֵאֹ֣יְבֵיהֶ֔ם וְהַחֹ֗דֶשׁ אֲשֶׁר֩ נֶהְפַּ֨ךְ לָהֶ֤ם מִיָּגוֹן֙
לְשִׂמְחָ֔ה וּמֵאֵ֖בֶל לְי֣וֹם ט֑וֹב לַעֲשׂ֣וֹת אוֹתָ֗ם יְמֵי֙
מִשְׁתֶּ֣ה וְשִׂמְחָ֔ה וּמִשְׁלֹ֤חַ מָנוֹת֙ אִ֣ישׁ לְרֵעֵ֔הוּ
וּמַתָּנ֖וֹת לָֽאֶבְיֹנִֽים: כג וְקִבֵּל֙ הַיְּהוּדִ֔ים אֵ֣ת אֲשֶׁר־

(וְהַיְּהוּדִיִּים כתיב)   (הַפְּרוֹזִים כתיב)

¹⁶The other Jews who were in the king's provinces gathered together and stood up for their lives, and had rest from their enemies. They slew seventy-five thousand of those who hated them; but they did not lay their hands on the spoil. ¹⁷On the thirteenth day of the month of Adar and on the fourteenth day of the same month they rested and made it a day of feasting and of gladness. ¹⁸But the Jews who were in Shushan assembled on the thirteenth and on the fourteenth, and they rested on the fifteenth day of the same month and made it a day of feasting and of gladness. ¹⁹Therefore, the Jews of the villages who dwelt in unwalled towns, made the fourteenth day of the month Adar a day of gladness and feasting, and a good day, and of sending gifts to one another.

²⁰Then Mordecai wrote down these things, and sent letters to all the Jews throughout the provinces of King Ahasuerus, near and far, ²¹charging them to observe the fourteenth and fifteenth days of Adar every year, ²²as the days on which the Jews had rest from their enemies, and the month which was changed for them from sorrow to joy, and from mourning into a good day: that they should make them days of feasting and joy, and of sending portions to one another, and gifts to the poor. ²³And the Jews undertook to do as they had begun, and as Mordecai had written to them.

הַחֵלּוּ לַעֲשׂוֹת וְאֵת אֲשֶׁר־כָּתַב מָרְדֳּכַי אֲלֵיהֶם:
כד כִּי הָמָן בֶּן־הַמְּדָתָא הָאֲגָגִי צֹרֵר כָּל־הַיְּהוּדִים
חָשַׁב עַל־הַיְּהוּדִים לְאַבְּדָם וְהִפִּל פּוּר הוּא
הַגּוֹרָל לְהֻמָּם וּלְאַבְּדָם: כה וּבְבֹאָהּ לִפְנֵי הַמֶּלֶךְ
אָמַר עִם־הַסֵּפֶר יָשׁוּב מַחֲשַׁבְתּוֹ הָרָעָה אֲשֶׁר־
חָשַׁב עַל־הַיְּהוּדִים עַל־רֹאשׁוֹ וְתָלוּ אֹתוֹ וְאֶת־
בָּנָיו עַל־הָעֵץ: כו עַל־כֵּן קָרְאוּ לַיָּמִים הָאֵלֶּה
פוּרִים עַל־שֵׁם הַפּוּר עַל־כֵּן עַל־כָּל־דִּבְרֵי
הָאִגֶּרֶת הַזֹּאת וּמָה־רָאוּ עַל־כָּכָה וּמָה הִגִּיעַ
אֲלֵיהֶם: כז קִיְּמוּ וְקִבְּלוּ* הַיְּהוּדִים׀ עֲלֵיהֶם׀ וְעַל־
זַרְעָם וְעַל כָּל־הַנִּלְוִים עֲלֵיהֶם וְלֹא יַעֲבוֹר לִהְיוֹת
עֹשִׂים אֵת־שְׁנֵי הַיָּמִים הָאֵלֶּה כִּכְתָבָם וְכִזְמַנָּם
בְּכָל־שָׁנָה וְשָׁנָה: כח וְהַיָּמִים הָאֵלֶּה נִזְכָּרִים
וְנַעֲשִׂים בְּכָל־דּוֹר וָדוֹר מִשְׁפָּחָה וּמִשְׁפָּחָה
מְדִינָה וּמְדִינָה וְעִיר וָעִיר וִימֵי הַפּוּרִים הָאֵלֶּה
לֹא יַעַבְרוּ מִתּוֹךְ הַיְּהוּדִים וְזִכְרָם לֹא־יָסוּף
מִזַּרְעָם:
כט וַתִּכְתֹּב* אֶסְתֵּר הַמַּלְכָּה בַת־אֲבִיחַיִל וּמָרְדֳּכַי
הַיְּהוּדִי אֶת־כָּל־תֹּקֶף לְקַיֵּם אֵת אִגֶּרֶת הַפֻּרִים
הַזֹּאת הַשֵּׁנִית: ל וַיִּשְׁלַח סְפָרִים אֶל־כָּל־הַיְּהוּדִים
אֶל־שֶׁבַע וְעֶשְׂרִים וּמֵאָה מְדִינָה מַלְכוּת
אֲחַשְׁוֵרוֹשׁ דִּבְרֵי שָׁלוֹם וֶאֱמֶת: לא לְקַיֵּם אֶת־יְמֵי
הַפֻּרִים הָאֵלֶּה בִּזְמַנֵּיהֶם כַּאֲשֶׁר קִיַּם עֲלֵיהֶם

(וְקִבֵּל כְּתִיב)   (תָּ׳ רַבָּתִי)

²⁴For Haman, the son of Hammedatha, the Agagite, the enemy of all the Jews, had plotted against the Jews to exterminate them, and had cast *pur*, that is 'the lot,' to destroy them and to exterminate them. ²⁵But when Esther came before the king, he commanded by letters that his wicked device which he had devised against the Jews should come upon his own head, and that he and his sons should be hanged on the gallows. ²⁶Therefore, they called these days Purim, after *pur*. Therefore, in accordance with all the words of this letter, and of what they had seen concerning this matter, and that which had come upon them, ²⁷the Jews established and took upon themselves and upon their descendants and upon all those who had joined them, so that it should not fail, that they should observe these two days according to their writing, and according to their appointed time, every year. ²⁸Therefore, these days are to be remembered and kept throughout every generation, every family, every province, and every city; and these days of Purim should never fail among the Jews, nor should the memory of them ever perish among their descendants. ²⁹The Queen Esther, the daughter of Abihail, and Mordecai the Jew wrote with all authority, to confirm this second letter of Purim. ³⁰He also sent letters to all the Jews, to the hundred and twenty-seven provinces of the kingdom of Ahasuerus, with words of peace and truth, ³¹to confirm these days of Purim in their appointed time as Mordecai the Jew and Queen Esther had established for them, and as they had established for themselves and for their descendants, the obligation

מָרְדֳּכַי הַיְּהוּדִי וְאֶסְתֵּר הַמַּלְכָּה וְכַאֲשֶׁר קִיְּמוּ
עַל־נַפְשָׁם וְעַל־זַרְעָם דִּבְרֵי הַצֹּמוֹת וְזַעֲקָתָם:
לב וּמַאֲמַר אֶסְתֵּר קִיַּם דִּבְרֵי הַפֻּרִים הָאֵלֶּה וְנִכְתָּב
בַּסֵּפֶר:

י א וַיָּשֶׂם הַמֶּלֶךְ אֲחַשְׁוֵרֹשׁ* ׀ מַס עַל־הָאָרֶץ וְאִיֵּי
הַיָּם: ב וְכָל־מַעֲשֵׂה תָקְפּוֹ וּגְבוּרָתוֹ וּפָרָשַׁת גְּדֻלַּת
מָרְדֳּכַי אֲשֶׁר גִּדְּלוֹ הַמֶּלֶךְ הֲלוֹא־הֵם כְּתוּבִים עַל־
סֵפֶר דִּבְרֵי הַיָּמִים לְמַלְכֵי מָדַי וּפָרָס: ג כִּי ׀ מָרְדֳּכַי
הַיְּהוּדִי מִשְׁנֶה לַמֶּלֶךְ אֲחַשְׁוֵרוֹשׁ וְגָדוֹל לַיְּהוּדִים
וְרָצוּי לְרֹב אֶחָיו דֹּרֵשׁ טוֹב לְעַמּוֹ וְדֹבֵר שָׁלוֹם
לְכָל־זַרְעוֹ:

(אחשרש כתיב)

of fasting and their cry of lamentation.
[32]And the decree of Esther established these matters of Purim; and it was recorded in the book.

10 [1]King Ahasuerus then imposed a tribute on the land and upon the isles of the sea. [2]And all the acts of his power and might, and the declaration of the greatness of Mordecai to which the king advanced him—are they not written in the Book of the Chronicles of the kings of Media and Persia? [3]For Mordecai the Jew was next in rank to King Ahasuerus, was great among the Jews and accepted by the multitude of his brethren; he sought the welfare of his people, and spoke peace for all his kindred.

THE SCROLL OF SONG OF SONGS

INTRODUCTION TO
THE SCROLL OF SONG OF SONGS

Who wrote the Five Scrolls? And why have they become part of our liturgy? For each scroll a different answer is needed; but for the Song of Songs, ancient Jewish tradition, as recorded in the Babylonian Talmud, has a ready answer: Solomon was the author, and the book is apparently a collection of songs about love, nature, kings and princesses, about shepherds and their dalliance. According to tradition, this is only the surface of the text. The book, according to ancient tradition, is an allegory. The love poems are the poetry of God's love for Israel and Israel's loving response. Since this love is the heart of prayer itself, the book deserves an honored place in Holy Scripture, perhaps even more than other works, especially in the liturgy, the text of worship of the community of Israel.

Taking its cue from allusions to Solomon's name in the text, an ancient authority also ascribes two other scriptural works to him, namely, the Book of Proverbs with its pragmatic and practical "wisdom for living," and the world-weary Scroll of Ecclesiastes whose tone, at best, is one of reverence for God arrived at only after resigned acceptance of the disappointments, inequities, and apparent emptiness of human existence.

But if Solomon is the author of all three works, how can one account for the difference in attitude between them? Rabbi Jonathan answered as follows:

> When a man is young, he sings songs [of love]. When he becomes an adult, he utters practical proverbs. When he becomes old, he speaks of the vanity of things.
>
> (*Song of Songs Rabbah* 1.1, no. 10)

Rabbi Jonathan's comment makes of Solomon a paradigm of the changing outlook in life that is characteristic of most human

beings in the course of a lifetime, a precursor of Shakespeare's seven stages of man.

Modern scholarship considers the text as dating from a far later period than that of Solomon, possibly edited ca. 400 B.C.E., even though some of the material may be older. In the end, such factual issues are of limited importance; the text is timeless, stronger than death, not to be quenched by the flow of the centuries. In his Theresienstadt midrash, Leo Baeck wrote:

> Two poetic works that tell of the love of man and woman have been incorporated in the Bible. One is the Song of Solomon, the Song of Songs, which sings of love as awakening in the young soul and in the young body; the other is the Book of Ruth, the book of the woman who hearkened to the voice of faithfulness, and for whom faithfulness then prepares marriage and a home.
>
> (Leo Baeck, *This People Israel,* p. 126)

The intensity of this love song, in its very celebration of physical love, is of such a nature that Rabbi Akiva's allegorical interpretation—God as the lover, Israel as the beloved—commends itself to all who encounter the text. Like Esther, the Song of Songs does not mention the name of God;* unlike Esther, the omission is ignored here because the reality of the Divine Presence, according to the religious interpretation, is felt in every line.

We look at the lyrics of this song; we turn and turn every word, and new interpretations flood into our lives. The Song of Songs is a composition in which elaborate imagery and the boldest of metaphors are joined together in a unique text of glowing beauty. Attempts have been made to structure the poetry into a straightforward drama with two or three protagonists (maiden and lover; or, king, maiden, and lover). Some Bible translations, recognizing that the text is made up of speeches, assign speakers to the lines. As Robert Gordis points out, the drama which is created by this method is achieved by artifice: "The entire plot must be read into the book and the natural

---

*Some authorities see punning light-hearted allusions in the text to designations for divinity. Also, there are the words *"shalhevet Yah,"* "flame of God."

intent of the words must be ignored again and again" (Robert Gordis, *The Song of Songs,* New York, 1954, p. 11).

Our need to bring order into what is an unstructured group of songs, poems, and perhaps even short librettos, can easily discover and extract out a wealthy king, a simple maiden, and her shepherd lover. The conflicts of this ancient triangle which test true love are finally resolved as maiden and lover are reunited and the virtue of faithfulness rewarded. But each component stands up on its own. This is a collection of lyric love songs in which love is celebrated for its own sake.

Some scholars view these texts as only secular in origin and intention. As inheritors of a sacred tradition, the religious dimension remains important for us. In ancient times, too, some must have viewed the songs merely as secular, and so the religious interpretation was more expressively reinforced by the authority of the scholars: "He who gives his voice a flourish in reading the Song of Songs in banquet halls and makes it a secular song has no share in the world to come" (Tosefta *Sanhedrin* 12:10).

Throughout Jewish history the text has been read by Jews on Passover, at a time when we are called from the bondage of utter servitude, to the freedom of the higher service of God. This freedom from bondage to which we are called is born of God's love for us, and we respond with loving gratitude. Freedom and the love and service of God thus are closely intertwined, and it is this note that the generations of our people heard in the Song of Songs. Thus, all is bound up together: feasts of love between man and woman and the celebration of a people which remembers the days of its youth, its betrothal to God in the wilderness.

A text of songs of springtime love and nature is in itself appropriate for the springtime Passover season, for we read the Song of Songs when

. . . the winter is past . . .
The flowers appear on the earth,
The time of singing has come,
And the voice of the turtledove is heard in our land.

The earth opens itself to humanity, the people respond in joy and in love for one another.

The Song of Songs has been accompanied throughout our generations not only by celebration, but cerebration as well. Endless allegories surround the text. The bride can become wisdom; the pathways of the shepherds turn into the courses of all of Jewish history from Egypt through the day of destruction and also the hope of messianic restitution. In all of this the love of God is imprinted as a seal upon the heart of Israel as, along with the older versions, we translate *"shalhevet Yah"* as "a blazing flame of God." Our love is a divine fire; it cannot be quenched.

In every generation we read these love poems in our own way. For those who wish to follow traditional interpretation, we might note the five major divisions cited in the Soncino Bible: 1:1-2:7; 2:8-3:5; 3:6-5:1; 5:2-6:3; 6:4-8:7; and an epilogue, 8:8-14. Yet almost every new translation and edition of this scroll makes its own divisions. Ultimately, once we have read these poems in our way, all come together as rejoicing in the human condition which dances and leaps over the mountain tops. They are a unity, proclaiming the unlimited dimensions of a human life which can experience love. That is why Akiva was right in setting himself against the strong opposition of colleagues who wanted to ban this text from the sacred writings, why he dared to say:

> The entire universe is not as worthy as the day on which the Song of Songs was given to Israel, for all the Writings are holy, but the Song of Songs is the Holy of Holies.
>
> (Mishnah *Yadayim* 3:5)

Beyond the wisdom of the neighbor who knew that nothing human was alien to him, Akiva had discovered that what was human was also holy. And so is the Song of Songs.

SERVICE FOR THE READING OF
THE SCROLL OF SONG OF SONGS

As lover to beloved, God calls to us,
in this season when our hearts yearn
for nature's renewal
and our spirits awaken
with stirrings of love.
As the rain to the grass of springtime,
as lover to beloved, God calls to us.

Arise my love, my fair one, and come away,
for, lo, the winter is passing,
flowers appear on the earth
and the time for singing is come.

קוּמִי לָךְ רַעְיָתִי יָפָתִי וּלְכִי לָךְ.
כִּי הִנֵּה הַסְּתָו עָבָר,
הַגֶּשֶׁם חָלַף הָלַךְ לוֹ.
הַנִּצָּנִים נִרְאוּ בָאָרֶץ,
עֵת הַזָּמִיר הִגִּיעַ.

Arise my love, my fair one, and come away.

For meditation or reading

Here am I, O Holy One, lonely for Your Presence.

Your Presence which fills Creation fills me with hope,

with hope of tenderness again and of our sharing,

of our sharing of renewed openness to love renewed.

To love renewed, here am I.

Here am I, O One whom I am to love with all my heart,

with all my heart ready to listen again to our song.

To our Song of Songs open my senses.

Open my senses to love blossoming.

To love blossoming, let me hear Your voice.

Let me hear Your voice again saying, "Arise my beloved!"

Arise my beloved, my fair one.

My fair one let me behold your watching presence,

Your watching presence behind the lattice of the world.

Behind the lattice of this world, let me again awaken,

let me again awaken to the sound of the bird of melody.

The sound of the bird of melody let me hear.

Let me hear, "Here am I!"

קוֹל דּוֹדִי הִנֵּה־זֶה בָּא, ¶

מְדַלֵּג עַל־הֶהָרִים,

מְקַפֵּץ עַל הַגְּבָעוֹת.

(The voice of my beloved!
Behold him as he comes,
dancing and skipping
over hills and mountains.)

We grow suspicious of love.

We have grown suspicious of love.

When ideals become an embarrassment to us,

We grow suspicious of love.

Where once there was fragrance and melody and form,

We grow suspicious of love.

Where once there was softness and sweetness,

We grow suspicious of love.

When all that remains is surface glamor,

We grow suspicious of love.

Exploiting or being exploited,

We grow suspicious of love.

Damaged in its selflessness, destructive in its selfishness,

We grow suspicious of love.

Let me trust again,

Let us trust again.

In love's innocent power to restore the soul,

Let us trust again.

For our own sake,

Let us trust again.

For the sake of the one I love,

Let us trust again.

For your sake, O beloved,

Let us trust again.

Many rivers cannot quench love,
nor waters sweep it away,

*Many rivers cannot quench love
nor waters sweep it away.*

> My beloved is mine,
> and I am his,
> the shepherd among the lilies.

Do-di li va-a-ni lo,   דּוֹדִי לִי וַאֲנִי לוֹ,

Ha-ro-eh ba-sho-sha-nim.   הָרֹעֶה בַּשּׁוֹשַׁנִּים.

May each uniting of man and woman fashion a like union in the highest order of being. May each uniting of man and woman bring to a higher fulfillment the Divine, Holy, Oneness:

Six days with the Sabbath,

Sun with Moon;

Daylight and Nightdark,

Right with Left;

Learning with Intuition,

Giving and Taking;

Having with Being,

What can be told with what cannot be told—

All the elements within myself,

All emanations of the Holy.

אַהֲבָה רַבָּה אֲהַבְתָּנוּ, יְיָ אֱלֹהֵינוּ,

אַהֲבַת עוֹלָם אֲהַבְתָּנוּ, יְיָ אֱלֹהֵינוּ.

Your love for us, O God, is great. Your love is everlasting. We know Your love in the work of Creation, O God, in the deliverance from Egypt, and in our covenant at Sinai. All our ways in love are also our way in Torah: affection and ecstasy, song and whisper, sharing and creating.

"All the writings are holy," said Rabbi Akiva, "and the Song of Songs is a Holy of Holies." May our reading from these songs of love awaken our love for one another, and awaken Israel in its love of God.

Blessings before reading from Song of Songs

בָּרוּךְ אַתָּה, יְיָ אֱלֹהֵינוּ, מֶלֶךְ הָעוֹלָם, אֲשֶׁר קִדְּשָׁנוּ בְּמִצְוֹתָיו וְצִוָּנוּ עַל מִקְרָא מְגִלָּה.

Ba-ruch a-ta, A-do-nai E-lo-hei-nu, me-lech ha-o-lam, a-sher ki-de-sha-nu be-mits-vo-tav ve-tsi-va-nu al mik-ra me-gila.

*We praise You, O God, Sovereign of existence, who has hallowed our lives
with commandments and commanded us to read this scroll.*

בָּרוּךְ אַתָּה, יְיָ אֱלֹהֵינוּ, מֶלֶךְ הָעוֹלָם, שֶׁהֶחֱיָנוּ וְקִיְּמָנוּ
וְהִגִּיעָנוּ לַזְּמַן הַזֶּה.

*Ba-ruch a-ta, A-do-nai E-lo-hei-nu, me-lech ha-olam, she-he-che-
ya-nu ve-ki-ye-ma-nu ve-hi-gi-a-nu la-ze-man ha-zeh.*

*We praise You, O God, Sovereign of existence, who has kept us alive,
sustained us, and enabled us to celebrate this festive day.*

READING FROM
THE SCROLL OF SONG OF SONGS

אׄ שִׁיר⋆ הַשִּׁירִים אֲשֶׁר לִשְׁלֹמֹה:

בׄ יִשָּׁקֵ֫נִי מִנְּשִׁיקוֹת פִּיהוּ

כִּי־טוֹבִים דֹּדֶ֫יךָ מִיָּ֫יִן:

גׄ לְרֵ֫יחַ שְׁמָנֶ֫יךָ טוֹבִ֫ים

שֶׁ֫מֶן תּוּרַק שְׁמֶ֫ךָ

עַל־כֵּ֫ן עֲלָמוֹת אֲהֵבֽוּךָ:

דׄ מָשְׁכֵ֫נִי אַחֲרֶ֫יךָ נָּר֫וּצָה

הֱבִיאַ֫נִי הַמֶּ֫לֶךְ חֲדָרָ֫יו נָגִ֫ילָה וְנִשְׂמְחָה֫ בָּ֫ךְ

נַזְכִּ֫ירָה דֹדֶ֫יךָ מִיַּ֫יִן

מֵישָׁרִ֫ים אֲהֵבֽוּךָ:

הׄ שְׁחוֹרָ֫ה אֲנִי֫ וְנָאוָ֫ה

בְּנוֹת יְרוּשָׁלָ֫ם

כְּאָהֳלֵ֫י קֵדָ֫ר

כִּירִיעוֹת שְׁלֹמֹֽה:

יׄ אַל־תִּרְאֻ֫נִי֫ שֶׁאֲנִי֫ שְׁחַרְחֹ֫רֶת

שֶׁשֱּׁזָפַ֫תְנִי הַשָּׁ֫מֶשׁ

בְּנֵ֫י אִמִּ֫י נִֽחֲרוּ־בִ֫י שָׂמֻ֫נִי֫ נֹטֵרָ֫ה אֶת־הַכְּרָמִ֫ים

כַּרְמִ֫י שֶׁלִּ֫י לֹ֫א נָטָֽרְתִּי:

זׄ הַגִּ֫ידָה לִּ֫י שֶׁאָהֲבָה֫ נַפְשִׁי֫

אֵיכָ֫ה תִרְעֶ֫ה

אֵיכָ֫ה תַּרְבִּ֫יץ בַּֽצָּהֳרָ֫יִם

שַׁלָּמָ֫ה אֶֽהְיֶה֫ כְּעֹֽטְיָ֫ה

עַל עֶדְרֵ֫י חֲבֵרֶֽיךָ:

(שׄ׳ רבתי)

I ¹The Song of Songs, which is Solomon's.
²Let him kiss me with the kisses of his mouth
For your love is better than wine.
³Your ointments have a delicate fragrance,
Your name is as oil poured out—
Therefore do the maidens love you.
⁴Draw me after you, let us hurry;
The king has brought me to his chambers, we will be
glad and rejoice in you.
We will remember your love more than wine;
How right it is to love you!
⁵I am black but comely,
O daughters of Jerusalem,
As the tents of Kedar,
As the curtains of Solomon.
⁶Do not look down upon me, because I am swarthy,
Because the sun has tanned me.
My mother's children were angry with me. They
made me keeper of the vineyard.
But my own vineyard I did not keep.
⁷Tell me then, you whom my heart loves:
Where do you pasture your flock,
Where will you make it rest at noon?
Why should I be a wanderer
Beside the flocks of your companions?
⁸If you yourself do not know,

"...a rose of Sharon."   2:1

ח אִם־לֹא תֵדְעִי לָךְ
הַיָּפָה בַּנָּשִׁים
צְאִי־לָךְ בְּעִקְבֵי הַצֹּאן וּרְעִי אֶת־גְּדִיֹּתַיִךְ
עַל מִשְׁכְּנוֹת הָרֹעִים:
ט לְסֻסָתִי בְּרִכְבֵי פַרְעֹה
דִּמִּיתִיךְ רַעְיָתִי:
י נָאווּ לְחָיַיִךְ בַּתֹּרִים
צַוָּארֵךְ בַּחֲרוּזִים:
יא תּוֹרֵי זָהָב נַעֲשֶׂה־לָּךְ
עִם נְקֻדּוֹת הַכָּסֶף:
יב עַד־שֶׁהַמֶּלֶךְ בִּמְסִבּוֹ
נִרְדִּי נָתַן רֵיחוֹ:
יג צְרוֹר הַמֹּר ׀ דּוֹדִי לִי
בֵּין שָׁדַי יָלִין:
יד אֶשְׁכֹּל הַכֹּפֶר ׀ דּוֹדִי לִי
בְּכַרְמֵי עֵין גֶּדִי:
טו הִנָּךְ יָפָה רַעְיָתִי
הִנָּךְ יָפָה עֵינַיִךְ יוֹנִים:
טז הִנְּךָ יָפֶה דוֹדִי אַף נָעִים
אַף־עַרְשֵׂנוּ רַעֲנָנָה:
יז קֹרוֹת בָּתֵּינוּ אֲרָזִים
רָהִיטֵנוּ* בְּרוֹתִים:
ב א אֲנִי חֲבַצֶּלֶת הַשָּׁרוֹן

(רחיטנו כתיב)

O fairest of women,
Go, follow the footprints of the sheep and feed
your kids
Near the tents of the shepherds.
⁹I have compared you, my love,
To a mare in Pharaoh's chariots:
¹⁰Your cheeks are lovely with rows of ringlets,
Your neck with strings of pearls.
¹¹We will make you golden wreaths
With studs of silver.
¹²While the king was on his couch,
My nard gave forth its fragrance.
¹³For me, my beloved is as a bag of myrrh
Lying between my breasts.
¹⁴My beloved to me is a bunch of cypress flowers
In the vineyard of Ein-Gedi.
¹⁵Behold, you are fair, my love,
Behold, you are fair with your eyes as doves.
¹⁶And, oh, you are handsome, my lover, oh, sweet.
Our bed is a bower of green.
¹⁷The beams of our house are cedar,
Cypresses are our rafters.
2 ¹I am a rose of Sharon,

שׁוֹשַׁנַּת הָעֲמָקִים:
ב כְּשׁוֹשַׁנָּה בֵּין הַחוֹחִים
כֵּן רַעְיָתִי בֵּין הַבָּנוֹת:
ג כְּתַפּוּחַ בַּעֲצֵי הַיַּעַר
כֵּן דּוֹדִי בֵּין הַבָּנִים
בְּצִלּוֹ חִמַּדְתִּי וְיָשַׁבְתִּי
וּפִרְיוֹ מָתוֹק לְחִכִּי:
ד הֱבִיאַנִי אֶל־בֵּית הַיַּיִן
וְדִגְלוֹ עָלַי אַהֲבָה:
ה סַמְּכוּנִי בָּאֲשִׁישׁוֹת
רַפְּדוּנִי בַּתַּפּוּחִים
כִּי־חוֹלַת אַהֲבָה אָנִי:
ו שְׂמֹאלוֹ תַּחַת לְרֹאשִׁי
וִימִינוֹ תְּחַבְּקֵנִי:
ז הִשְׁבַּעְתִּי אֶתְכֶם בְּנוֹת יְרוּשָׁלַם בִּצְבָאוֹת
אוֹ בְּאַיְלוֹת הַשָּׂדֶה
אִם־תָּעִירוּ ׀ וְאִם־תְּעוֹרְרוּ אֶת־הָאַהֲבָה
עַד שֶׁתֶּחְפָּץ:
ח קוֹל דּוֹדִי
הִנֵּה־זֶה בָּא
מְדַלֵּג עַל־הֶהָרִים
מְקַפֵּץ עַל־הַגְּבָעוֹת:
ט דּוֹמֶה דוֹדִי לִצְבִי
אוֹ לְעֹפֶר הָאַיָּלִים
הִנֵּה־זֶה עוֹמֵד אַחַר כָּתְלֵנוּ

A lily of the valleys.
²As a lily among thorns,
So is my love among the daughters.
³As an apple tree among the trees of the forest,
So is my beloved among the sons.
I sat down under its shadow with great delight,
And its fruit was sweet to my taste.
⁴He brought me to the banqueting house
And his banner over me was love.
⁵Strengthen me with dainties,
Comfort me with apples,
For I am faint with love.
⁶His left hand is under my head,
And his right hand embraces me.
⁷I adjure you, O daughters of Jerusalem, by the
gazelles,
And by the hinds of the field,
Lest you stir up or arouse my love . . . Until it please!
⁸Hark! The voice of my beloved!
Behold! He comes
Leaping over the mountains
Bounding over the hills.
⁹My beloved is like a gazelle
Or a young wild stag.
See where he stands behind our wall,

מַשְׁגִּיחַ מִן־הַחַלֹּנוֹת
מֵצִיץ מִן־הַחֲרַכִּים:
'עָנָה דוֹדִי וְאָמַר לִי
קוּמִי לָךְ רַעְיָתִי יָפָתִי וּלְכִי־לָךְ:
יא כִּי־הִנֵּה הַסְּתָו עָבָר
הַגֶּשֶׁם חָלַף הָלַךְ לוֹ:
יב הַנִּצָּנִים נִרְאוּ בָאָרֶץ
עֵת הַזָּמִיר הִגִּיעַ
וְקוֹל הַתּוֹר נִשְׁמַע בְּאַרְצֵנוּ:
יג הַתְּאֵנָה חָנְטָה פַגֶּיהָ
וְהַגְּפָנִים | סְמָדַר נָתְנוּ רֵיחַ
קוּמִי לָךְ* רַעְיָתִי יָפָתִי וּלְכִי־לָךְ:
יד יוֹנָתִי בְּחַגְוֵי הַסֶּלַע בְּסֵתֶר הַמַּדְרֵגָה
הַרְאִינִי אֶת־מַרְאַיִךְ
הַשְׁמִיעִנִי אֶת־קוֹלֵךְ
כִּי־קוֹלֵךְ עָרֵב וּמַרְאֵיךְ נָאוֶה:
טו אֶחֱזוּ־לָנוּ שׁוּעָלִים
שֻׁעָלִים קְטַנִּים מְחַבְּלִים כְּרָמִים
וּכְרָמֵינוּ סְמָדַר:
טז דוֹדִי לִי וַאֲנִי לוֹ
הָרֹעֶה בַּשּׁוֹשַׁנִּים:
יז עַד שֶׁיָּפוּחַ הַיּוֹם
וְנָסוּ הַצְּלָלִים

(לכי כתיב)

Looking in through the windows,
Gazing through the lattice.
¹⁰My beloved answered and said to me:
"Rise up, my love, my fair one, and come away.
¹¹For lo, the winter is past,
The rains are over and gone.
¹²The flowers appear on the earth,
The time of singing has come,
And the voice of the turtle dove is heard in our land.
¹³The fig tree sweetens her green figs
And the vines are in blossom, giving their fragrance.
Rise up, my love, my fair one, and come away!
¹⁴My dove, hiding in the clefts of the rock, in the
secret places of the cliff,
Let me see your face,
Let me hear your voice;
For your voice is sweet and your face is lovely."
¹⁵Catch us the foxes,
The little foxes that spoil our vineyards;
For our vineyards are in blossom.
¹⁶My beloved is mine, and I am his
Who feeds among the lilies.
¹⁷Before the dawn wind rises,
Before the shadows flee,

סב דְּמֵה־לְךָ דוֹדִי לִצְבִי אוֹ לְעֹפֶר הָאַיָּלִים
עַל־הָרֵי בָתֶר:
ג אעַל־מִשְׁכָּבִי בַּלֵּילוֹת
בִּקַּשְׁתִּי אֵת שֶׁאָהֲבָה נַפְשִׁי
בִּקַּשְׁתִּיו וְלֹא מְצָאתִיו:
באָקוּמָה נָּא וַאֲסוֹבְבָה בָעִיר בַּשְּׁוָקִים וּבָרְחֹבוֹת
אֲבַקְשָׁה אֵת שֶׁאָהֲבָה נַפְשִׁי
בִּקַּשְׁתִּיו וְלֹא מְצָאתִיו:
גמְצָאוּנִי הַשֹּׁמְרִים
הַסֹּבְבִים בָּעִיר
אֵת שֶׁאָהֲבָה נַפְשִׁי רְאִיתֶם:
דכִּמְעַט שֶׁעָבַרְתִּי מֵהֶם
עַד שֶׁמָּצָאתִי
אֵת שֶׁאָהֲבָה נַפְשִׁי
אֲחַזְתִּיו וְלֹא אַרְפֶּנּוּ
עַד־שֶׁהֲבֵיאתִיו אֶל־בֵּית אִמִּי
וְאֶל־חֶדֶר הוֹרָתִי:
ההִשְׁבַּעְתִּי אֶתְכֶם בְּנוֹת יְרוּשָׁלַם בִּצְבָאוֹת
אוֹ בְּאַיְלוֹת הַשָּׂדֶה
אִם־תָּעִירוּ ׀ וְאִם־תְּעוֹרְרוּ אֶת־הָאַהֲבָה
עַד שֶׁתֶּחְפָּץ:
ימִי זֹאת עֹלָה מִן־הַמִּדְבָּר
כְּתִימֲרוֹת עָשָׁן
מְקֻטֶּרֶת מֹר וּלְבוֹנָה

Turn my love, be like a gazelle or a young stag
upon the mountain of spices.
3 ¹By night upon my couch
I sought him whom I love;
I sought him, but I found him not.
²"I will rise now, and go about the city, through the
streets and through the broad ways,
Seeking my true love."
I sought him, but I found him not.
³The watchmen who go about the city
Found me.
"Have you seen my true love?"
⁴Scarcely had I passed them,
When I found
My true love.
I held him, and I would not let him go,
Until I had brought him into my mother's house,
Into the chamber of her who conceived me.
⁵I adjure you, O daughters of Jerusalem, by the gazelles
And by the hinds of the field,
Lest you stir up or arouse my love, until it please . . .
⁶Who is this coming up from the desert
Like pillars of smoke
From burning myrrh and frankincense,

"And gaze upon King Solomon." 3:11

מִכֹּל אַבְקַת רוֹכֵל:

ז הִנֵּה מִטָּתוֹ שֶׁלִּשְׁלֹמֹה

שִׁשִּׁים גִּבֹּרִים סָבִיב לָהּ

מִגִּבֹּרֵי יִשְׂרָאֵל:

ח כֻּלָּם אֲחֻזֵי חֶרֶב

מְלֻמְּדֵי מִלְחָמָה

אִישׁ חַרְבּוֹ עַל־יְרֵכוֹ

מִפַּחַד בַּלֵּילוֹת:

ט אַפִּרְיוֹן עָשָׂה לוֹ הַמֶּלֶךְ שְׁלֹמֹה

מֵעֲצֵי הַלְּבָנוֹן:

י עַמּוּדָיו עָשָׂה כֶסֶף

רְפִידָתוֹ זָהָב

מֶרְכָּבוֹ אַרְגָּמָן

תּוֹכוֹ רָצוּף אַהֲבָה

מִבְּנוֹת יְרוּשָׁלָ͏ִם:

יא צְאֶינָה ׀ וּרְאֶינָה בְּנוֹת צִיּוֹן בַּמֶּלֶךְ שְׁלֹמֹה

בָּעֲטָרָה שֶׁעִטְּרָה־לּוֹ אִמּוֹ בְּיוֹם חֲתֻנָּתוֹ

וּבְיוֹם שִׂמְחַת לִבּוֹ:

ד א הִנָּךְ יָפָה רַעְיָתִי הִנָּךְ יָפָה

עֵינַיִךְ יוֹנִים

מִבַּעַד לְצַמָּתֵךְ

שַׂעְרֵךְ כְּעֵדֶר הָעִזִּים

שֶׁגָּלְשׁוּ מֵהַר גִּלְעָד:

ב שִׁנַּיִךְ כְּעֵדֶר הַקְּצוּבוֹת

שֶׁעָלוּ מִן־הָרַחְצָה

With all the powders of the merchant?
⁷Behold, it is the litter of Solomon;
Three score mighty men are about it,
Of the mighty men of Israel.
⁸They all handle the sword,
They are expert in war:
Each has sword upon thigh
Because of dread in the night.
⁹King Solomon made himself a palanquin
Of the wood of Lebanon.
¹⁰He has made its pillars of silver,
Its top of gold,
The seat of it is purple.
Inside, it is—love,
Paved by the daughters of Jerusalem.
¹¹Go forth, O daughters of Zion, and gaze
upon King Solomon
Wearing the crown with which his mother crowned
him, on the day of his espousal,
On the day of the gladness of his heart.
4 ¹Behold, you are fair, my love,
Behold, you are fair with your eyes as doves
Behind your veil.
Your hair is like a flock of goats,
Trailing down Mount Gilead.
²Your teeth are like a flock of ewes just shorn
Come up from the washing,

שֶׁכֻּלָּם֙ מַתְאִימ֔וֹת
וְשַׁכֻּלָ֖ה אֵ֥ין בָּהֶֽם:
ג כְּח֤וּט הַשָּׁנִי֙ שִׂפְתוֹתַ֔יִךְ
וּמִדְבָּרֵ֖ךְ נָאוֶ֑ה
כְּפֶ֤לַח הָרִמּוֹן֙ רַקָּתֵ֔ךְ
מִבַּ֖עַד לְצַמָּתֵֽךְ:
ד כְּמִגְדַּ֤ל דָּוִיד֙ צַוָּארֵ֔ךְ
בָּנ֖וּי לְתַלְפִּיּ֑וֹת
אֶ֤לֶף הַמָּגֵן֙ תָּל֣וּי עָלָ֔יו
כֹּ֖ל שִׁלְטֵ֥י הַגִּבֹּרִֽים:
ה שְׁנֵ֥י שָׁדַ֛יִךְ כִּשְׁנֵ֥י עֳפָרִ֖ים תְּאוֹמֵ֣י צְבִיָּ֑ה
הָרֹעִ֖ים בַּשּׁוֹשַׁנִּֽים:
י עַ֤ד שֶׁיָּפ֙וּחַ֙ הַיּ֔וֹם
וְנָ֖סוּ הַצְּלָלִ֑ים
אֵ֤לֶךְ לִי֙ אֶל־הַ֣ר הַמּ֔וֹר
וְאֶל־גִּבְעַ֖ת הַלְּבוֹנָֽה:
ז כֻּלָּ֤ךְ יָפָה֙ רַעְיָתִ֔י
וּמ֖וּם אֵ֥ין בָּֽךְ:
ח אִתִּ֤י מִלְּבָנוֹן֙ כַּלָּ֔ה
אִתִּ֖י מִלְּבָנ֣וֹן תָּב֑וֹאִי
תָּשׁ֣וּרִי ׀ מֵרֹ֣אשׁ אֲמָנָ֗ה מֵרֹ֤אשׁ שְׂנִיר֙ וְחֶרְמ֔וֹן
מִמְּעֹנ֣וֹת אֲרָי֔וֹת
מֵהַֽרְרֵ֖י נְמֵרִֽים:
ט לִבַּבְתִּ֖נִי אֲחֹתִ֣י כַלָּ֑ה

All paired alike,
None missing among them.
³Your lips are like a thread of scarlet,
And your mouth is lovely.
Your temples behind your veil
Are like a pomegranate split open.
⁴Your neck is like the tower of David,
Turreted as a fortress,
A thousand shields hanging upon it,
All the armor of the mighty men.
⁵Your breasts are like two fawns, twins of a gazelle,
Which feed among the lilies.
⁶Before the dawn wind rises
Before the shadows flee
I will get me to the mountain of myrrh,
And to the hill of frankincense.
⁷You are all fair, my love;
There is no blemish in you.
⁸With me from Lebanon, my bride,
O, come with me from Lebanon!
Hurry down from the top of Amana, from the top of
Senir and of Hermon,
From the lions' dens,
From the mountain of panthers.
⁹You have ravished my heart, my sister, my bride,

"Your limbs are an orchard of pomegranates." 4:13

לִבַּבְתִּ֫נִי֙ בְּאַחַ֣ת* מֵעֵינַ֔יִךְ
בְּאַחַ֥ד עֲנָ֖ק מִצַּוְּרֹנָֽיִךְ:
יֹ מַה־יָּפ֥וּ דֹדַ֛יִךְ אֲחֹתִ֥י כַלָּ֑ה
מַה־טֹּ֤בוּ דֹדַ֙יִךְ֙ מִיַּ֔יִן
וְרֵ֥יחַ שְׁמָנַ֖יִךְ מִכָּל־בְּשָׂמִֽים:
יא נֹ֣פֶת תִּטֹּ֤פְנָה שִׂפְתוֹתַ֙יִךְ֙ כַּלָּ֔ה
דְּבַ֥שׁ וְחָלָב֙ תַּ֣חַת לְשׁוֹנֵ֔ךְ
וְרֵ֥יחַ שַׂלְמֹתַ֖יִךְ כְּרֵ֥יחַ לְבָנֽוֹן:
יב גַּ֥ן ׀ נָע֖וּל אֲחֹתִ֣י כַלָּ֑ה
גַּ֥ל נָע֖וּל מַעְיָ֥ן חָתֽוּם:
יג שְׁלָחַ֙יִךְ֙ פַּרְדֵּ֣ס רִמּוֹנִ֔ים
עִ֖ם פְּרִ֥י מְגָדִ֑ים
כְּפָרִ֖ים עִם־נְרָדִֽים:
יד נֵ֣רְדְּ ׀ וְכַרְכֹּ֗ם קָנֶה֙ וְקִנָּמ֔וֹן
עִ֖ם כָּל־עֲצֵ֣י לְבוֹנָ֑ה
מֹ֖ר וַאֲהָל֔וֹת
עִ֖ם כָּל־רָאשֵׁ֥י בְשָׂמִֽים:
טו מַעְיַ֣ן גַּנִּ֔ים
בְּאֵ֖ר מַ֣יִם חַיִּ֑ים
וְנֹזְלִ֖ים מִן־לְבָנֽוֹן:
טז ע֤וּרִי צָפוֹן֙ וּב֣וֹאִי תֵימָ֔ן
הָפִ֤יחִי גַנִּי֙ יִזְּל֣וּ בְשָׂמָ֔יו
יָבֹ֤א דוֹדִי֙ לְגַנּ֔וֹ
וְיֹאכַ֖ל פְּרִ֥י מְגָדָֽיו:

(באחד כתיב)

You have ravished my heart with one glance of your
eyes,
With one jewel of your necklace.
¹⁰How fair is your love, my sister, my bride.
How much better is your love than wine,
The fragrance of your ointments than all spices.
¹¹Sweet honey drops from your lips, my bride,
Honey and milk are under your tongue;
The scent of your garments is like the scent of
Lebanon.
¹²A closed garden is my sister, my bride;
A closed spring, a sealed fountain.
¹³Your limbs are an orchard of pomegranates,
With precious fruit,
Henna and spikenard—
¹⁴Spikenard and saffron, calamus and cinnamon,
With all trees of frankincense;
Myrrh and aloes—
All special spices.
¹⁵You are a garden's fountain,
A well of living waters,
Streams from the Lebanon.
¹⁶Awake, O North wind, come, O South wind.
Blow upon my garden, that its spices may flow out.
Let my beloved come into his garden,
And eat its delicious fruit.

ה ^א בָּ֣אתִי לְגַנִּי֮ אֲחֹתִ֣י כַלָּה֒

אָרִ֤יתִי מוֹרִי֙ עִם־בְּשָׂמִ֔י

אָכַ֤לְתִּי יַעְרִי֙ עִם־דִּבְשִׁ֔י

שָׁתִ֥יתִי יֵינִ֖י עִם־חֲלָבִ֑י

אִכְל֣וּ רֵעִ֔ים

שְׁת֥וּ וְשִׁכְר֖וּ דּוֹדִֽים:

^ב אֲנִ֥י יְשֵׁנָ֖ה וְלִבִּ֣י עֵ֑ר

ק֣וֹל ׀ דּוֹדִ֣י דוֹפֵ֗ק פִּתְחִי־לִ֞י אֲחֹתִ֤י רַעְיָתִי֙

יוֹנָתִ֣י תַמָּתִ֔י

שֶׁרֹּאשִׁי֙ נִמְלָא־טָ֔ל

קְוֻּצּוֹתַ֖י רְסִ֥יסֵי לָֽיְלָה:

^ג פָּשַׁ֙טְתִּי֙ אֶת־כֻּתָּנְתִּ֔י

אֵיכָ֖כָה אֶלְבָּשֶׁ֑נָּה

רָחַ֥צְתִּי אֶת־רַגְלַ֖י אֵיכָ֥כָה אֲטַנְּפֵֽם:

^ד דּוֹדִ֗י שָׁלַ֤ח יָדוֹ֙ מִן־הַחֹ֔ר

וּמֵעַ֖י הָמ֥וּ עָלָֽיו:

^ה קַ֥מְתִּֽי אֲנִ֖י לִפְתֹּ֣חַ לְדוֹדִ֑י

וְיָדַ֣י נָֽטְפוּ־מ֗וֹר וְאֶצְבְּעֹתַי֙ מ֣וֹר עֹבֵ֔ר

עַ֖ל כַּפּ֥וֹת הַמַּנְעֽוּל:

^ו פָּתַ֤חְתִּֽי אֲנִי֙ לְדוֹדִ֔י

וְדוֹדִ֖י חָמַ֣ק עָבָ֑ר

נַפְשִׁי֙ יָֽצְאָ֣ה בְדַבְּר֔וֹ

בִּקַּשְׁתִּ֙יהוּ֙ וְלֹ֣א מְצָאתִ֔יהוּ

קְרָאתִ֖יו וְלֹ֥א עָנָֽנִי:

^ז מְצָאֻ֧נִי הַשֹּׁמְרִ֛ים הַסֹּבְבִ֥ים בָּעִ֖יר הִכּ֣וּנִי פְצָע֑וּנִי

5 ¹'I have come into my garden, my sister, my bride.
I have gathered my myrrh and my spice.
I have eaten my honeycomb with my honey.
I have drunk my wine and my milk.
Eat, O friends,
And drink, drink deep, O love.
²I sleep, but my heart is awake.
Hark, my beloved knocks: "Open to me, my sister,
my love, my dove, my perfect one.
For my head is drenched with dew,
My locks with drops of the night."
³I have taken off my robe;
How shall I put it on?
I have washed my feet; how shall I soil them?
⁴My beloved drew his hand from the door hole,
And my heart was stirred for him:
⁵I rose to open to my beloved,
And my hand dropped myrrh, my fingers,
with flowing myrrh,
Upon the handles of the bolt.
⁶I opened to my beloved,
But my beloved had turned away and gone.
My soul departed when he spoke:
I sought him, but I found him not;
I called him, but he answered me not.
⁷The watchmen that went about the city found me,

"His head is as the finest gold..." 5:11

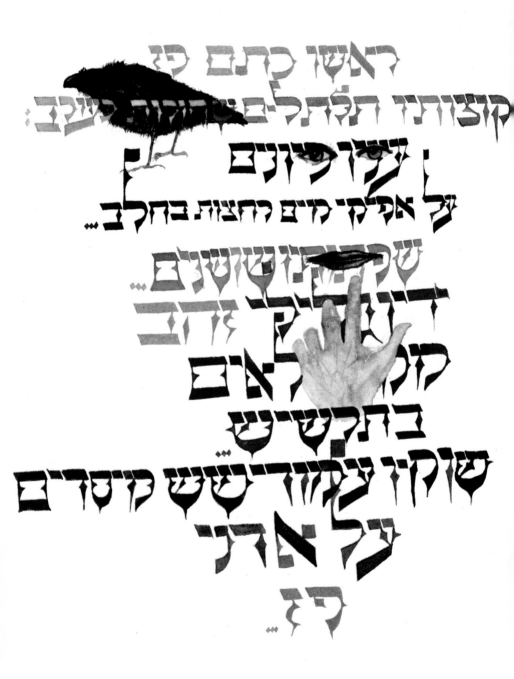

ראשו כתם פז

קצותיו תלתלים ...שחורות כעורב:

עיניו כיונים

על אפיקי מים רחצות בחלב...

שפתותיו שושנים...

ידיו ...זהב

מעיו ...אש

בתקשיש

שוקיו עמודי שש מיסדים

על אדני

פז...

נָשְׂאוּ אֶת־רְדִידִי מֵעָלַי
שֹׁמְרֵי הַחֹמוֹת:
ח הִשְׁבַּעְתִּי אֶתְכֶם בְּנוֹת יְרוּשָׁלָ͏ִם
אִם־תִּמְצְאוּ אֶת־דּוֹדִי
מַה־תַּגִּידוּ לוֹ
שֶׁחוֹלַת אַהֲבָה אָנִי:
ט מַה־דּוֹדֵךְ מִדּוֹד
הַיָּפָה בַּנָּשִׁים
מַה־דּוֹדֵךְ מִדּוֹד
שֶׁכָּכָה הִשְׁבַּעְתָּנוּ:
י דּוֹדִי צַח וְאָדוֹם
דָּגוּל מֵרְבָבָה:
יא רֹאשׁוֹ כֶּתֶם פָּז
קְוֻצּוֹתָיו תַּלְתַּלִּים
שְׁחֹרוֹת כָּעוֹרֵב:
יב עֵינָיו כְּיוֹנִים עַל־אֲפִיקֵי מָיִם
רֹחֲצוֹת בֶּחָלָב
יֹשְׁבוֹת עַל־מִלֵּאת:
יג לְחָיָו כַּעֲרוּגַת הַבֹּשֶׂם
מִגְדְּלוֹת מֶרְקָחִים
שִׂפְתוֹתָיו שׁוֹשַׁנִּים
נֹטְפוֹת מוֹר עֹבֵר:
יד יָדָיו גְּלִילֵי זָהָב
מְמֻלָּאִים בַּתַּרְשִׁישׁ
מֵעָיו עֶשֶׁת שֵׁן

they struck me, they wounded me.
The keepers of the ramparts
Took away my veil.
⁸I adjure you, O daughters of Jerusalem:
If you find my beloved
Will you not tell him
That I am faint with love?
⁹"What is your beloved more than any other,
O fairest among women?
What is your beloved more than any other
That you adjure us so?"
¹⁰My beloved is fair and ruddy,
A paragon among ten thousand.
¹¹His head is as the finest gold
His locks are flowing,
Black as a raven.
¹²His eyes, like doves on water streams,
Are bathed in milk
And fitly set.
¹³His cheeks are like beds of spices
Or towers filled with perfume.
His lips are as lilies
Dropping with flowing myrrh.
¹⁴His hands are golden cylinders
Inlaid with beryl.
His body is as polished ivory,

מְעֻלֶּפֶת סַפִּירִים:

טו שׁוֹקָיו֙ עַמּ֣וּדֵי שֵׁ֔שׁ

מְיֻסָּדִים עַל־אַדְנֵי־פָ֑ז

מַרְאֵ֙הוּ֙ כַּלְּבָנ֔וֹן

בָּח֖וּר כָּאֲרָזִֽים:

טז חִכּוֹ֙ מַֽמְתַקִּ֔ים

וְכֻלּ֖וֹ מַחֲמַדִּ֑ים

זֶ֤ה דוֹדִי֙ וְזֶ֣ה רֵעִ֔י

בְּנ֖וֹת יְרוּשָׁלָֽ͏ִם:

ו א אָ֚נָה הָלַ֣ךְ דּוֹדֵ֔ךְ

הַיָּפָ֖ה בַּנָּשִׁ֑ים

אָ֚נָה פָּנָ֣ה דוֹדֵ֔ךְ

וּנְבַקְשֶׁ֖נּוּ עִמָּֽךְ:

ב דּוֹדִי֙ יָרַ֣ד לְגַנּ֔וֹ

לַעֲרוּג֖וֹת הַבֹּ֑שֶׂם

לִרְעוֹת֙ בַּגַּנִּ֔ים

וְלִלְקֹ֖ט שֽׁוֹשַׁנִּֽים:

ג אֲנִ֤י לְדוֹדִי֙ וְדוֹדִ֣י לִ֔י

הָרוֹעֶ֖ה בַּשּׁוֹשַׁנִּֽים:

ד יָפָ֨ה אַ֤תְּ רַעְיָתִי֙ כְּתִרְצָ֔ה

נָאוָ֖ה כִּירוּשָׁלָ֑͏ִם

אֲיֻמָּ֖ה כַּנִּדְגָּלֽוֹת:

ה הָסֵ֤בִּי עֵינַ֙יִךְ֙ מִנֶּגְדִּ֔י

שֶׁהֵ֖ם הִרְהִיבֻ֑נִי

שַׂעְרֵךְ֙ כְּעֵ֣דֶר הָֽעִזִּ֔ים

Covered with sapphires.
¹⁵His legs are as pillars of marble
In sockets of finest gold.
He is majestic as Lebanon,
Noble as the cedars.
¹⁶His mouth is most sweet,
Yes, he is altogether lovely.
This is my beloved, and this is my friend,
O daughters of Jerusalem.

6 ¹"Where is your beloved gone,
O fairest among women?
Which way did your beloved turn
That we may help you seek him?"
²My beloved has gone down to his garden,
To the beds of spices,
To feed in the gardens,
And to gather lilies.
³I am my beloved's, and my beloved is mine,
Who feeds among the lilies.
⁴You are beautiful, O my love, as Tirza,
Comely as Jerusalem,
Awe-inspiring as bannered hosts.
⁵Turn your eyes away from me,
For they have overcome me.
Your hair is like a flock of goats

שֶׁגָּלְשׁוּ מִן־הַגִּלְעָד:
י שִׁנַּיִךְ כְּעֵדֶר הָרְחֵלִים
שֶׁעָלוּ מִן־הָרַחְצָה
שֶׁכֻּלָּם מַתְאִימוֹת
וְשַׁכֻּלָה אֵין בָּהֶם:
י כְּפֶלַח הָרִמּוֹן רַקָּתֵךְ
מִבַּעַד לְצַמָּתֵךְ:
ח שִׁשִּׁים הֵמָּה מְלָכוֹת
וּשְׁמֹנִים פִּילַגְשִׁים
וַעֲלָמוֹת אֵין מִסְפָּר:
ט אַחַת הִיא יוֹנָתִי תַמָּתִי
אַחַת הִיא לְאִמָּהּ
בָּרָה הִיא לְיוֹלַדְתָּהּ
רָאוּהָ בָנוֹת וַיְאַשְּׁרוּהָ
מְלָכוֹת וּפִילַגְשִׁים וַיְהַלְלוּהָ:
י מִי־זֹאת הַנִּשְׁקָפָה כְּמוֹ־שָׁחַר
יָפָה כַלְּבָנָה בָּרָה כַּחַמָּה
אֲיֻמָּה כַּנִּדְגָּלוֹת:
יא אֶל־גִּנַּת אֱגוֹז יָרַדְתִּי
לִרְאוֹת בְּאִבֵּי הַנָּחַל
לִרְאוֹת הֲפָרְחָה הַגֶּפֶן
הֵנֵצוּ הָרִמֹּנִים:
יב לֹא יָדַעְתִּי
נַפְשִׁי שָׂמַתְנִי
מַרְכְּבוֹת עַמִּי נָדִיב:

Trailing down Mount Gilead.
⁶Your teeth are like a flock of ewes
Come up from the washing,
All paired alike,
None missing among them.
⁷Your temples behind your veil
Are like a pomegranate split open.
⁸There are threescore queens
And fourscore concubines
And young women without number.
⁹My dove is the only one, the perfect beauty.
The only one of her mother,
The choice one of her who bore her.
Daughters saw her, and praised her,
Queens and concubines also, and extolled her.
¹⁰Who is she gazing forth like the dawn,
Fair as the moon, clear as the sun,
Awe-inspiring as bannered armies?
¹¹I went down into the nut garden,
To look at the green shoots of the valley,
To see whether the vine budded,
Whether the pomegranates were in bloom.
¹²Before I was aware,
My soul carried me
Among the chariots of my princely people.

"Return, return, O Shulammite."   7:1

ז יא שׁוּבִי שׁוּבִי הַשּׁוּלַמִּית

שׁוּבִי שׁוּבִי וְנֶחֱזֶה־בָּךְ

מַה־תֶּחֱזוּ בַּשּׁוּלַמִּית

כִּמְחֹלַת הַמַּחֲנָיִם:

ב מַה־יָּפוּ פְעָמַיִךְ בַּנְּעָלִים בַּת־נָדִיב

חַמּוּקֵי יְרֵכַיִךְ

כְּמוֹ חֲלָאִים

מַעֲשֵׂה יְדֵי אׇמָּן:

ג שָׁרְרֵךְ אַגַּן הַסַּהַר

אַל־יֶחְסַר הַמָּזֶג

בִּטְנֵךְ עֲרֵמַת חִטִּים

סוּגָה בַּשּׁוֹשַׁנִּים:

ד שְׁנֵי שָׁדַיִךְ כִּשְׁנֵי עֳפָרִים תׇּאֳמֵי צְבִיָּה:

ה צַוָּארֵךְ כְּמִגְדַּל הַשֵּׁן

עֵינַיִךְ בְּרֵכוֹת בְּחֶשְׁבּוֹן עַל־שַׁעַר בַּת־רַבִּים

אַפֵּךְ כְּמִגְדַּל הַלְּבָנוֹן

צוֹפֶה פְּנֵי דַמָּשֶׂק:

י רֹאשֵׁךְ עָלַיִךְ כַּכַּרְמֶל

וְדַלַּת רֹאשֵׁךְ כָּאַרְגָּמָן

מֶלֶךְ אָסוּר בָּרְהָטִים:

ז מַה־יָּפִית וּמַה־נָּעַמְתְּ

אַהֲבָה בַּתַּעֲנוּגִים:

ח זֹאת קוֹמָתֵךְ דָּמְתָה לְתָמָר

וְשָׁדַיִךְ לְאַשְׁכֹּלוֹת:

ט אָמַרְתִּי אֶעֱלֶה בְתָמָר

7 ¹Return, return, O Shulammite;
Return, return, that we may look at you.
What will you see in the Shulammite,
As she moves between the line of dancers?
²How beautiful are your steps in sandals, O daughter
of nobles!
The curves of your thighs
Are like jewels,
The handwork of a skilled craftsman.
³Your navel is like a round goblet
Where spiced wine will not be lacking.
Your body is like a heap of wheat
Set about with lilies.
⁴Your breasts are like two young fawns, twins of a
gazelle.
⁵Your neck is as a tower of ivory;
Your eyes, as the pools in Heshbon, by the gate
of a great concourse.
Your nose is as the tower of Lebanon,
Looking toward Damascus.
⁶You carry your head like Carmel
And the tresses of your hair are as purple—
A king held captive in its locks!
⁷How fair you are, how pleasant,
O love, for delights.
⁸You are as stately as a palm tree,
Your breasts are like a cluster of grapes.
⁹I said: "I will climb up into the palm tree,

אֹחֲזָה בְּסַנְסִנָּיו

וְיִהְיוּ־נָא שָׁדַ֫יִךְ֙ כְּאֶשְׁכְּלוֹת הַגֶּ֫פֶן

וְרֵיחַ אַפֵּךְ כַּתַּפּוּחִים:

י וְחִכֵּךְ כְּיֵין הַטּוֹב הוֹלֵךְ לְדוֹדִי לְמֵישָׁרִים

דּוֹבֵב שִׂפְתֵי יְשֵׁנִים:

יא אֲנִי לְדוֹדִי

וְעָלַי תְּשׁוּקָתוֹ:

יב לְכָה דוֹדִי נֵצֵא הַשָּׂדֶה

נָלִינָה בַּכְּפָרִים:

יג נַשְׁכִּ֫ימָה֙ לַכְּרָמִים

נִרְאֶה אִם־פָּרְחָה הַגֶּ֫פֶן֙ פִּתַּח הַסְּמָדַר

הֵנֵצוּ הָרִמּוֹנִים

שָׁם אֶתֵּן אֶת־דֹּדַי לָךְ:

יד הַדּוּדָאִים נָתְנוּ־רֵ֫יחַ וְעַל־פְּתָחֵ֫ינוּ֙ כָּל־מְגָדִים

חֲדָשִׁים גַּם־יְשָׁנִים

דּוֹדִי צָפַנְתִּי לָךְ:

ח א מִי יִתֶּנְךָ֙ כְּאָח לִי

יוֹנֵק שְׁדֵי אִמִּי

אֶמְצָאֲךָ֤ בַחוּץ֙ אֶשָּׁקְךָ֔

גַּם לֹא־יָבֻ֫זוּ לִי:

ב אֶנְהָגֲךָ֗ אֲבִיאֲךָ֛ אֶל־בֵּית אִמִּי תְּלַמְּדֵ֑נִי

אַשְׁקְךָ֙ מִיַּ֫יִן הָרֶ֫קַח

מֵעֲסִיס רִמֹּנִי:

ג שְׂמֹאלוֹ֙ תַּחַת רֹאשִׁי

וִימִינוֹ תְּחַבְּקֵנִי:

I will take hold of its branches."
Now your breasts will be as clusters of the vine,
And the fragrance of your breath as apples.
[10]Let your mouth be like the best wine which glides
down smoothly for my beloved,
Moving gently the lips of those who sleep.
[11]I am my beloved's,
And his desire is for me.
[12]Come, my beloved, let us go forth into the field.
Let us lodge in the villages.
[13]Let us get up early to the vineyards.
Let us see if the vine has flowered, if its blossoms
have opened,
If the pomegranates are in flower.
There I will give you my love.
[14]The mandrakes give forth fragrance, and at your
doors are all choice fruits,
New and old,
Which I have kept for you, O my beloved.

8 [1]Would that you were as my brother,
Who sucked the breasts of my mother.
I could kiss you then, when I met you outside,
And would not be despised by anyone.
[2]I would lead you, would bring you to the house of
my mother, for you to instruct me.
I would let you drink of the spiced wine,
Of the juice of my pomegranate.
[3]His left hand is under my head,
And his right hand embraces me.

ז הִשְׁבַּ֤עְתִּי אֶתְכֶם֙ בְּנ֣וֹת יְרוּשָׁלַ֔͏ִם

מַה־תָּעִ֥ירוּ ׀ וּֽמַה־תְּעֹֽרְר֛וּ אֶת־הָאַהֲבָ֖ה

עַ֥ד שֶׁתֶּחְפָּֽץ׃

ח מִ֣י זֹ֗את עֹלָה֙ מִן־הַמִּדְבָּ֔ר

מִתְרַפֶּ֖קֶת עַל־דּוֹדָ֑הּ

תַּ֤חַת הַתַּפּ֙וּחַ֙ עֽוֹרַרְתִּ֔יךָ

שָׁ֚מָּה חִבְּלַ֣תְךָ אִמֶּ֔ךָ

שָׁ֥מָּה חִבְּלָ֖ה יְלָדַֽתְךָ׃

ט שִׂימֵ֨נִי כַֽחוֹתָ֜ם עַל־לִבֶּ֗ךָ כַּֽחוֹתָם֙ עַל־זְרוֹעֶ֔ךָ

כִּֽי־עַזָּ֤ה כַמָּ֙וֶת֙ אַהֲבָ֔ה

קָשָׁ֥ה כִשְׁא֖וֹל קִנְאָ֑ה

רְשָׁפֶ֕יהָ רִשְׁפֵּ֕י אֵ֖שׁ שַׁלְהֶ֥בֶתְיָֽה׃

י מַ֣יִם רַבִּ֗ים לֹ֤א יֽוּכְלוּ֙ לְכַבּ֣וֹת אֶת־הָֽאַהֲבָ֔ה

וּנְהָר֖וֹת לֹ֣א יִשְׁטְפ֑וּהָ

אִם־יִתֵּ֨ן אִ֜ישׁ אֶת־כָּל־ה֤וֹן בֵּיתוֹ֙ בָּאַהֲבָ֔ה

בּ֖וֹז יָב֥וּזוּ לֽוֹ׃

יא אָח֥וֹת לָ֙נוּ֙ קְטַנָּ֔ה

וְשָׁדַ֖יִם אֵ֣ין לָ֑הּ

מַֽה־נַּעֲשֶׂה֙ לַֽאֲחֹתֵ֔נוּ

בַּיּ֖וֹם שֶׁיְּדֻבַּר־בָּֽהּ׃

יב אִם־חוֹמָ֣ה הִ֔יא

נִבְנֶ֥ה עָלֶ֖יהָ טִ֣ירַת כָּ֑סֶף

וְאִם־דֶּ֣לֶת הִ֔יא

נָצ֥וּר עָלֶ֖יהָ ל֥וּחַ אָֽרֶז׃

⁴I adjure you, O daughters of Jerusalem,
Lest you stir up or arouse my love . . . until it please.
⁵Who is she coming up from the wilderness
Leaning upon her beloved?
I roused you under the apple tree.
There your mother brought you forth,
There she who bore you, brought you forth.
⁶Set me as a seal upon your heart, as a seal upon your
arm.
For love is strong as death,
Jealousy is cruel as the grave.
Its flashes are flashes of fire, a blazing flame of the
Lord.
⁷Many waters cannot quench love,
Neither can rivers sweep it away.
If a man would give all the substances of his house for
love,
He would be utterly condemned.
⁸We have a little sister
And she has no breasts.
What shall we do for our sister
On the day she is spoken for?
⁹If she be a rampart
We will build upon her a turret of silver.
And if she be a door
We will enclose her with boards of cedar.

יֹ אֲנִי חוֹמָ֔ה

וְשָׁדַ֖י כַּמִּגְדָּל֑וֹת

אָ֤ז הָיִ֙יתִי֙ בְעֵינָ֔יו כְּמוֹצְאֵ֖ת שָׁלֽוֹם׃

יאֹ כֶּ֣רֶם הָיָ֤ה לִשְׁלֹמֹה֙ בְּבַ֣עַל הָמ֔וֹן

נָתַ֥ן אֶת־הַכֶּ֖רֶם לַנֹּטְרִ֑ים

אִ֛ישׁ יָבִ֥א בְּפִרְי֖וֹ אֶ֥לֶף כָּֽסֶף׃

יבֹ כַּרְמִ֥י שֶׁלִּ֖י לְפָנָ֑י

הָאֶ֤לֶף לְךָ֙ שְׁלֹמֹ֔ה

וּמָאתַ֖יִם לְנֹטְרִ֥ים אֶת־פִּרְיֽוֹ׃

יגֹ הַיּוֹשֶׁ֣בֶת בַּגַּנִּ֗ים חֲבֵרִ֛ים מַקְשִׁבִ֥ים לְקוֹלֵ֖ךְ

הַשְׁמִיעִֽנִי׃

ידֹ בְּרַ֣ח ׀ דּוֹדִ֗י וּֽדְמֵה־לְךָ֤ לִצְבִי֙ א֚וֹ לְעֹ֣פֶר הָֽאַיָּלִ֔ים

עַ֖ל הָרֵ֥י בְשָׂמִֽים׃

[10]I am a rampart
And my breasts are like towers.
Then I was in his eyes as one who found peace.
[11]Solomon had a vineyard at Baal Hamon.
He let out the vineyard to keepers.
For its fruit one would give a thousand pieces of silver.
[12]My vineyard, which is mine, is before me.
Let the thousand be yours, O Solomon,
And the two hundred to the keepers of fruit.
[13]O you who dwell in the gardens, while your
companions are listening, let me hear your voice:
[14]"Make haste, my beloved, and be like a gazelle,
or a young stag
Upon the mountain of spices."

AFTER READING FROM
THE SCROLL OF SONG OF SONGS

Creator of all worlds, manifest and hidden:
We have read from the Song of Songs,
    sacred poetry of love.
Our ancestors, trusting in the value
    of each phrase, of every word,
    of each letter and vowel,
    sought awesome mysteries in every nuance of its sentences,
    Your presence in meanings manifest and hidden.
May our reading of the Song of Songs open our hearts to You.
O God, help us also to find Your Presence,
    in meanings both manifest and hidden.
Guide us in our thoughts,
    fulfill our yearnings for goodness.
O God, renew us with Your love,
    that all Your children may still yet rejoice together
    in a Zion of love and peace. Amen.

בָּרוּךְ אַתָּה, יְיָ אֱלֹהֵינוּ, מֶלֶךְ הָעוֹלָם, אֲשֶׁר בָּרָא שָׂשׂוֹן וְשִׂמְחָה,
אַהֲבָה וְאַחְוָה, שָׁלוֹם וְרֵעוּת. בָּרוּךְ אַתָּה, יְיָ, מְשַׂמֵּחַ צִיּוֹן בְּבָנֶיהָ.

THE SCROLL OF RUTH

INTRODUCTION TO
THE SCROLL OF RUTH

Ruth is the nightingale song of love and trust in our tradition. Out of the biblical text there rises a lyrical tale told to perfection, simplicity blending with profound meaning. A song moves through the lives presented in the text.

> Perhaps the self-same song that found a path
> Through the sad heart of Ruth, when, sick for home,
> She stood in tears amid the alien corn . . .
> (John Keats, *Ode to a Nightingale*, st. 6)

Perhaps the greatest line in Keats' poetry, though not the most accurate one, it does bring us into the heart of an experience which still dominates our covenant of marriage, our treatment of strangers, our reception of proselytes. Ruth is a book for all times, whether written in post-exilic days or based upon very old oral traditions. It is set in the time of the Judges—not the best ones, if we assign it to the period of Gideon and Samson—and it attempts to define the rights of widows and aliens within a society fallen upon hard times. The Book of Leviticus comes to life here, with its injunctions to leave part of the harvest for the needy, and with all of its concern and compassion for the underprivileged within the society. The text contains complexities; yet these fade away against the simple message of a Divine plan fulfilling itself among decent people: Ruth, Naomi and Boaz all occupy the stage in turn, and God's purpose is fulfilled through their actions.

We read the Scroll of Ruth on Shavuot, the time of the Giving of the Law. The authority for this is found in *Soferim* (xiv, 3ff), an 8th century Palestinian text; and the rabbis find many reasons why Ruth and Shavuot are linked: harvest time, the Giving of the Torah and its acceptance as we see it in the life of Ruth and David, the offspring of Ruth, who died on Shavuot; and it is a

happy book for a season of joy.

The opening paragraph, with a marvelous economy of words, sets the stage: the characters are presented, the situation is clear. Elimelech, Naomi, and their two sons become refugees in an alien land, losing all rights and status in fleeing from a famine—a major disaster in their homeland. Mahlon and Chilion have a role to play in the story. "Sick" and "Ailing," as their names describe them, they are still paired against one another. Mahlon's name will survive through Ruth; Chilion disappears from view. Even then, rabbinic imagination makes Orpah the ancestor of Goliath who will meet Ruth's descendant, David, in a final confrontation of these branches of the family. Elimelech and the sons die. The rabbis see the death as caused by their leaving of Canaan. In this they touch on a clear theme within the book: the love for this land, a rich and sensuous feeling rising out of the story and out of the loving descriptions of the land at harvest time. Naomi returns to Bethlehem, the "sweet one" made "bitter" by adversity.

Ruth remains with Naomi, while the realistic Orpah accepts Naomi's reasoning that the daughters-in-law need not become refugees in turn. The text needs no embellishments:

> Entreat me not to leave you, or to return from following after you. For wherever you go, I will go. Wherever you lodge, I will lodge. Your people shall be my people, and your God my God. Where you die, I will die; and there will I be buried . . .

It is a statement of loyalty and faith which endures through all generations. And the loyalty is soon put to the test, as Ruth goes out to glean in strange fields. There, in the field of Boaz, several patterns converge. Naomi has a plan which will obligate the kinsman to support her. Ruth has her own ideas which will, if realized, change her own position as well. And Boaz moves from an initial position of utter correctness and minimum courtesy to a granting of extra privileges which reflect a change within himself of which he is not fully aware at this point. He acknowledges her right to glean behind his handmaidens and to remain unmolested in his fields, but he does not yet accede to her request to glean among the sheaves. By meal time, he is a changed person: she is to eat with him, she may glean among the sheaves, and his men

are to drop part of their harvest for Ruth to acquire. Ruth returns home with "an *eifa* of barley" (between 30 and 50 pounds according to modern authorities), and Naomi realizes that their future might be brighter than she had dared to hope.

The harvest comes to an end, and Naomi instructs Ruth in a new plan: she is to join Boaz at the threshing floor during his night of vigil. The vigil had cultic and ceremonial significance; and Ruth's preparations for the night are preparations of marriage. Whether or not the marriage was consummated on that night is debated, although the story is clear enough here: the consummation took place after the marriage (4:13) and was blessed by God with a son, Obed. The whole thrust of the narrative, of Boaz as 'the redeemer,' of Obed declared to be the son of Naomi, would lose its point had the relationship between Ruth and Boaz been other than a proper marriage between equals. The court scene, between Boaz and the other unnamed claimant, establishes this as it resolves the underlying patterns with a happy ending. And time and history place another dimension into this pattern: the covenant of love between Boaz and Ruth reminded the people Israel, in times of exile and need, that a similar covenant exists and continues between Israel and God.

All of the story is brought to a successful conclusion. First, there is the matter of redeeming Elimelech's property, Naomi's only possibility of re-establishing herself in the land. The anonymous kinsman is anxious to purchase the land. Since Naomi has no male descendants, the property would then become part of his permanent family holding. Then Boaz reminds him that marriage to Ruth would be part of the obligation. The son of that marriage would be assigned to Naomi, and the final outcome of the contract would see the land revert to Naomi and her family. The kinsman demurs, and Boaz happily accepts the privilege and obligation of marrying Ruth and raising a family for Naomi. Professor Herbert Brichto points out that the welfare of the dead depended upon descendants retaining ancestral property, and that the unknown kinsman had no desire to raise a son who would continue Mahlon's name. The irony is clear: it is the kinsman whose name is forgotten!

The Scroll of Ruth is not a legal document giving instruction on levirate marriage and land redemption. As Jack Sassoon has

pointed out, it is a folk tale, with the structure and logic of the storyteller's art. It takes the legalities of the time for granted, as incidental to the unfolding of a Divine pattern within human lives, in the creation of a family tree for King David, with possible intimations of a messianic kingdom. It began with the suffering of Naomi, and ends with her joy. The declaration of Ruth is fulfilled: the destinies of Naomi and Ruth are interlocked, they are now one family and one faith. Boaz has fulfilled both of their hopes; he has been the redeemer to Naomi, the true husband to Ruth. And the community rejoices.

Some scholars have argued that the book was written to defend intermarriage. It was, they contend, a kind of tract put out against the demand made by Ezra on the return from exile that Jews who had remained in the land must divorce their non-Jewish wives. Certainly, it gives full rights to a Moabite woman who then becomes the ancestress of the royal house of the Jewish people, of King David who comes to represent the messianic ideal, the unity and peace which will embrace all humanity. Loyalty to the faith of Israel is fused with the love of humanity for whom the Torah was revealed. As this text becomes part of Shavuot, the festival of that revelation, the convert who joins Ruth freely, with all her love and loyalty given freely, stands before Sinai and receives the Torah.

But the Scroll of Ruth exists in its own right, alone, as a simple, beautiful story. Stories can exist without special justification; beautiful stories are also part of Torah. They are there, and they have a right to be there. We are taught:

> Rabbi Ze'ira said: "This scroll is not concerned with either purity or defilement, either prohibition or permission. Why, then, was it written? To teach you of a magnificent reward to those who practice and dispense *chesed* (steadfast kindness)."
>
> (*Ruth Rabba*, 2:15)

Placed into our liturgy, at the season of the giving of the Torah, we thus rediscover the heart of the matter: the steadfast love, the *chesed,* which assures the eternity of the covenant made at Sinai between God and Israel to the commemoration of which we devote the festival of Shavuot.

SERVICE FOR THE READING OF
THE SCROLL OF RUTH

אַל־תִּפְגְּעִי־בִי לְעָזְבֵךְ, לָשׁוּב מֵאַחֲרָיִךְ.

Entreat me not to leave thee, nor to return from following thee.

בָּרוּךְ יְיָ אֲשֶׁר לֹא־עָזַב חַסְדּוֹ אֶת־הַחַיִּים וְאֶת־הַמֵּתִים.

Blessed be God who has not ceased in loving faithfulness with the living and with the dead.

כִּי אֶל־אֲשֶׁר תֵּלְכִי, אֵלֵךְ.

For whither thou goest, I will go.

בָּרוּךְ יְיָ אֲשֶׁר לֹא עֲזָבֵךְ הַיּוֹם הַזֶּה.

Blessed be God who has not forsaken you today.

עַמֵּךְ עַמִּי, וֵאלֹהַיִךְ אֱלֹהָי.

Thy people shall be my people, and thy God my God.

בָּרוּךְ יְיָ אֲשֶׁר לֹא־עָזַב חַסְדּוֹ וַאֲמִתּוֹ, אָנֹכִי בַּדֶּרֶךְ נָחַנִי יְיָ.

Blessed be God who has not withheld steadfast kindness, for I have been guided on my way by God.

For Obed begot Jesse, and Jesse begot David, and from David came forth the dream of Messianic days.

215

בָּרוּךְ יְיָ אֲשֶׁר לֹא־עָזַב חַסְדּוֹ אֶת־הַחַיִּים וְאֶת־הַמֵּתִים.

Praised be God who has not ceased in loving faithfulness
with the living and with the dead.

READING FROM
THE SCROLL OF RUTH

א א וַיְהִ֗י בִּימֵי֙ שְׁפֹ֣ט הַשֹּׁפְטִ֔ים וַיְהִ֥י רָעָ֖ב בָּאָ֑רֶץ וַיֵּ֨לֶךְ
אִ֜ישׁ מִבֵּ֧ית לֶ֣חֶם יְהוּדָ֗ה לָגוּר֙ בִּשְׂדֵ֣י מוֹאָ֔ב ה֥וּא
וְאִשְׁתּ֖וֹ וּשְׁנֵ֥י בָנָֽיו: ² וְשֵׁ֣ם הָאִ֣ישׁ אֱלִימֶ֗לֶךְ וְשֵׁם֩
אִשְׁתּ֨וֹ נׇעֳמִ֜י וְשֵׁ֥ם שְׁנֵֽי־בָנָ֣יו ׀ מַחְל֤וֹן וְכִלְיוֹן֙
אֶפְרָתִ֔ים מִבֵּ֥ית לֶ֖חֶם יְהוּדָ֑ה וַיָּבֹ֥אוּ שְׂדֵי־מוֹאָ֖ב
וַיִּֽהְיוּ־שָֽׁם:
³ וַיָּ֥מׇת אֱלִימֶ֖לֶךְ אִ֣ישׁ נׇעֳמִ֑י וַתִּשָּׁאֵ֥ר הִ֖יא וּשְׁנֵ֥י
בָנֶֽיהָ: ⁴ וַיִּשְׂא֣וּ לָהֶ֗ם נָשִׁים֙ מֹ֣אֲבִיּ֔וֹת שֵׁ֤ם הָֽאַחַת֙
עׇרְפָּ֔ה וְשֵׁ֥ם הַשֵּׁנִ֖ית ר֑וּת וַיֵּ֥שְׁבוּ שָׁ֖ם כְּעֶ֥שֶׂר שָׁנִֽים:
⁵ וַיָּמ֣וּתוּ גַם־שְׁנֵיהֶ֖ם מַחְל֣וֹן וְכִלְי֑וֹן וַתִּשָּׁאֵר֙ הָֽאִשָּׁ֔ה
מִשְּׁנֵ֥י יְלָדֶ֖יהָ וּמֵאִישָֽׁהּ:
⁶ וַתָּ֤קׇם הִיא֙ וְכַלֹּתֶ֔יהָ וַתָּ֖שׇׁב מִשְּׂדֵ֣י מוֹאָ֑ב כִּ֤י
שָֽׁמְעָה֙ בִּשְׂדֵ֣ה מוֹאָ֔ב כִּֽי־פָקַ֤ד יְהֹוָה֙ אֶת־עַמּ֔וֹ
לָתֵ֥ת לָהֶ֖ם לָֽחֶם: ⁷ וַתֵּצֵ֗א מִן־הַמָּקוֹם֙ אֲשֶׁ֣ר הָיְתָה־
שָׁ֔מָּה וּשְׁתֵּ֥י כַלֹּתֶ֖יהָ עִמָּ֑הּ וַתֵּלַ֣כְנָה בַדֶּ֔רֶךְ לָשׁ֖וּב
אֶל־אֶ֥רֶץ יְהוּדָֽה:
⁸ וַתֹּ֤אמֶר נׇעֳמִי֙ לִשְׁתֵּ֣י כַלֹּתֶ֔יהָ לֵ֣כְנָה שֹּׁ֔בְנָה אִשָּׁ֖ה
לְבֵ֣ית אִמָּ֑הּ יַ֣עַשׂ* יְהֹוָ֤ה עִמָּכֶם֙ חֶ֔סֶד כַּאֲשֶׁ֧ר
עֲשִׂיתֶ֛ם עִם־הַמֵּתִ֖ים וְעִמָּדִֽי: ⁹ יִתֵּ֤ן יְהֹוָה֙ לָכֶ֔ם
וּמְצֶ֣אןָ מְנוּחָ֔ה אִשָּׁ֖ה בֵּ֣ית אִישָׁ֑הּ וַתִּשַּׁ֣ק לָהֶ֔ן
וַתִּשֶּׂ֥אנָה קוֹלָ֖ן וַתִּבְכֶּֽינָה: ¹⁰ וַתֹּאמַ֖רְנָה לָּ֑הּ כִּי־אִתָּ֥ךְ
נָשׁ֖וּב לְעַמֵּֽךְ:

(יעשה כתיב)

I   ¹Now it came to pass in the days when the judges ruled, that there was a famine in the land. And a certain man of Bethlehem in Judah went to sojourn in the field of Moab; he, and his wife, and his two sons. ²The name of the man was Elimelech, and the name of his wife was Naomi. His two sons were named Mahlon and Chilion—Ephrathites of Bethlehem in Judah. They came into the fields of Moab; and there they stayed.

³Then Elimelech, Naomi's husband, died; and she was left alone with her two sons. ⁴They married Moabite women; one of them was named Orpah, and the name of the other was Ruth; and they lived there for about ten years. ⁵And Mahlon and Chilion also died, both of them. So the woman was left without her two sons and her husband.

⁶Then she started out with her daughters-in-law, to return from the fields of Moab; for she had heard in the fields of Moab that the Lord had cared for His people in giving them food. ⁷She therefore went forth from the place where she had been staying, together with her two daughters-in-law; and they took the road back to the land of Judah.

⁸Naomi then said to her two daughters-in-law: "Go, return—each of you—to her mother's house. May the Lord deal kindly with you, as you have dealt with the dead, and with me. ⁹May the Lord grant that you will find security, each of you in the house of her husband." Then she kissed them; and they lifted up their voices and wept. ¹⁰And they said to her: "We will certainly return with you to your people."

Ruth, Naomi, and Orpah   1:4

יא וַתֹּאמֶר נָעֳמִי שֹׁבְנָה בְנֹתַי לָמָּה תֵלַכְנָה עִמִּי הַעוֹד־לִי בָנִים בְּמֵעַי וְהָיוּ לָכֶם לַאֲנָשִׁים: יב שֹׁבְנָה בְנֹתַי לֵכְןָ כִּי זָקַנְתִּי מִהְיוֹת לְאִישׁ כִּי אָמַרְתִּי יֶשׁ־ לִי תִקְוָה גַּם הָיִיתִי הַלַּיְלָה לְאִישׁ וְגַם יָלַדְתִּי בָנִים: יג הֲלָהֵן ׀ תְּשַׂבֵּרְנָה עַד אֲשֶׁר יִגְדָּלוּ הֲלָהֵן תֵּעָגֵנָה לְבִלְתִּי הֱיוֹת לְאִישׁ אַל בְּנֹתַי כִּי־מַר־לִי מְאֹד מִכֶּם כִּי־יָצְאָה בִי יַד־יְהֹוָה: יד וַתִּשֶּׂנָה קוֹלָן וַתִּבְכֶּינָה עוֹד וַתִּשַּׁק עָרְפָּה לַחֲמוֹתָהּ וְרוּת דָּבְקָה בָּהּ: טו וַתֹּאמֶר הִנֵּה שָׁבָה יְבִמְתֵּךְ אֶל־עַמָּהּ וְאֶל־אֱלֹהֶיהָ שׁוּבִי אַחֲרֵי יְבִמְתֵּךְ: טז וַתֹּאמֶר רוּת אַל־תִּפְגְּעִי־בִי לְעָזְבֵךְ לָשׁוּב מֵאַחֲרָיִךְ כִּי אֶל־אֲשֶׁר תֵּלְכִי אֵלֵךְ וּבַאֲשֶׁר תָּלִינִי אָלִין עַמֵּךְ עַמִּי וֵאלֹהַיִךְ אֱלֹהָי: יז בַּאֲשֶׁר תָּמוּתִי אָמוּת וְשָׁם אֶקָּבֵר כֹּה יַעֲשֶׂה יְהֹוָה לִי וְכֹה יוֹסִיף כִּי הַמָּוֶת יַפְרִיד בֵּינִי וּבֵינֵךְ: יח וַתֵּרֶא כִּי־ מִתְאַמֶּצֶת הִיא לָלֶכֶת אִתָּהּ וַתֶּחְדַּל לְדַבֵּר אֵלֶיהָ: יט וַתֵּלַכְנָה שְׁתֵּיהֶם עַד־בּוֹאָנָה בֵּית לָחֶם וַיְהִי כְּבוֹאָנָה בֵּית לֶחֶם וַתֵּהֹם כָּל־הָעִיר עֲלֵיהֶן וַתֹּאמַרְנָה הֲזֹאת נָעֳמִי: כ וַתֹּאמֶר אֲלֵיהֶן אַל־ תִּקְרֶאנָה לִי נָעֳמִי קְרֶאןָ לִי מָרָא כִּי־הֵמַר שַׁדַּי לִי מְאֹד: כא אֲנִי מְלֵאָה הָלַכְתִּי וְרֵיקָם הֱשִׁיבַנִי יְהֹוָה

[11]But Naomi replied: "Return, my daughters. Why should you go with me? Are there any more sons in my body who might be husbands for you? [12]Return, my daughters, go your way; for I am too old to have a husband. Even if I should say, 'I have hope,' even if I should have a husband tonight and should also bear sons— [13]would you tarry for them until they were grown? Would you tie yourselves down for them and have no husbands? Oh no, my daughters. I would be all the more bitter on your behalf; for the hand of the Lord has gone out against me."

[14]They lifted up their voices and wept again; and Orpah kissed her mother-in-law farewell, but Ruth clung to her. [15]So she said: "Look, your sister-in-law has returned to her people and to her gods. Go, follow your sister-in-law." [16]But Ruth said: "Entreat me not to leave you, or to return from following after you. For wherever you go, I will go. Wherever you lodge, I will lodge. Your people shall be my people, and your God my God. [17]Where you die, I will die; and there will I be buried. The Lord do thus to me—and more as well—if anything but death parts me from you." [18]When she (Naomi) saw how determined she was to go with her, she said no more to her. [19]So the two went on until they came to Bethlehem.

And it came to pass, when they arrived in Bethlehem, that all the city was astir concerning them; and the women said: "Is this Naomi?" [20]She replied: "Do not call me Naomi ('Pleasantness'); call me Mara ('Bitterness'): for the Almighty has dealt very bitterly with me. [21]I went out full, and the Lord brought me

Ruth and Naomi   1:16

לָמָּה תִקְרֶאנָה לִי נָעֳמִי וַיהוָה עָנָה בִי וְשַׁדַּי
הֵרַע־לִי:

כּב וַתָּשָׁב נָעֳמִי וְרוּת הַמּוֹאֲבִיָּה כַלָּתָהּ עִמָּהּ
הַשָּׁבָה מִשְּׂדֵי מוֹאָב וְהֵמָּה בָּאוּ בֵּית לֶחֶם
בִּתְחִלַּת קְצִיר שְׂעֹרִים:

ב א וּלְנָעֳמִי מוֹדָע* לְאִישָׁהּ אִישׁ גִּבּוֹר חַיִל
מִמִּשְׁפַּחַת אֱלִימֶלֶךְ וּשְׁמוֹ בֹּעַז:

ב וַתֹּאמֶר רוּת הַמּוֹאֲבִיָּה אֶל־נָעֳמִי אֵלְכָה־נָּא
הַשָּׂדֶה וַאֲלַקֳטָה בַשִּׁבֳּלִים אַחַר אֲשֶׁר אֶמְצָא־חֵן
בְּעֵינָיו וַתֹּאמֶר לָהּ לְכִי בִתִּי: ג וַתֵּלֶךְ וַתָּבוֹא
וַתְּלַקֵּט בַּשָּׂדֶה אַחֲרֵי הַקֹּצְרִים וַיִּקֶר מִקְרֶהָ
חֶלְקַת הַשָּׂדֶה לְבֹעַז אֲשֶׁר מִמִּשְׁפַּחַת אֱלִימֶלֶךְ:

ד וְהִנֵּה־בֹעַז בָּא מִבֵּית לֶחֶם וַיֹּאמֶר לַקּוֹצְרִים
יְהוָה עִמָּכֶם וַיֹּאמְרוּ לוֹ יְבָרֶכְךָ יְהוָה: ה וַיֹּאמֶר
בֹּעַז לְנַעֲרוֹ הַנִּצָּב עַל־הַקּוֹצְרִים לְמִי הַנַּעֲרָה
הַזֹּאת: ו וַיַּעַן הַנַּעַר הַנִּצָּב עַל־הַקּוֹצְרִים וַיֹּאמַר
נַעֲרָה מוֹאֲבִיָּה הִיא הַשָּׁבָה עִם־נָעֳמִי מִשְּׂדֵי
מוֹאָב: ז וַתֹּאמֶר אֲלַקֳטָה־נָּא וְאָסַפְתִּי בָעֳמָרִים
אַחֲרֵי הַקּוֹצְרִים וַתָּבוֹא וַתַּעֲמוֹד מֵאָז הַבֹּקֶר
וְעַד־עַתָּה זֶה שִׁבְתָּהּ הַבַּיִת מְעָט:

ח וַיֹּאמֶר בֹּעַז אֶל־רוּת הֲלוֹא שָׁמַעַתְּ בִּתִּי אַל־
תֵּלְכִי לִלְקֹט בְּשָׂדֶה אַחֵר וְגַם לֹא תַעֲבוּרִי מִזֶּה
וְכֹה תִדְבָּקִין עִם־נַעֲרֹתָי: ט עֵינַיִךְ בַּשָּׂדֶה אֲשֶׁר־

(מידע כתיב)

home again empty. Why do you call me Naomi, since the Lord has testified against me, and the Almighty has brought misfortune upon me!"

²²So Naomi returned. And Ruth, the Moabitess, her daughter-in-law, returned with her out of the field of Moab. And they came to Bethlehem at the beginning of the barley harvest.

2 ¹Now Naomi had a kinsman of her husband's, a mighty man of wealth, of the family of Elimelech, whose name was Boaz.

²And Ruth the Moabitess said to Naomi: "Let me now go to the field and glean ears of corn behind someone in whose sight I might find grace." She said to her: "Go, my daughter." ³And she went, and came and gleaned in the field behind the reapers. As it happened, she came to a piece of the field belonging to Boaz, who was of the family of Elimelech.

⁴Lo and behold, Boaz came from Bethlehem and said to the reapers: "The Lord be with you," and they answered him: "The Lord bless you." ⁵Then Boaz said to the servant who was appointed over the reapers: "Whose girl is that?" ⁶And the servant who was appointed over the reapers answered and said: "She is a Moabite girl who came back with Naomi out of the fields of Moab. ⁷She said: 'Please let me glean and gather behind the reapers among the sheaves.' So she came, and stood at work from the morning until now, except for her resting in the hut for a little while."

⁸Boaz then said to Ruth: "Hear me, my daughter. Do not go to glean in another field, and do not go away from here; but stay here, close to my maidens. ⁹Keep

Boaz   2:1

יִקְצֹרוּן וְהָלַכְתְּ אַחֲרֵיהֶן הֲלֹוא צִוִּיתִי אֶת־
הַנְּעָרִים לְבִלְתִּי נָגְעֵךְ וְצָמִת וְהָלַכְתְּ אֶל־הַכֵּלִים
וְשָׁתִית מֵאֲשֶׁר יִשְׁאֲבוּן הַנְּעָרִים:
י וַתִּפֹּל עַל־פָּנֶיהָ וַתִּשְׁתַּחוּ אָרְצָה וַתֹּאמֶר אֵלָיו
מַדּוּעַ מָצָאתִי חֵן בְּעֵינֶיךָ לְהַכִּירֵנִי וְאָנֹכִי נָכְרִיָּה:
יא וַיַּעַן בֹּעַז וַיֹּאמֶר לָהּ הֻגֵּד הֻגַּד לִי כֹּל אֲשֶׁר־
עָשִׂית אֶת־חֲמוֹתֵךְ אַחֲרֵי מוֹת אִישֵׁךְ וַתַּעַזְבִי
אָבִיךְ וְאִמֵּךְ וְאֶרֶץ מוֹלַדְתֵּךְ וַתֵּלְכִי אֶל־עַם אֲשֶׁר
לֹא־יָדַעַתְּ תְּמוֹל שִׁלְשׁוֹם: יב יְשַׁלֵּם יְהֹוָה פָּעֳלֵךְ
וּתְהִי מַשְׂכֻּרְתֵּךְ שְׁלֵמָה מֵעִם יְהֹוָה אֱלֹהֵי יִשְׂרָאֵל
אֲשֶׁר־בָּאת לַחֲסוֹת תַּחַת־כְּנָפָיו:
יג וַתֹּאמֶר אֶמְצָא־חֵן בְּעֵינֶיךָ אֲדֹנִי כִּי נִחַמְתָּנִי וְכִי
דִבַּרְתָּ עַל־לֵב שִׁפְחָתֶךָ וְאָנֹכִי לֹא אֶהְיֶה כְּאַחַת
שִׁפְחֹתֶיךָ:
יד וַיֹּאמֶר לָהּ בֹעַז לְעֵת הָאֹכֶל גֹּשִׁי הֲלֹם וְאָכַלְתְּ
מִן־הַלֶּחֶם וְטָבַלְתְּ פִּתֵּךְ בַּחֹמֶץ וַתֵּשֶׁב מִצַּד
הַקֹּצְרִים וַיִּצְבָּט־לָהּ קָלִי וַתֹּאכַל וַתִּשְׂבַּע וַתֹּתַר:
טו וַתָּקָם לְלַקֵּט וַיְצַו בֹּעַז אֶת־נְעָרָיו לֵאמֹר גַּם בֵּין
הָעֳמָרִים תְּלַקֵּט וְלֹא תַכְלִימוּהָ: טז וְגַם שֹׁל־תָּשֹׁלּוּ

your eyes on the field that they reap, and follow them. Have I not commanded the young men not to touch you? And when you are thirsty, go to the vessels and drink of that which the young men have drawn."

[10]Then she fell on her face, prostrating herself to the ground, and said to him: "Why have I found grace in your sight, for you to take notice of me, when I am only an alien?"

[11]And Boaz answered her and said: "I have had a full report of all that you have done for your mother-in-law since the death of your husband: how you left your father and mother, and the land where you were born, and came to a people whom you had never known before. [12]May the Lord reward your work, and may you have a full recompense from the Lord God of Israel under whose wings you have come to take refuge."

[13]Then she said: "Let me find grace in your sight, my lord, for you have comforted me, and you have spoken to the heart of your handmaid—even though I am not really one of your handmaidens!"

[14]At mealtime, Boaz said to her: "Come over here, and have some of the bread, and dip your morsel in the sour wine." So she sat beside the reapers; and he gave her parched corn, and she ate and was satisfied, and had food left over.

[15]When she rose up again to glean, Boaz gave orders to his young men, saying: "Let her glean even among the sheaves, and do not put her to shame. [16]You must even pull some stalks out of the bundles deliberately, and

Ruth in the Field   2:3

לָהּ מִן־הַצְּבָתִים וַעֲזַבְתֶּם וְלִקְּטָה וְלֹא תִגְעֲרוּ־
בָהּ:

יֹז וַתְּלַקֵּט בַּשָּׂדֶה עַד־הָעָרֶב וַתַּחְבֹּט אֵת אֲשֶׁר־
לִקֵּטָה וַיְהִי כְּאֵיפָה שְׂעֹרִים: יֹח וַתִּשָּׂא וַתָּבוֹא
הָעִיר וַתֵּרֶא חֲמוֹתָהּ אֵת אֲשֶׁר־לִקֵּטָה וַתּוֹצֵא
וַתִּתֶּן־לָהּ אֵת אֲשֶׁר־הוֹתִרָה מִשָּׂבְעָהּ: יֹט וַתֹּאמֶר
לָהּ חֲמוֹתָהּ אֵיפֹה לִקַּטְתְּ הַיּוֹם וְאָנָה עָשִׂית יְהִי
מַכִּירֵךְ בָּרוּךְ וַתַּגֵּד לַחֲמוֹתָהּ אֵת אֲשֶׁר־עָשְׂתָה
עִמּוֹ וַתֹּאמֶר שֵׁם הָאִישׁ אֲשֶׁר עָשִׂיתִי עִמּוֹ הַיּוֹם
בֹּעַז:

כֹ וַתֹּאמֶר נָעֳמִי לְכַלָּתָהּ בָּרוּךְ הוּא לַיהוָֹה אֲשֶׁר
לֹא־עָזַב חַסְדּוֹ אֶת־הַחַיִּים וְאֶת־הַמֵּתִים וַתֹּאמֶר
לָהּ נָעֳמִי קָרוֹב לָנוּ הָאִישׁ מִגֹּאֲלֵנוּ הוּא:
כֹּא וַתֹּאמֶר רוּת הַמּוֹאֲבִיָּה גַּם ׀ כִּי־אָמַר אֵלַי עִם־
הַנְּעָרִים אֲשֶׁר־לִי תִּדְבָּקִין עַד אִם־כִּלּוּ אֵת כָּל־
הַקָּצִיר אֲשֶׁר־לִי: כֹּב וַתֹּאמֶר נָעֳמִי אֶל־רוּת כַּלָּתָהּ
טוֹב בִּתִּי כִּי תֵצְאִי עִם־נַעֲרוֹתָיו וְלֹא יִפְגְּעוּ־בָךְ
בְּשָׂדֶה אַחֵר: כֹּג וַתִּדְבַּק בְּנַעֲרוֹת בֹּעַז לְלַקֵּט עַד־
כְּלוֹת קְצִיר־הַשְּׂעֹרִים וּקְצִיר הַחִטִּים וַתֵּשֶׁב אֶת־
חֲמוֹתָהּ:

ג ֹא וַתֹּאמֶר לָהּ נָעֳמִי חֲמוֹתָהּ בִּתִּי הֲלֹא אֲבַקֶּשׁ־לָךְ
מָנוֹחַ אֲשֶׁר יִיטַב־לָךְ: ֹב וְעַתָּה הֲלֹא בֹעַז מֹדַעְתָּנוּ
אֲשֶׁר הָיִית אֶת־נַעֲרוֹתָיו הִנֵּה־הוּא זֹרֶה אֶת־גֹּרֶן

leave them for her to glean; and you must not rebuke her."

[17]So she gleaned in the field until evening, and she beat out what she had gleaned, and it was about an *eifa* of barley. [18]She took it, and she went to the city. Her mother-in-law saw what she had gleaned; and, when Ruth brought out what she had saved from her meal and gave it to her, [19]her mother-in-law said to her: "Where did you glean today? And where did you work? Blessed be he who took such kind notice of you!" So she told her mother-in-law with whom she had worked, and said: "The name of the man with whom I worked today is Boaz."

[20]And Naomi said to her daughter-in-law: "Blessings upon him from the Lord, who has kept faith with the living and the dead." And Naomi said to her: "This man is closely related to us; he is one of our redeeming kinsmen." [21]Ruth the Moabitess said: "He even told me to stay close to his men until they have finished all his harvest!" [22]And Naomi said to Ruth, her daughter-in-law: "It is best for you, my daughter, to go out with his girls. Let no one catch you in another field." [23]So she kept close to the girls of Boaz, and gleaned until the end of the barley harvest and the wheat harvest. And she lived with her mother-in-law.

3 [1]Then Naomi, her mother-in-law, said to her: "My daughter, I must seek rest for you, so that all will be well with you. [2]Now: Boaz, with whose maidens you have been, is our next-of-kin. He will be winnowing barley tonight on the threshing floor. [3]Therefore, bathe and anoint yourself. Put on your cloak, and go down

הַשְּׁעָרִים הַלָּיְלָה: ³וְרָחַצְתְּ ׀ וָסַכְתְּ וְשַׂמְתְּ*
שִׂמְלֹתַיִךְ* עָלַיִךְ וְיָרַדְתִּי הַגֹּרֶן אַל־תִּוָּדְעִי לָאִישׁ
עַד כַּלֹּתוֹ לֶאֱכֹל וְלִשְׁתּוֹת: ⁴וִיהִי בְשָׁכְבוֹ וְיָדַעַתְּ
אֶת־הַמָּקוֹם אֲשֶׁר יִשְׁכַּב־שָׁם וּבָאת וְגִלִּית
מַרְגְּלֹתָיו וְשָׁכָבְתְּ* וְהוּא יַגִּיד לָךְ אֵת אֲשֶׁר
תַּעֲשִׂין: ⁵וַתֹּאמֶר אֵלֶיהָ כֹּל אֲשֶׁר־תֹּאמְרִי אֵלַי*
אֶעֱשֶׂה:
⁶וַתֵּרֶד הַגֹּרֶן וַתַּעַשׂ כְּכֹל אֲשֶׁר־צִוַּתָּה חֲמוֹתָהּ:
⁷וַיֹּאכַל בֹּעַז וַיֵּשְׁתְּ וַיִּיטַב לִבּוֹ וַיָּבֹא לִשְׁכַּב בִּקְצֵה
הָעֲרֵמָה וַתָּבֹא בַלָּט וַתְּגַל מַרְגְּלֹתָיו וַתִּשְׁכָּב:
⁸וַיְהִי בַּחֲצִי הַלַּיְלָה וַיֶּחֱרַד הָאִישׁ וַיִּלָּפֵת וְהִנֵּה
אִשָּׁה שֹׁכֶבֶת מַרְגְּלֹתָיו:
⁹וַיֹּאמֶר מִי־אָתְּ וַתֹּאמֶר אָנֹכִי רוּת אֲמָתֶךָ
וּפָרַשְׂתָּ כְנָפֶךָ עַל־אֲמָתְךָ כִּי גֹאֵל אָתָּה:
¹⁰וַיֹּאמֶר בְּרוּכָה אַתְּ לַיהוָה בִּתִּי הֵיטַבְתְּ חַסְדֵּךְ
הָאַחֲרוֹן מִן־הָרִאשׁוֹן לְבִלְתִּי־לֶכֶת אַחֲרֵי
הַבַּחוּרִים אִם־דַּל וְאִם־עָשִׁיר: ¹¹וְעַתָּה בִּתִּי אַל־
תִּירְאִי כֹּל אֲשֶׁר־תֹּאמְרִי אֶעֱשֶׂה־לָּךְ כִּי יוֹדֵעַ כָּל־
שַׁעַר עַמִּי כִּי אֵשֶׁת חַיִל אָתְּ: ¹²וְעַתָּה כִּי אָמְנָם כִּי*
גֹאֵל אָנֹכִי וְגַם יֵשׁ גֹּאֵל קָרוֹב מִמֶּנִּי: ¹³לִינִי* ׀
הַלַּיְלָה וְהָיָה בַבֹּקֶר אִם־יִגְאָלֵךְ טוֹב יִגְאָל וְאִם־

(ושמתי כתיב)   (שמלתך כתיב)   (וירדתי כתיב)

(ושכבתי כתיב)   (אלי קרי ולא כתיב)

(אם כתיב ולא קרי)   (נ' רבתי)

to the threshing floor; but do not make yourself
known to the man until he has finished eating and
drinking. ⁴Then, when he lies down, take note of the
place where he lies. And go over, uncover his feet,
and lie down. He will tell you what to do." ⁵And she
said to her: "I will do all that you have said to me."
⁶She went down to the threshing floor, and did exactly
what her mother-in-law had told her to do. ⁷Boaz ate
and drank, and his heart was merry. He went to lie
down at the end of a heap of corn; and she came
softly, and uncovered his feet, and lay down. ⁸And it
happened at midnight that the man was startled and
turned over—a woman was lying at his feet!
⁹And he said: "Who are you?" She answered: "I am
Ruth, your hand-maiden. Spread your robe over your
hand-maiden, for you are our next-of-kin."
¹⁰He said: "The Lord bless you, my daughter. Your
latest act of kindness is even greater than the first, in
that you have not gone after the young men, whether
poor or rich. ¹¹And now, my daughter, do not be
afraid. I will do for you whatever you say; for all the
elders of my people know that you are a virtuous
woman. ¹²Now: is it true that I am next-of-kin? There
is a kinsman even closer than I. ¹³Stay the night. In the
morning, if he will redeem you, fine; let him redeem!
But if he does not want to redeem you, then—as the
Lord lives!—I shall redeem you! Now, lie down until
morning."

לֹא יַחְפֹּץ לְגָאֳלֵךְ וּגְאַלְתִּיךְ אָנֹכִי חַי־יְהֹוָה שִׁכְבִי
עַד־הַבֹּקֶר:

י וַתִּשְׁכַּב מַרְגְּלוֹתָו* עַד־הַבֹּקֶר וַתָּקָם בְּטֶרֶם*
יַכִּיר אִישׁ אֶת־רֵעֵהוּ וַיֹּאמֶר אַל־יִוָּדַע כִּי־בָאָה
הָאִשָּׁה הַגֹּרֶן: טו וַיֹּאמֶר הָבִי הַמִּטְפַּחַת אֲשֶׁר־
עָלַיִךְ וְאֶחֳזִי־בָהּ וַתֹּאחֶז בָּהּ וַיָּמָד שֵׁשׁ־שְׂעֹרִים
וַיָּשֶׁת עָלֶיהָ וַיָּבֹא הָעִיר:

טז וַתָּבוֹא אֶל־חֲמוֹתָהּ וַתֹּאמֶר מִי־אַתְּ בִּתִּי וַתַּגֶּד־
לָהּ אֵת כָּל־אֲשֶׁר עָשָׂה־לָהּ הָאִישׁ: יז וַתֹּאמֶר שֵׁשׁ־
הַשְּׂעֹרִים הָאֵלֶּה נָתַן לִי כִּי אָמַר אֵלַי* אַל־תָּבוֹאִי
רֵיקָם אֶל־חֲמוֹתֵךְ: יח וַתֹּאמֶר שְׁבִי בִתִּי עַד אֲשֶׁר
תֵּדְעִין אֵיךְ יִפֹּל דָּבָר כִּי לֹא יִשְׁקֹט הָאִישׁ כִּי אִם־
כִּלָּה הַדָּבָר הַיּוֹם:

ד א וּבֹעַז עָלָה הַשַּׁעַר וַיֵּשֶׁב שָׁם וְהִנֵּה הַגֹּאֵל עֹבֵר
אֲשֶׁר דִּבֶּר־בֹּעַז וַיֹּאמֶר סוּרָה שְׁבָה־פֹּה פְּלֹנִי
אַלְמֹנִי וַיָּסַר וַיֵּשֵׁב: ב וַיִּקַּח עֲשָׂרָה אֲנָשִׁים מִזִּקְנֵי
הָעִיר וַיֹּאמֶר שְׁבוּ־פֹה וַיֵּשֵׁבוּ:

ג וַיֹּאמֶר לַגֹּאֵל חֶלְקַת הַשָּׂדֶה אֲשֶׁר לְאָחִינוּ
לֶאֱלִימֶלֶךְ מָכְרָה נָעֳמִי הַשָּׁבָה מִשְּׂדֵה מוֹאָב:
ד וַאֲנִי אָמַרְתִּי אֶגְלֶה אָזְנְךָ לֵאמֹר קְנֵה נֶגֶד
הַיֹּשְׁבִים וְנֶגֶד זִקְנֵי עַמִּי אִם־תִּגְאַל גְּאָל וְאִם־לֹא
יִגְאַל הַגִּידָה לִּי וְאֵדְעָה* כִּי אֵין זוּלָתְךָ לִגְאוֹל

(מרגלותו כתיב)   (בטרום כתיב)

(אלי קרי ולא כתיב)   (ואדע כתיב)

¹⁴And she lay at his feet until the morning. Then, before a person could recognize another, she arose; for he said: "Let it not be known that the woman came to the threshing floor." ¹⁵He said: "Bring me the shawl you are wearing, and hold it firmly." And when she held it, he measured out six measures of barley, and placed them upon her, and went into the city.

¹⁶She came to her mother-in-law, and Naomi asked: "How are things, my daughter?" And she told her all that the man had done for her. ¹⁷Then she said: "He gave me these six measures of barley, for he said to me: 'Do not go empty-handed to your mother-in-law.'" ¹⁸Then Naomi said: "Wait, my daughter, until you know how the matter will turn out. The man will not rest; he will surely settle the matter today."

4 ¹Now Boaz had gone up to the city gate and had sat down there. Presently, the next-of-kin whom he had mentioned passed by. He said to him: "Come, sit down!" calling him by his name. And he came over and sat down. ²Then Boaz took ten men of the elders of the city and said: "Sit here!" And they sat. ³And he said to the next-of-kin: "Naomi, who has returned out of the fields of Moab, must sell the parcel of land which belonged to our brother Elimelech. ⁴I decided to inform you and to say: 'Buy it in the presence of those sitting here and in the presence of the elders of my people. If you are willing to redeem it, redeem! But if you will not redeem it, then tell me, so that I may know. For there is none to redeem it except you, and I after you!'" And he said: "I will

וְאָנֹכִי אַחֲרֶיךָ וַיֹּאמֶר אָנֹכִי אֶגְאָל: ⁴וַיֹּאמֶר בֹּעַז
בְּיוֹם־קְנוֹתְךָ הַשָּׂדֶה מִיַּד נָעֳמִי וּמֵאֵת רוּת
הַמּוֹאֲבִיָּה אֵשֶׁת־הַמֵּת קָנִיתִי* לְהָקִים שֵׁם־הַמֵּת
עַל־נַחֲלָתוֹ: ⁵וַיֹּאמֶר הַגֹּאֵל לֹא אוּכַל לִגְאָל*־לִי
פֶּן־אַשְׁחִית אֶת־נַחֲלָתִי גְּאַל־לְךָ אַתָּה אֶת־
גְּאֻלָּתִי כִּי לֹא־אוּכַל לִגְאֹל:
⁶וְזֹאת לְפָנִים בְּיִשְׂרָאֵל עַל־הַגְּאוּלָּה וְעַל־
הַתְּמוּרָה לְקַיֵּם כָּל־דָּבָר שָׁלַף אִישׁ נַעֲלוֹ וְנָתַן
לְרֵעֵהוּ וְזֹאת הַתְּעוּדָה בְּיִשְׂרָאֵל: ⁷וַיֹּאמֶר הַגֹּאֵל
לְבֹעַז קְנֵה־לָךְ וַיִּשְׁלֹף נַעֲלוֹ: ⁹וַיֹּאמֶר בֹּעַז לַזְּקֵנִים
וְכָל־הָעָם עֵדִים אַתֶּם הַיּוֹם כִּי קָנִיתִי אֶת־כָּל־
אֲשֶׁר לֶאֱלִימֶלֶךְ וְאֵת כָּל־אֲשֶׁר לְכִלְיוֹן וּמַחְלוֹן
מִיַּד נָעֳמִי: ¹וְגַם אֶת־רוּת הַמֹּאֲבִיָּה אֵשֶׁת מַחְלוֹן
קָנִיתִי לִי לְאִשָּׁה לְהָקִים שֵׁם־הַמֵּת עַל־נַחֲלָתוֹ
וְלֹא־יִכָּרֵת שֵׁם־הַמֵּת מֵעִם אֶחָיו וּמִשַּׁעַר מְקוֹמוֹ
עֵדִים אַתֶּם הַיּוֹם:
¹¹וַיֹּאמְרוּ כָּל־הָעָם אֲשֶׁר־בַּשַּׁעַר וְהַזְּקֵנִים עֵדִים
יִתֵּן יְהוָה אֶת־הָאִשָּׁה הַבָּאָה אֶל־בֵּיתֶךָ כְּרָחֵל |
וּכְלֵאָה אֲשֶׁר בָּנוּ שְׁתֵּיהֶם אֶת־בֵּית יִשְׂרָאֵל
וַעֲשֵׂה־חַיִל בְּאֶפְרָתָה וּקְרָא־שֵׁם בְּבֵית לָחֶם:
¹²וִיהִי בֵיתְךָ כְּבֵית פֶּרֶץ אֲשֶׁר־יָלְדָה תָמָר
לִיהוּדָה מִן־הַזֶּרַע אֲשֶׁר יִתֵּן יְהוָה לְךָ מִן־הַנַּעֲרָה
הַזֹּאת:

(קָנִיתִי כְּתִיב)　　(לִגְאוֹל כְּתִיב)

redeem it!'" ⁵Then Boaz said: "On the day you acquire
the field from Naomi, you will also acquire Ruth the
Moabitess, the dead man's wife, to perpetuate the
name of the deceased upon his inheritance." ⁶The
next-of-kin said: "Then I cannot redeem it for
myself, for I would impair my own patrimony. You
take over my right of redemption; I cannot exercise
it."

⁷Now this is what was done in former times in Israel
concerning redemption and exchanging, to confirm
every matter: a man pulled off his shoe, and gave it to
his neighbor; this was a form of testifying in Israel. ⁸So
the next-of-kin said to Boaz: "Acquire it for yourself," and he pulled off his shoe. ⁹And Boaz said to the
elders, and to all the people: "You are witnesses this
day that I have acquired from Naomi all that belonged
to Elimelech and all that belonged to Mahlon and
Chilion. ¹⁰And further, that I have myself acquired as
my wife Ruth the Moabitess, the wife of Mahlon, to
perpetuate the name of the deceased upon his
inheritance, so that his name may not be missing
among his brothers and from the gate of his place: you
are witnesses today."

¹¹Then all the people who were at the gate and the
elders said: "We are witnesses! May the Lord make
this woman who is coming into your house like
Rachel and like Leah, the two who built up the House
of Israel! May you prosper in Ephrathah and be
famous in Bethlehem! ¹²And let your house be like the
house of Perez whom Tamar bore to Judah, through
the seed which the Lord will give you by this young
woman."

"There is a son born to Naomi." 4:17

יג וַיִּקַּח בֹּעַז אֶת־רוּת וַתְּהִי־לוֹ לְאִשָּׁה וַיָּבֹא אֵלֶיהָ
וַיִּתֵּן יְהֹוָה לָהּ הֵרָיוֹן וַתֵּלֶד בֵּן: יד וַתֹּאמַרְנָה
הַנָּשִׁים אֶל־נָעֳמִי בָּרוּךְ יְהֹוָה אֲשֶׁר לֹא הִשְׁבִּית
לָךְ גֹּאֵל הַיּוֹם וְיִקָּרֵא שְׁמוֹ בְּיִשְׂרָאֵל: טו וְהָיָה לָךְ
לְמֵשִׁיב נֶפֶשׁ וּלְכַלְכֵּל אֶת־שֵׂיבָתֵךְ כִּי כַלָּתֵךְ
אֲשֶׁר־אֲהֵבָתֶךְ יְלָדַתּוּ אֲשֶׁר־הִיא טוֹבָה לָךְ
מִשִּׁבְעָה בָּנִים:
טז וַתִּקַּח נָעֳמִי אֶת־הַיֶּלֶד וַתְּשִׁתֵהוּ בְחֵיקָהּ וַתְּהִי־
לוֹ לְאֹמֶנֶת: יז וַתִּקְרֶאנָה לוֹ הַשְּׁכֵנוֹת שֵׁם לֵאמֹר
יֻלַּד־בֵּן לְנָעֳמִי וַתִּקְרֶאנָה שְׁמוֹ עוֹבֵד הוּא אֲבִי־
יִשַׁי אֲבִי דָוִד:
יח וְאֵלֶּה תּוֹלְדוֹת פָּרֶץ פֶּרֶץ הוֹלִיד אֶת־חֶצְרוֹן:
יט וְחֶצְרוֹן הוֹלִיד אֶת־רָם וְרָם הוֹלִיד אֶת־
עַמִּינָדָב: כ וְעַמִּינָדָב הוֹלִיד אֶת־נַחְשׁוֹן וְנַחְשׁוֹן
הוֹלִיד אֶת־שַׂלְמָה: כא וְשַׂלְמוֹן הוֹלִיד אֶת־בֹּעַז
וּבֹעַז הוֹלִיד אֶת־עוֹבֵד: כב וְעוֹבֵד הוֹלִיד אֶת־יִשָׁי
וְיִשַׁי הוֹלִיד אֶת־דָּוִד:

¹³So Boaz took Ruth, and she was his wife. When they came together, the Lord caused her to conceive and she bore a son. ¹⁴Then the women said to Naomi: "Blessed be the Lord who has not left you without a kinsman today. May his name be famous in Israel. ¹⁵He will be a restorer of your life to you, and he will sustain your old age; for your daughter-in-law who loves you has borne him, and she is better to you than seven sons."

¹⁶And Naomi took the child and laid it in her bosom and became his nurse. ¹⁷And the women neighbors gave him a name, saying: "There is a son born to Naomi!" They called his name Obed. He was the father of Jesse, father of David.

¹⁸Now these are the generations of Perez: Perez begot Hezron, ¹⁹and Hezron begot Ram, and Ram begot Amminadab. ²⁰And Amminadab begot Nahshon, and Nahshon begot Salmon, ²¹and Salmon begot Boaz. Boaz begot Obed, ²²and Obed begot Jesse, and Jesse begot David.

AFTER READING FROM
THE SCROLL OF RUTH

Those who call to God from whatever place
will hear the voice of commandment.

Those who seek God will not be weary.

Whither thou goest, I will go—

to wait at the gates of the House of the Book,
to serve at the Gates of Righteousness.

Thy people shall be my people.

Blessed be those who come to us in the Name of God.

And thy God, my God.

The Torah is given in a place unpossessed, open to all.
All may hear the call to the service of God.
All may turn from the idols of place and possession.
All may enter God's covenant of the Peoples.

When the harvest comes, let us go to the field
and glean among the sheaves.

Grant abundant harvest, O God,
of whatever seeds of Your spirit we sow,
that all may glean together
in the fields of that Kingdom
extolled from the throne of David.

THE SCROLL OF LAMENTATIONS

INTRODUCTION TO
THE SCROLL OF LAMENTATIONS

Writing about one illustration for the Scroll of Lamentations, Leonard Baskin said:

> . . . the suggestion of a pestilential, fox-and-jackal infested ruin is manifest, made almost palpable. The specific *derush* in the drawing is . . . five (!) nights. First night: the actual night and moon; second night: the black embrace of the surround; third night: the night blue of Eicha, the letters; the fourth night: the foxes who are night creatures (unless disturbed); the fifth night: all the elements combined so that the resultant meaning is . . . the final night!

Reading the text, we are captured by a sense of desolation, from the first word of bitter outrage to the final longing for renewal and return. This is the Scroll of Lamentations, the text for our time of destroyed cities and slaughtered populace. It is universal in its description of the aftermath of war, of human suffering. And it is a very particular text, dealing with an historical event—the destruction of Jerusalem in 586 B.C.E. by the Babylonians.

Tradition views Jeremiah as the author of these *kinot,* laments which mourn the destroyed city and the vanquished people. The Christian Bible automatically places these writings at the end of the Book of Jeremiah and lists him as the author. But Jeremiah was not the author. Jeremiah had believed in his visions to the end, while the author of Lamentations says (2:9): "Her prophets also find no vision from the Lord." Jeremiah would not have praised King Tzedekiah as does the author here (4:20). He opposed the king and had seen the needs and the future of Israel in different ways. He had pronounced the fall of Jerusalem as an outcome of evil leadership and not as the result of the common

people's failings (as does Lamentations). Nor does Jeremiah's flowing style accord with the tightly organized acrostics which, in Lamentations, marshall the reality of anguish into lines of formal expression. The author of the Scroll of Lamentations, in fact, often used acrostics, poetry organized around the progression of the letters of the alphabet. Our translation maintains this, so that we can ourselves read these five elegies, four of them acrostics, as formal mourning texts, limping along in their special cadence which is so appropriate to the liturgy of Tish-ah Be-Av. In accordance with the Hebrew text, the acrostic is reversed for the letters 'P' and 'Q' in chapters two, three, and four. The letters *peh* and *ayin* in these chapters are reversed, and the Midrash (Lam. R. 2) cites Rabbah in the name of R. Yochanan to the effect that "the letters are reversed because of the spies who spoke with their mouths what they had not seen with their eyes" (*peh* means mouth and *ayin* means the eye). It is a dimension of the Hebrew text which should not be ignored, meaning placed upon meaning in the struggle to let language cope with grief.

Formal expressions of grief do not deny pain. The situation breaks through the lines in countless ways, individuals come to live with their own situation: the "man who has seen affliction" stands alongside the mother listening to her dying child's "where is corn and wine?" And behind all the individual happenings, there are the death throes of the city. More than a city dies: the future, the dream, the sanctuary—all are in ruins. It is a religious text which tries to deal with the crumbling of faith in a world where the center, the foundation of existence itself, does not hold and turns to dust. But our text speaks of a God who can and will forgive, who will make restitution, who will renew our days as of old. Lamentations is a word of faith in God, faith found in darkest times and therefore particularly suited to our days. We read it on Tish-ah Be-av, with the megillah blessing chanted in some communities as a whispered incantation, or omitted. But on that dark day, our people also experience the hope which has not been forced beyond the boundaries of existence. Faith is reconstituted as it senses, on another level, the continuing struggle with evil which has not ended in surrender or total silence. In this way, the Scroll of Lamentations can become part of our personal affirmation.

After Auschwitz, Theodor Adorno had written that no more poems could now be written. And he was wrong. Had he read the Scroll of Lamentations, he might have realized that after destruction there must be an opportunity to express anguish and pain, that there must be the reassertion of the self, the rediscovery of hope. When the rabbis assigned the scriptural reading for the Sabbath, they did not permit the prophetic reading to end on a negative note. Some verses of affirmation, hope, and renewed vision had to be added. And Lamentations has to follow that rule.

> Turn us unto You, O Lord,
> and we shall be turned;
> Renew our days as of old.

This is more than a matter of ancient convention. It is a statement in which affirmation beyond despair becomes an essential component of our faith. And it is the final statement of faith in a text written by those who had seen unspeakable affliction. This affirmation is central to our Scroll of Lamentations.

> Turn us unto You, O Lord,
> and we shall be turned;
> Renew our days as of old.

סֵדֶר עֲבוֹדַת תִּשְׁעָה־בְאָב

SERVICE FOR THE READING OF
THE SCROLL OF LAMENTATIONS

יְרוּשָׁלַיִם הָרִים סָבִיב לָהּ,
זָהָב יְסוֹדָתָם וַעֲטַרְתָּם זָהָב.
כִּי שָׁם הִתְהַלְּכוּ הוֹזֵי יָהּ,
לְוִיִּים דָּרְכוּ הוֹד,
פַּעֲמֵי נָדִיב פַּעֲמֵיהֶם כְּסַהֲרוּרִים בַּקֹּדֶשׁ.

Jerusalem is a hill city.
Its foundations are gold, and gold is its crown.
For there God's seers once walked,
Levites strode in glory.
And their tread was of nobles,
as if moon-struck in the Holy Service.

How were Thy lovely corners ravaged,
the precious quarters exceedingly despoiled,
O City of the Book,
Abode of Peace,
built with turrets.

Gazelle of Israel!
How they plotted to hew down your antlers!

"Remembrance leads to redemption," said the Baal Shem Tov.

According to the sage's word, O God, may our Remembrance of Jerusalem
lead to Redemption, that out of Zion may again come forth the Law, and
the word of God from Jerusalem.

We are told that the place where two brothers embraced in love
became the place of the Temple's altar.

253

That Your love, O God, may embrace the world, turn us towards Remembrance. That our will toward Redemption be not forsworn, turn us toward Remembrance. That the path toward Redemption not be forlorn, turn us toward Remembrance, as it is written:

אִם אֶשְׁכָּחֵךְ, יְרוּשָׁלַיִם, תִּשְׁכַּח יְמִינִי.

Im esh-ka-cheich, Ye-ru-she-la-yim, tish-kach ye-mi-ni.

If I forget thee, O Jerusalem, let the use of my hand be forgotten . . . if I remember thee not!

⅟ אִם אֶשְׁכָּחֵךְ, יְרוּשָׁלַיִם, תִּשְׁכַּח יְמִינִי.

Zion! Wilt thou not ask if Peace's wing
shadows the captives that beseech thy peace,
left lonely from thine ancient shepherding?

*Lo! West and east and north and south, worldwide,
all those from far and near without surcease
salute thee. Peace and peace from every side.*

With thee, O Zion, God's Presence dwelt. To thee was given
thy Maker's Presence when God opened there
the gates of thee towards the gates of Heaven.

*Lo! West and east and north and south, worldwide,
all those from far and near without surcease
salute thee. Peace and peace from every side.*

Where the Ark rested in the place most dear,
where the Spirit of God, revealing, oft drew near,
showing light to messenger and seer.

*Lo! West and east and north and south, worldwide,
all those from far and near without surcease
salute thee. Peace and peace from every side.*

Return us, O God, unto Thee, and we will return.
Renew our days as of old.

Return us, O God, unto Thee, and we will return.
Renew our days as of old.

הֲשִׁיבֵנוּ, יְיָ, אֵלֶיךָ וְנָשׁוּבָה, ♪

חַדֵּשׁ יָמֵינוּ כְּקֶדֶם.

Ha-shi-vei-nu, A-do-nai, ei-le-cha ve-na-shu-va,
cha-deish, cha-deish ya-mei-nu,
cha-deish ya-mei-nu ke-ke-dem.

It is told: On Tish-ah Be-Av these events occurred; remember and
do not forget.

Help us to remember and not forget.

It was decreed upon the retrograde generations of the wilderness
that they would not enter the Land.

Return us, O God, unto Thee, and we will return.

The Temple of Solomon was put to the torch.

We have remembered and will not forget.

The Second Temple was destroyed and the Temple Mount was
plowed. The words of Jeremiah came to pass: "Zion will be
plowed as a field. . . ."

Return us, O God, unto Thee, and we will return.

On Tish-ah Be-Av, the shining Jewry of a golden Spain was
expelled by the foe into the darkness of yet further exile, and the
Divine Unity further sundered.

We have learned to remember and will not forget.

On the ninth of Av the fire was kindled;
on the tenth of Av the fire destroyed.
On the ninth of Av the First World War began;
the Great Burning was still to come.

We must remember and never forget.

הֲשִׁיבֵנוּ, יְיָ, אֵלֶיךָ וְנָשׁוּבָה, ♪

חַדֵּשׁ יָמֵינוּ כְּקֶדֶם.

Ha-shi-vei-nu, A-do-nai, ei-le-cha ve-na-shu-va,
cha-deish, cha-deish ya-mei-nu,
cha-deish ya-mei-nu ke-ke-dem.

When we conclude the story of the Exodus, we remember,
as we celebrate our journey away from servitude
and towards the service of God.

לְשָׁנָה הַבָּאָה בִּירוּשָׁלָיִם.

Next year in Jerusalem.

At the conclusion of Atonement we remember,
at the closing of the gates.

לְשָׁנָה הַבָּאָה בִּירוּשָׁלָיִם.

Next year in Jerusalem.

In our comfort to the mourner we remember,
as we console the bereaved.

הַמָּקוֹם יְנַחֵם אֶתְכֶם בְּתוֹךְ אֲבֵלֵי צִיּוֹן וִירוּשָׁלָיִם.

May God comfort you among those who mourn
Zion and Jerusalem.

At the consecration of our love we remember,
as we rejoice with bride and groom.

בָּרוּךְ אַתָּה, יְיָ, מְשַׂמֵּחַ צִיּוֹן בְּבָנֶיהָ.

We praise Thee, O God,
who makes Zion rejoice through these, her children.

Remembering, our people have muted the fullness of joy,
of music, of song.

By the waters of Babylon we sat, weeping,
as we remembered Zion.

Al na-ha-rot Ba-vel,	❧ עַל נַהֲרוֹת בָּבֶל,
sham ya-shav-nu gam ba-chi-nu,	שָׁם יָשַׁבְנוּ גַּם בָּכִינוּ,
be-zoch-rei-nu et Tsi-yon.	בְּזָכְרֵנוּ אֶת־צִיּוֹן.
Shi-ru la-nu mi-shi-rei Tsi-yon,	שִׁירוּ לָנוּ מִשִּׁירֵי צִיּוֹן,
eich na-shir et shir A-do-nai	אֵיךְ נָשִׁיר אֶת שִׁיר יְיָ
al ad-mat nei-char?	עַל אַדְמַת נֵכָר?

And on this day of Tish-ah Be-Av above all we remember.

We are those who have seen desolation:
The crafted stones shattered to rubble,
the holy places filled with offal,
the sacred vessels debased to informer's hire;
the lovelabor of artisans endowed by Heaven
melted down for the wages of the courtesan;
the ravaged virgins, battered babes, savaged elders;
the Temple become a den of jackals and thieves;
and the shackled princes of Judah
endlessly trudging the blazing plains of Babylon,
bearing in sacks sewn from Torah scroll strips,
a burden of rock and rubble.

אֲנִי הַגֶּבֶר אֲקוֹנֵן
בְּלֵיל זֶה בְּמַר וְאֶתְבּוֹנֵן
וְתַחַת וִיהִי נֹעַם זָהָב יוּעָם.

I am one who has seen destruction,
I am one who must mourn in lamentation.
Instead of comfort, the pleasant, the sweet,
the gold has turned into terror.

And in the destruction of the Temple
we remember other destructions, we count other ruins:

In the destruction of the Temple,
the ruin from within of Babel's Tower,
a great thrust into space wasted,
and human discourse become a babble.

In the destruction of the Temple,
the fertile green and fruitful vale of Sodom and Gomorrah
withered by brimstone into dust and ashes.

In the destruction of the Temple,
the tearing of covenants, sundering of faiths.

In the destruction of the Temple,
the banner of God's kingdom torn,
a fissure of tragedy in the wholeness of life.

In the destruction of the Temple,
the revolving spheres broken from the moral orbit,
vessels of light shattered, the Throne of Glory cracked.

And in the destruction of the Temple,
an image of the thrusting out
of God's Presence from among us.

אֱלֵי צִיּוֹן וְעָרֶיהָ כְּמוֹ אִשָּׁה בְּצִירֶיהָ
וְכִבְתוּלָה חֲגוּרַת־שַׂק עַל בַּעַל נְעוּרֶיהָ.

(For Zion we mourn and for her cities,
like a woman in her pains we mourn for Zion,
for Zion we mourn like a young maid in sackcloth doth mourn,
weeping for the husband of her youth.)

And so we remember the destruction of the walls of Jerusalem, the Temple of Solomon, of Ezra, of the Levites, of the Princes of Judah, of the Prophets of Israel, the Jerusalem of the sages, the Jerusalem of Torah; the Jerusalem of the altar. Jerusalem: a center from which, towards which, broken harmonies could be restored, where fire could be rekindled against the harsh chaos of the cold, a spark preserved to renew the light.

"Raze it! Raze it!" they said, "Even to the foundations thereof."

The First Temple was destroyed because of idolatry, lust, and murder, so, the sages; while the Second Temple fell from within because of baseless hatreds, needless conflict, trivial jealousies, petty meanness. And both were battered by the boundless greed of arrogant power, by the monstrous wreckings of Babylon, of Rome.

We have seen the place of sanctity desecrated, the altar-fire scattered, the words of ordering prayer lost in whirlwinds of destruction; the ritual abandoned, forgotten, lost.

We bring into the recollection of the realm of Moloch, Bel, and Mammon, a sense of the place of sanctity; the awareness of a flawed humanity, of wholeness scorched by terror.

"Things fall apart, the center will not hold,
Mere anarchy is loosed upon the world,
The blood-dimmed tide is loosed,
And everywhere the ceremony of innocence is drowned."

And this our shadowed remembrance-rite serves now for the ordering prayer of the priest, the restoring vision of the prophet, the preserving doctrine of the sage; at the altar, center, place of light, thrice-holy from Above.

Pray for the peace of Jerusalem.
Tranquil be those who bear you love.
Peace! Peace within your palaces . . .

We bring this remembrance into the realm of Moloch, of Bel, and of Mammon. In remembrance we redeem something of the sorrow and the pity of the suffering. We remember so as not to forget the place of access to God. We remember in order to renew our hope, the human hope, the hope Divine:

יְפֵה נוֹף מְשׂוֹשׂ כָּל הָאָרֶץ!

O beautiful height, joy of the whole world's gladness!
O Great Sovereign's city, mountain-blest!

Before God who is the Place of the universe, we turn in meditation upon a parable of place. Before God in whom space without end is finite beyond imagination, we probe imagination to ask, conceive, and ponder: Why Jerusalem, why Zion, why the Temple Mount?

MEDITATION

Brothers.
Two brothers dwell on either side of a hill. Each cultivates fields near the bottom of opposite slopes. On the moon-bright night of the harvest's completion each has gone home to rest, to sleep. Each has labored strenuously. The garner of each is rich, yet neither brother can sleep. Each lies awake in worry over the other brother.

The one thinks: My brother is a bachelor, alone. He has no family to help him in the work. How could he possibly have reaped enough to sustain him through the year?

The other brother, too, lies anxiously awake in worry over the large family that is his brother's care. Will they have enough to sustain them through the year from hunger, from want?

In the middle of a moon-bright night each arises; each yokes an ox to a large cart; each heaps his cart to overflowing with all manner of the goods of harvest; each ascends his side of the hill with the aim of secretly storing this provender in the barn of his brother on the other side.

But at the hill-top they meet. At once they understand. Understanding, they wordlessly embrace, weeping in the joy of love.

At that very spot does God purpose to build the Sacred Sanctuary. There it arises. There the people worship.

At that place the Temple arises:
where love and truth embrace each other,
where goodness and peace kiss one another.

When God renews our Restoration,
we will be as those who dream.
Our mouths will be full of laughter then,
our mouths with song.

◆　◆

שִׁיר הַמַּעֲלוֹת. ♪

בְּשׁוּב יְיָ אֶת־שִׁיבַת צִיּוֹן הָיִינוּ כְּחֹלְמִים.

אָז יִמָּלֵא שְׂחוֹק פִּינוּ, וּלְשׁוֹנֵנוּ רִנָּה.

אָז יֹאמְרוּ בַגּוֹיִם: הִגְדִּיל יְיָ לַעֲשׂוֹת עִם־אֵלֶּה.

הִגְדִּיל יְיָ לַעֲשׂוֹת עִמָּנוּ, הָיִינוּ שְׂמֵחִים.

הָלוֹךְ יֵלֵךְ וּבָכֹה נֹשֵׂא מֶשֶׁךְ־הַזָּרַע,

בֹּא־יָבֹא בְרִנָּה, נֹשֵׂא אֲלֻמֹּתָיו.

Now through this service of remembrance
we renew the dream of harmony.
We mend the broken sphere of hope;
to restore a center among us,
a dwelling place of God.

הוֹי, יִבָּנֶה הַמִּקְדָּשׁ. ♪

Hoi, yi-ba-neh ha-mik-dash.

O may that sanctuary be rebuilt.

Guard me, O God, from hating man my brother.
Guard me from recalling what,
from my earlier youth, he did to me.
Even when all the stars in my sky are quenched,
even when my soul's voice grows mute—
When I am overcome by disaster,
let me not lay bare his guilt.

For he is my hidden dwelling-place,
in him am I reflected again,
like a wayfarer from the planets,
beholding his face in a pool.

When the gates are locked,
darkness over the city reclining,
and emptied of love, rejected,
I am bound to my rock—
permit me to see in my brother a spark,
only a spark still shining,
that I may know that in me, myself,
all is not yet extinguished.

Blessings before reading from the Scroll of Lamentations

בָּרוּךְ אַתָּה, יְיָ אֱלֹהֵינוּ, מֶלֶךְ הָעוֹלָם, אֲשֶׁר עָשָׂנוּ אֲסִירֵי־תִּקְוָה.

Ba-ruch a-ta, A-do-nai E-lo-hei-nu, me-lech ha-o-lam, a-sher a-sa-nu
a-si-rei tik-vah.

We praise You, O God, Sovereign of existence, who has made us captives
of Hope.

בָּרוּךְ אַתָּה, יְיָ אֱלֹהֵינוּ, מֶלֶךְ הָעוֹלָם, אֲשֶׁר קִדְּשָׁנוּ בְּמִצְוֹתָיו
וְצִוָּנוּ עַל מִקְרָא מְגִלָּה.

Ba-ruch a-ta, A-do-nai E-lo-hei-nu, me-lech ha-o-lam, a-sher ki-de-
sha-nu be-mits-vo-tav ve-tsi-va-nu al mik-ra me-gi-la.

We praise You, O God, Sovereign of existence, who has hallowed our lives
with commandments and commanded us to read this scroll.

READING FROM
THE SCROLL OF LAMENTATIONS

Blessing following the reading

נַחֵם, יְיָ אֱלֹהֵינוּ, אֶת אֲבֵלֵי צִיּוֹן וְאֶת אֲבֵלֵי יְרוּשָׁלָיִם,
הָעִיר אֲשֶׁר בָּלְעוּ לְגִיוֹנוֹת

וַיֵּירָשׁוּהָ עוֹבְדֵי פְסִילִים

וַיַּטִּילוּ אֶת עַמְּךָ יִשְׂרָאֵל לֶחָרֶב,

וַיַּהַרְגוּ בְזָדוֹן חֲסִידֵי עֶלְיוֹן.

כִּי בָאֵשׁ הִצַּתָּהּ, וּבָאֵשׁ אַתָּה עָתִיד לִבְנוֹתָהּ.

כָּאָמוּר: וַאֲנִי אֶהְיֶה לָהּ, נְאֻם יְיָ,

חוֹמַת אֵשׁ סָבִיב,

וּלְכָבוֹד אֶהְיֶה בְתוֹכָהּ.

בָּרוּךְ אַתָּה, יְיָ, מְנַחֵם צִיּוֹן וּבוֹנֶה יְרוּשָׁלָיִם.

Na-cheim, A-do-nai E-lo-hei-nu, et a-vei-lei Tsi-yon ve-et a-vei-lei
Ye-ru-sha-la-yim, ha-ir a-sher ba-le-u lig-yo-not va-yi-ra-shu-ha
o-ve-dei pe-si-lim, va-ya-ti-lu et a-me-cha Yis-ra-eil le-cha-rev, va-
ya-har-gu be-za-don cha-si-dei el-yon. Ki ba-eish hi-tsa-tah u-va-
eish a-ta a-tid liv-no-tah. Ka-a-mur: va-ani eh-yeh lah, ne-um
A-do-nai, cho-mat eish sa-viv, u-le-cha-vod eh-yeh be-to-chah.

Ba-ruch a-ta, A-do-nai, me-na-cheim Tsi-yon u-vo-nei Ye-ru-sha-
la-yim.

Comfort, O God, the mourners of Zion, the mourners of Jerusalem.
Legions devoured her;
idolators took possession of her;
they put Thy people Israel to the sword
and wantonly slaughtered the faithful servants of God Most High.
With fire was Zion destroyed,
but with fire wilt Thou, O God, rebuild her;
as it is said: "I will be to her," says God,
"a wall of fire round about,
and for as it is glory I will be in the midst of her."
We praise You, O God, who comforts Zion and is rebuilding Jerusalem.

CONCLUSION OF WORSHIP

The world of God is great and holy. Every land is holy, but the
holiest of lands is the Land of Israel; the holiest of its cities is
Jerusalem; and in Jerusalem the holiest place was the Temple.

And in the Temple the holiest place was the Holy of Holies.

God called Israel to be a holy people. Among these, of old, the holiest were the Levites; of the Levites, the priests were holiest.

And the holiest of these was the High Priest.

All time is holy; the holiest of times are the Holy Days, and of these the holiest is the Sabbath.

And of the Sabbaths, the Sabbath of Sabbaths, the Day of Atonement, is holiest.

Hebrew is called a holy tongue, and of all the words in the holy tongue the words of the Torah are holiest.

And in the Torah, the word of Transcendent Holiness is the ineffable Name of God.

In ancient times—in one place, at one time, in one person, in one word, all these supernal holinesses were met:

At the Holy of Holies, on the Day of Atonement, when the High Priest spoke—as only he, in fear and trembling, was permitted to do—the Name of God.

And if the hearts of the priest and of the people
were at that moment truly directed to heaven,
it was an instant of highest grace,
full of the promise of harmony and order and peace.
But if, God forbid, the priest himself
and with him the people were impure,
their motives unworthy,
it was a moment of peril for the entire world.

Each person ought to consider himself a priest;
each of whose days is a Sabbath of Sabbaths;
and the place where one stands,
heart turned to God,
a Holy of Holies;

and each of one's deeds
as bearing within it the order or the ruin of worlds.

It shall come to pass at the end of days
that the mountain of the Lord's House
shall be exalted above all the hills,
and all the nations shall flow unto it.

They shall not hurt nor destroy
in all My holy mountain.
For the earth shall be full
of the knowledge of God
as the waters cover the sea.

Lo! It shall pass, shall change,
the power of the vain-crowned kingdoms;
not all time subdues Thy strength;
Thy crown endures from age to age.

Happy are the ones who wait!
They shall go to Thee,
and Thine arising radiance see
when over all shall break Thy morning glow.

Thy God desired thee for a dwelling-place;
and happy is the one whom God shall choose
and draw nigh to rest within thy space.

Happy are the ones who wait!
They shall go to Thee,
and Thine arising radiance see
when over all shall break Thy morning glow.

And see rest for Thy chosen;
and sublime rejoicing find amid the joy of Thy flock
returned unto Thine olden youthful time.

Happy are the ones who wait!
They shall go to Thee,
and Thy arising radiance see
when over all shall break Thy morning glow.

Return us unto Thee, O God,
and we shall return.
Renew our days as of old.

Renew our days as of old,
and we shall return unto Thee, O God.

הֲשִׁיבֵנוּ, יְיָ, אֵלֶיךָ וְנָשׁוּבָה,
חַדֵּשׁ יָמֵינוּ כְּקֶדֶם.

Ha-shi-vei-nu, A-do-nai, ei-le-cha ve-na-shu-va,
cha-deish, cha-deish ya-mei-nu,
cha-deish ya-mei-nu ke-ke-dem.

אא אֵיכָה ׀ יָשְׁבָה בָדָד הָעִיר רַבָּתִי עָם
הָיְתָה כְּאַלְמָנָה
רַבָּתִי בַגּוֹיִם שָׂרָתִי בַּמְּדִינוֹת
הָיְתָה לָמַס:
ב בָּכוֹ תִבְכֶּה בַּלַּיְלָה וְדִמְעָתָהּ עַל לֶחֱיָהּ
אֵין־לָהּ מְנַחֵם מִכָּל־אֹהֲבֶיהָ
כָּל־רֵעֶיהָ בָּגְדוּ בָהּ
הָיוּ לָהּ לְאֹיְבִים:
ג גָּלְתָה יְהוּדָה מֵעֹנִי וּמֵרֹב עֲבֹדָה
הִיא יָשְׁבָה בַגּוֹיִם
לֹא מָצְאָה מָנוֹחַ
כָּל־רֹדְפֶיהָ הִשִּׂיגוּהָ בֵּין הַמְּצָרִים:
ד דַּרְכֵי צִיּוֹן אֲבֵלוֹת מִבְּלִי בָּאֵי מוֹעֵד
כָּל־שְׁעָרֶיהָ שׁוֹמֵמִין
כֹּהֲנֶיהָ נֶאֱנָחִים
בְּתוּלֹתֶיהָ נּוּגוֹת וְהִיא מַר־לָהּ:
ה הָיוּ צָרֶיהָ לְרֹאשׁ אֹיְבֶיהָ שָׁלוּ
כִּי־יְהוָה הוֹגָהּ עַל־רֹב פְּשָׁעֶיהָ
עוֹלָלֶיהָ הָלְכוּ שְׁבִי לִפְנֵי־צָר:
ו וַיֵּצֵא מִבַּת־צִיּוֹן כָּל־הֲדָרָהּ
הָיוּ שָׂרֶיהָ כְּאַיָּלִים לֹא־מָצְאוּ מִרְעֶה

(מִן־בַּת כתיב)

1 ¹**A**las, how solitary does the city sit that was
so full of people.
How is she become as a widow.
She that was great among the nations, and princess
among the provinces,
How is she become tributary.
²**B**itterly does she weep at night, and her tears are
on her cheeks:
Among her lovers she has none to comfort her;
All her friends have dealt treacherously with her,
They are become her enemies.
³**C**aptivity is Judah's fate because of affliction,
and because of great servitude.
She dwells among the nations,
She finds no rest,
All her persecutors overtook her in her sore straits.
⁴**D**ark mourning covers Zion's roads, because
none come
to the solemn feasts.
All her gates are desolate.
Her priests sigh,
Her virgins are afflicted, she is in bitterness.
⁵**E**nemies are become the masters now, her adversaries
are at ease.
For the Lord has afflicted her for the multitude
of her transgressions.
Her children are gone into captivity, before
the adversary.
⁶**F**rom the daughter of Zion has departed all of
her splendor.
Her princes are become like deer that find no pasture,

"Bitterly does she weep at night." 1:2

וַיֵּלְכוּ בְלֹא־כֹחַ לִפְנֵי רוֹדֵף:

ז זָכְרָה יְרוּשָׁלַם יְמֵי עָנְיָהּ וּמְרוּדֶיהָ

כֹּל מַחֲמֻדֶיהָ

אֲשֶׁר הָיוּ מִימֵי קֶדֶם

בִּנְפֹל עַמָּהּ בְּיַד־צָר וְאֵין עוֹזֵר לָהּ

רָאוּהָ צָרִים

שָׂחֲקוּ עַל־מִשְׁבַּתֶּהָ:

ח חֵטְא חָטְאָה יְרוּשָׁלַם

עַל־כֵּן לְנִידָה הָיָתָה

כָּל־מְכַבְּדֶיהָ הִזִּילוּהָ כִּי־רָאוּ עֶרְוָתָהּ

גַּם־הִיא נֶאֶנְחָה וַתָּשָׁב אָחוֹר:

ט טֻמְאָתָהּ בְּשׁוּלֶיהָ לֹא זָכְרָה אַחֲרִיתָהּ

וַתֵּרֶד פְּלָאִים

אֵין מְנַחֵם לָהּ

רְאֵה יְהֹוָה אֶת־עָנְיִי

כִּי הִגְדִּיל אוֹיֵב:

י יָדוֹ פָּרַשׂ צָר

עַל כָּל־מַחֲמַדֶּיהָ

כִּי־רָאֲתָה גוֹיִם בָּאוּ מִקְדָּשָׁהּ

אֲשֶׁר צִוִּיתָה

לֹא־יָבֹאוּ בַקָּהָל לָךְ:

יא כָּל־עַמָּהּ נֶאֱנָחִים מְבַקְשִׁים לֶחֶם

נָתְנוּ מַחֲמַדֵּיהֶם* בְּאֹכֶל לְהָשִׁיב נָפֶשׁ

(מחמודיהם כתיב)

And they are gone without strength before the pursuer.
⁷Great treasures Jerusalem now recalls,
Those from the old days are remembered
In the days of her affliction and her anguish;
Now that her people fall by the hand of the adversary,
And no one helps her,
The adversaries have seen her,
They have mocked at her calamities.
⁸How grievously Jerusalem has sinned,
Therefore she is become as one unclean.
All that honored her vilify her, because they have seen
her nakedness.
What could she do but sigh, and turn away.
⁹Into her skirts her filthiness has crept, she gave no
thought to her future.
Her fall was beyond belief,
And she has no one to comfort her.
"Behold, O Lord, my affliction;
For the enemy has magnified himself!"
¹⁰Jutting hands of the adversary
Are spread upon all her treasures.
For she has seen that nations have entered her sanctuary,
Nations forbidden by You
To enter Your congregation.
¹¹Keeping themselves alive they barter all,
Their treasures go for food.
All of her people sigh as they seek bread.

רְאֵ֤ה יְהֹוָה֙ וְהַבִּ֔יטָה
כִּ֥י הָיִ֖יתִי זוֹלֵלָֽה׃
יב לֹ֣וא אֲלֵיכֶם֮ כׇּל־עֹ֣בְרֵי דֶ֒רֶךְ֒
הַבִּ֣יטוּ וּרְא֔וּ אִם־יֵ֤שׁ מַכְאוֹב֙ כְּמַכְאֹבִ֔י
אֲשֶׁ֥ר עוֹלַ֖ל לִ֑י
אֲשֶׁר֙ הוֹגָ֣ה יְהֹוָ֔ה
בְּי֖וֹם חֲר֥וֹן אַפּֽוֹ׃
יג מִמָּר֛וֹם שָֽׁלַח־אֵ֥שׁ בְּעַצְמֹתַ֖י וַיִּרְדֶּ֑נָּה
פָּרַ֨שׂ רֶ֤שֶׁת לְרַגְלַי֙ הֱשִׁיבַ֣נִי אָח֔וֹר
נְתָנַ֙נִי֙ שֹֽׁמֵמָ֔ה
כׇּל־הַיּ֖וֹם דָּוָֽה׃
יד נִשְׂקַד֩ עֹ֨ל פְּשָׁעַ֜י בְּיָד֗וֹ יִשְׂתָּֽרְגוּ֙ עָל֣וּ עַל־צַוָּארִ֔י
הִכְשִׁ֖יל כֹּחִ֑י
נְתָנַ֣נִי אֲדֹנָ֔י
בִּידֵ֖י לֹא־אוּכַ֥ל קֽוּם׃
טו סִלָּ֨ה כׇל־אַבִּירַ֤י ׀ אֲדֹנָי֙ בְּקִרְבִּ֔י
קָרָ֥א עָלַ֛י מוֹעֵ֖ד לִשְׁבֹּ֣ר בַּחוּרָ֑י
גַּ֚ת דָּרַ֣ךְ אֲדֹנָ֔י
לִבְתוּלַ֖ת בַּת־יְהוּדָֽה׃
טז עַל־אֵ֣לֶּה ׀ אֲנִ֣י בוֹכִיָּ֗ה עֵינִ֤י ׀ עֵינִי֙ יֹ֣רְדָה מַּ֔יִם
כִּֽי־רָחַ֥ק מִמֶּ֛נִּי מְנַחֵ֖ם מֵשִׁ֣יב נַפְשִׁ֑י
הָי֤וּ בָנַי֙ שֽׁוֹמֵמִ֔ים
כִּ֥י גָבַ֖ר אוֹיֵֽב׃

(ל׳ זעירא)

"See, O Lord, and behold,
How abject I am become."
¹²Let it not come unto you,
all you who pass by!
Behold and see if there is any pain resembling my pain
Which is inflicted upon me,
With which the Lord has grieved me
In the day of His fierce anger.
¹³My bones are filled with fire which He sent down
from on high, and it prevails against them.
He has spread a net for my feet, He has turned me back.
He has turned me desolate
And faint all the day.
¹⁴Now is the yoke of my transgressions bound by His
hand. They are wreathed, and come up to my neck,
He has made my strength to stumble.
The Lord has delivered me into their hands,
I am not able to rise up against them.
¹⁵Of all the mighty in the midst of me, not one
can stand.
He has called a solemn assembly against me
to crush my young men.
The Lord has trodden the virgin, the daughter of Judah,
As in a winepress.
¹⁶Pour out your tears, my eyes; for these things
do I weep:
Because the comforter is far from me, He who
should relieve my soul.
My children are desolate,
Because the enemy prevails.

יז פֵּרְשָׂה צִיּוֹן בְּיָדֶיהָ אֵין מְנַחֵם לָהּ
צִוָּה יְהֹוָה לְיַעֲקֹב סְבִיבָיו צָרָיו
הָיְתָה יְרוּשָׁלַ͏ִם לְנִדָּה בֵּינֵיהֶם:
יח צַדִּיק הוּא יְהֹוָה כִּי פִיהוּ מָרִיתִי
שִׁמְעוּ־נָא כָל־הָעַמִּים* וּרְאוּ מַכְאֹבִי
בְּתוּלֹתַי וּבַחוּרַי הָלְכוּ בַשֶּׁבִי:
יט קָרָאתִי לַמְאַהֲבַי הֵמָּה רִמּוּנִי
כֹּהֲנַי וּזְקֵנַי בָּעִיר גָּוָעוּ
כִּי־בִקְשׁוּ אֹכֶל לָמוֹ
וְיָשִׁיבוּ אֶת־נַפְשָׁם:
כ רְאֵה יְהֹוָה כִּי־צַר־לִי מֵעַי חֳמַרְמָרוּ
נֶהְפַּךְ לִבִּי בְּקִרְבִּי
כִּי מָרוֹ מָרִיתִי
מִחוּץ שִׁכְּלָה־חֶרֶב בַּבַּיִת כַּמָּוֶת:
כא שָׁמְעוּ כִּי נֶאֱנָחָה אָנִי אֵין מְנַחֵם לִי
כָּל־אֹיְבַי שָׁמְעוּ רָעָתִי שָׂשׂוּ
כִּי אַתָּה עָשִׂיתָ
הֵבֵאתָ יוֹם־קָרָאתָ וְיִהְיוּ כָמֹנִי:
כב תָּבֹא כָל־רָעָתָם לְפָנֶיךָ וְעוֹלֵל לָמוֹ
כַּאֲשֶׁר עוֹלַלְתָּ לִי עַל כָּל־פְּשָׁעָי
כִּי־רַבּוֹת אַנְחֹתַי וְלִבִּי דַוָּי:
ב א אֵיכָה יָעִיב בְּאַפּוֹ | אֲדֹנָי אֶת־בַּת־צִיּוֹן
הִשְׁלִיךְ מִשָּׁמַיִם אֶרֶץ

(עמים כתיב)

¹⁷Quiet comfort is not here for Zion, as she spreads out
her hands.
The Lord has commanded concerning Jacob, that
his adversaries should be round about him.
Jerusalem is as an unclean one amongst them.
¹⁸Righteous is the Lord. For I have rebelled
against His commandment.
Listen, O listen, all you nations, and behold my agony:
My virgins and my young men are gone into captivity.
¹⁹So I called for my lovers, but they deceived me.
My priests and my elders expired in the city,
While they sought food for themselves,
To relieve their souls.
²⁰Then see, O Lord, that I am in distress.
My bowels burn.
My heart is turned within me.
For I have grievously rebelled.
Abroad the sword bereaves, as death at home.
²¹Upon hearing that I sigh, none came to comfort me.
All my enemies heard of my trouble: they are glad
That You have done it.
But You will bring the day You have proclaimed, and
they shall be like unto me.
²²View all their wickedness before Yourself, and do
to them
As You have done to me for all my transgressions.
For my sighs are many, and my heart is faint.

2 ¹Alas! The Lord has covered with a cloud
the daughter of Zion in His anger.

תִּפְאֶ֣רֶת יִשְׂרָאֵ֑ל

וְלֹא־זָכַ֥ר הֲדֹם־רַגְלָ֖יו בְּי֥וֹם אַפּֽוֹ׃

בִּלַּ֨ע אֲדֹנָ֜י וְלֹ֣א* חָמַ֗ל אֵ֚ת כָּל־נְא֣וֹת יַעֲקֹ֔ב

הָרַ֧ס בְּעֶבְרָת֛וֹ מִבְצְרֵ֥י בַת־יְהוּדָ֖ה הִגִּ֣יעַ לָאָ֑רֶץ

חִלֵּ֥ל מַמְלָכָ֖ה וְשָׂרֶֽיהָ׃

גָּדַ֣ע בָּֽחֳרִי־אַ֗ף כֹּ֚ל קֶ֣רֶן יִשְׂרָאֵ֔ל

הֵשִׁ֥יב אָח֛וֹר יְמִינ֖וֹ מִפְּנֵ֣י אוֹיֵ֑ב

וַיִּבְעַ֤ר בְּיַעֲקֹב֙ כְּאֵ֣שׁ לֶֽהָבָ֔ה

אָכְלָ֖ה סָבִֽיב׃

דָּרַ֨ךְ קַשְׁתּ֜וֹ כְּאוֹיֵ֗ב נִצָּ֤ב יְמִינוֹ֙ כְּצָ֔ר

וַֽיַּהֲרֹ֔ג

כֹּ֖ל מַחֲמַדֵּי־עָ֑יִן

בְּאֹ֙הֶל֙ בַּת־צִיּ֔וֹן

שָׁפַ֥ךְ כָּאֵ֖שׁ חֲמָתֽוֹ׃

הָיָ֨ה אֲדֹנָ֤י ׀ כְּאוֹיֵב֙ בִּלַּ֣ע יִשְׂרָאֵ֔ל

בִּלַּע֙ כָּל־אַרְמְנוֹתֶ֔יהָ

שִׁחֵ֖ת מִבְצָרָ֑יו

וַיֶּ֙רֶב֙ בְּבַת־יְהוּדָ֔ה

תַּאֲנִיָּ֖ה וַאֲנִיָּֽה׃

וַיַּחְמֹ֤ס כַּגַּן֙ שֻׂכּ֔וֹ

שִׁחֵ֖ת מוֹעֲד֑וֹ

שִׁכַּ֣ח יְהֹוָ֣ה ׀ בְּצִיּוֹן֙ מוֹעֵ֣ד וְשַׁבָּ֔ת

וַיִּנְאַ֥ץ בְּזַֽעַם־אַפּ֖וֹ מֶ֥לֶךְ וְכֹהֵֽן׃

(לֹא כְּתִיב)

He has cast down from heaven unto earth
The splendor of Israel.
He has not remembered His footstool in the day
of His anger.
²Brought waste without pity by the Lord are
all of Jacob's habitations.
He has thrown down in His wrath the stronghold
of the daughters of Judah. He has brought them down
to the ground,
He has polluted the kingdom and its princes.
³Cut off by Him in fierce anger is all the horn of Israel.
He has withdrawn His right hand in the presence
of the foe.
He has burned in Jacob like a flaming fire
Which consumes everything.
⁴Drawn has He now His bow like an enemy,
standing with His right hand like a foe.
He slew
All who were pleasant to the eye.
In the tent of the daughter of Zion
He has poured out His fury like fire.
⁵Enemy is the Lord become. He has swallowed
up Israel;
He has swallowed up all her palaces:
He has destroyed His strongholds,
Has increased in the daughter of Judah
Wailing and lamentation.
⁶Fences have been removed from His booth, His garden,
He has destroyed His place of assembly.
The Lord has caused His solemn feasts and sabbaths
to be forgotten in Zion.

"They have cast dust upon their heads..." 2:10

ישבו לארץ ידמו זקני בת־ציון העלו עפר על ראשם חגרו שקים

זָנַ֨ח אֲדֹנָ֤י ׀ מִזְבְּחוֹ֙ נִאֵ֣ר מִקְדָּשׁ֔וֹ
הִסְגִּיר֙ בְּיַד־אוֹיֵ֔ב
חוֹמֹ֣ת אַרְמְנוֹתֶ֑יהָ
ק֛וֹל נָתְנ֥וּ בְּבֵית־יְהֹוָ֖ה כְּי֥וֹם מוֹעֵֽד׃
ח חָשַׁ֨ב יְהֹוָ֤ה ׀ לְהַשְׁחִית֙ חוֹמַ֣ת בַּת־צִיּ֔וֹן
נָ֣טָה קָ֔ו
לֹא־הֵשִׁ֥יב יָד֖וֹ מִבַּלֵּ֑עַ
וַיַּֽאֲבֶל־חֵ֥ל וְחוֹמָ֖ה יַחְדָּ֥ו אֻמְלָֽלוּ׃
ט טָבְע֤וּ* בָאָ֙רֶץ֙ שְׁעָרֶ֔יהָ
אִבַּ֥ד וְשִׁבַּ֖ר בְּרִיחֶ֑יהָ
מַלְכָּ֨הּ וְשָׂרֶ֤יהָ בַגּוֹיִם֙ אֵ֣ין תּוֹרָ֔ה
גַּם־נְבִיאֶ֕יהָ לֹא־מָצְא֥וּ חָז֖וֹן מֵיְהֹוָֽה׃
י יֵשְׁב֤וּ לָאָ֙רֶץ֙ יִדְּמ֔וּ זִקְנֵ֖י בַת־צִיּ֑וֹן
הֶעֱל֤וּ עָפָר֙ עַל־רֹאשָׁ֔ם
חָגְר֖וּ שַׂקִּ֑ים
הוֹרִ֤ידוּ לָאָ֙רֶץ֙ רֹאשָׁ֔ן
בְּתוּלֹ֖ת יְרוּשָׁלָֽ͏ִם׃
יא כָּל֨וּ בַדְּמָע֤וֹת עֵינַי֙ חֳמַרְמְר֣וּ מֵעַ֔י
נִשְׁפַּ֤ךְ לָאָ֙רֶץ֙ כְּבֵדִ֔י
עַל־שֶׁ֖בֶר בַּת־עַמִּ֑י
בֵּֽעָטֵ֤ף עוֹלֵל֙ וְיוֹנֵ֔ק
בִּרְחֹב֖וֹת קִרְיָֽה׃
יב לְאִמֹּתָם֙ יֹ֣אמְר֔וּ

(ט׳ זעירא)

In the indignation of His anger, He has scorned
king and priest.
⁷Given away has God His own altar, He has disdained
His sanctuary.
He has given into the hand of the enemy,
The walls of her palaces;
They have shouted their victory in the House of the
Lord, as in the day of a solemn feast.
⁸How is the Lord minded to bring down in ruins
the wall of the daughter of Zion.
He has stretched out a line,
He has not withdrawn His hand from destroying:
Therefore He has made trench and rampart to lament,
they languished together.
⁹Into the ground her gates are sunk.
He has destroyed and broken her bar.
Her king and her princes are among the nations,
without law;
Her prophets also find no vision from the Lord.
¹⁰Judicious silence do they keep, and sit upon the ground,
the elders of the daughter of Zion.
They have cast dust upon their heads,
And clothed themselves in sackcloth.
The virgins of Jerusalem
Hang down their heads upon the ground.
¹¹Kept full of tears, my eyes do fail, my bowels burn,
My bile is spilled upon the ground,
For the destruction of the daughter of my people;
Because infants and sucklings swoon
In the broad places of the city.
¹²Languishing as the wounded in the broad places

אַיֵּ֖ה דָּגָ֣ן וָיָ֑יִן

בְּהִֽתְעַטְּפָ֤ם כֶּֽחָלָל֙ בִּרְחֹב֣וֹת עִ֔יר

בְּהִשְׁתַּפֵּ֣ךְ נַפְשָׁ֔ם

אֶל־חֵ֖יק אִמֹּתָֽם:

יג מָֽה־אֲעִידֵ֞ךְ* מָ֣ה אֲדַמֶּה־לָּ֗ךְ הַבַּת֙ יְר֣וּשָׁלַ֔͏ִם

מָ֤ה אַשְׁוֶה־לָּךְ֙ וַאֲנַֽחֲמֵ֔ךְ

בְּתוּלַ֖ת בַּת־צִיּ֑וֹן

כִּֽי־גָד֥וֹל כַּיָּ֛ם שִׁבְרֵ֖ךְ מִ֥י יִרְפָּא־לָֽךְ:

יד נְבִיאַ֗יִךְ חָ֤זוּ לָךְ֙ שָׁ֣וְא וְתָפֵ֔ל

וְלֹֽא־גִלּ֤וּ עַל־עֲוֺנֵךְ֙ לְהָשִׁ֣יב שְׁבוּתֵ֔ךְ*

וַיֶּ֣חֱזוּ לָ֔ךְ

מַשְׂא֥וֹת שָׁ֖וְא וּמַדּוּחִֽים:

טו סָֽפְק֨וּ עָלַ֤יִךְ כַּפַּ֙יִם֙ כָּל־עֹ֣בְרֵי דֶ֔רֶךְ

שָֽׁרְקוּ֙ וַיָּנִ֣עוּ רֹאשָׁ֔ם

עַל־בַּ֖ת יְר֣וּשָׁלָ֑͏ִם

הֲזֹ֣את הָעִ֗יר שֶׁיֹּֽאמְרוּ֙ כְּלִ֣ילַת יֹ֔פִי

מָשׂ֖וֹשׂ לְכָל־הָאָֽרֶץ:

טז פָּצ֨וּ עָלַ֤יִךְ פִּיהֶם֙ כָּל־אֹ֣יְבַ֔יִךְ

שָֽׁרְקוּ֙ וַיַּֽחַרְקוּ־שֵׁ֔ן

אָמְר֖וּ בִּלָּ֑עְנוּ

אַ֣ךְ זֶ֥ה הַיּ֛וֹם שֶׁקִּוִּינֻ֖הוּ מָצָ֥אנוּ רָאִֽינוּ:

יז עָשָׂ֨ה יְהֹוָ֜ה אֲשֶׁ֣ר זָמָ֗ם בִּצַּ֤ע אֶמְרָתוֹ֙ אֲשֶׁ֣ר צִוָּ֣ה

מִֽימֵי־קֶ֔דֶם

(אֵעִידֵךְ כתיב)   (שְׁבִיתֵךְ כתיב)

of the city,
They say to their mothers:
"Where is corn and wine?"
As their life runs out
In their mother's bosom.
¹³Must I find something to compare with you?
To what shall I liken you, daughter of Jerusalem?
What shall I equal to you, that I might comfort you,
O virgin daughter of Zion?
For your wound gapes wide as the sea: who can
heal you?
¹⁴Night visions have your prophets seen of you,
of vanity and delusion.
But they have not uncovered your iniquity,
to bring back your captivity.
The prophecies they gave you
Were delusions, vanities and deceptions.
¹⁵Oh, those who pass by clap their hands at you,
They hiss and shake their head
At the daughter of Jerusalem:
"Is this the city that men call the perfection of beauty?
The joy of the whole earth?"
¹⁶Pulled wide, their mouth is set against you.
They hiss and gnash their teeth.
They say: "We have swallowed her up.
Certainly, this is the day that we have looked for;
we have found, we have seen it."
¹⁷Quickly, the Lord did that which He had planned.
He has performed His word which He commanded
in the days of old.

הָרַס וְלֹא חָמֵל

וַיְשַׂמַּח עָלַיִךְ אוֹיֵב

הֵרִים קֶרֶן צָרָיִךְ:

יח **צָעַק** לִבָּם אֶל־אֲדֹנָי

חוֹמַת בַּת־צִיּוֹן הוֹרִידִי כַנַּחַל דִּמְעָה יוֹמָם וָלַיְלָה

אַל־תִּתְּנִי פוּגַת לָךְ

אַל־תִּדֹּם בַּת־עֵינֵךְ:

יט **קוּמִי** ׀ רֹנִּי בַלַּיְלָה* לְרֹאשׁ אַשְׁמֻרוֹת

שִׁפְכִי כַמַּיִם לִבֵּךְ

נֹכַח פְּנֵי אֲדֹנָי

שְׂאִי אֵלָיו כַּפַּיִךְ עַל־נֶפֶשׁ עוֹלָלַיִךְ

הָעֲטוּפִים בְּרָעָב בְּרֹאשׁ כָּל־חוּצוֹת:

כ **רְאֵה** יְהֹוָה וְהַבִּיטָה

לְמִי עוֹלַלְתָּ כֹּה

אִם־תֹּאכַלְנָה נָשִׁים פִּרְיָם עֹלֲלֵי טִפֻּחִים

אִם־יֵהָרֵג בְּמִקְדַּשׁ אֲדֹנָי כֹּהֵן וְנָבִיא:

כא **שָׁכְבוּ** לָאָרֶץ חוּצוֹת נַעַר וְזָקֵן

בְּתוּלֹתַי וּבַחוּרַי נָפְלוּ בֶחָרֶב

הָרַגְתָּ בְּיוֹם אַפֶּךָ

טָבַחְתָּ לֹא חָמָלְתָּ:

כב **תִּקְרָא** כְיוֹם מוֹעֵד מְגוּרַי מִסָּבִיב

וְלֹא הָיָה בְּיוֹם אַף־יְהֹוָה פָּלִיט וְשָׂרִיד

אֲשֶׁר־טִפַּחְתִּי וְרִבִּיתִי אֹיְבִי כִלָּם:

(בליל כתיב)

He has thrown down, and has not pitied.
He has caused your enemy to rejoice over you,
He has lifted up the horn of your adversaries.
¹⁸Reaching the Lord their heart cried out:
O wall of the daughter of Zion, let tears run down
like a river day and night.
Give yourself no rest;
Let not the apple of your eye cease.
¹⁹So rise, cry in the night, at the beginning
of the watches;
Pour out your heart like water
Before the face of the Lord.
Lift up your hands towards Him, for the life of
your infants
Who faint from hunger in the top of every street.
²⁰Then see, O Lord, consider:
Whom have You tortured thus?
Shall women eat their fruit, their children
borne and loved?
Shall priest and prophet be slain in the sanctuary
of the Lord?
²¹Unto the ground of streets have fallen
both young and old.
My virgins and my young men fallen by the sword.
You slew them in the day of Your anger;
You killed, and did not pity.
²²Violence all around me You did call, as in the day
of solemn assembly.
Thus there was none in the day of the Lord's anger
who escaped or who remained.
Those tenderly nursed and reared by me
the enemy consumed.

ג ‏א אֲנִי הַגֶּבֶר רָאָה עֳנִי
בְּשֵׁבֶט עֶבְרָתוֹ:
‏ב אוֹתִי נָהַג וַיֹּלַךְ חֹשֶׁךְ וְלֹא־אוֹר:
‏ג אַךְ בִּי יָשֻׁב יַהֲפֹךְ יָדוֹ כָּל־הַיּוֹם:
‏ד בִּלָּה בְשָׂרִי וְעוֹרִי
שִׁבַּר עַצְמוֹתָי:
‏ה בָּנָה עָלַי וַיַּקַּף רֹאשׁ וּתְלָאָה:
‏ו בְּמַחֲשַׁכִּים הוֹשִׁיבַנִי כְּמֵתֵי עוֹלָם:
‏ז גָּדַר בַּעֲדִי וְלֹא אֵצֵא הִכְבִּיד נְחָשְׁתִּי:
‏ח גַּם כִּי אֶזְעַק וַאֲשַׁוֵּעַ
שָׂתַם תְּפִלָּתִי:
‏ט גָּדַר דְּרָכַי בְּגָזִית
נְתִיבֹתַי עִוָּה:
‏י דֹּב אֹרֵב הוּא לִי
אֲרִי* בְּמִסְתָּרִים:
‏יא דְּרָכַי סוֹרֵר וַיְפַשְּׁחֵנִי שָׂמַנִי שֹׁמֵם:
‏יב דָּרַךְ קַשְׁתּוֹ וַיַּצִּיבֵנִי
כַּמַּטָּרָא לַחֵץ:
‏יג הֵבִיא בְּכִלְיֹתָי
בְּנֵי אַשְׁפָּתוֹ:
‏יד הָיִיתִי שְּׂחֹק לְכָל־עַמִּי
נְגִינָתָם כָּל־הַיּוֹם:
‏טו הִשְׂבִּיעַנִי בַמְּרוֹרִים הִרְוַנִי לַעֲנָה:

(אריה כתיב)

3 ¹Ah! I am the man who has seen affliction
By the rod of His wrath.
²Am I not driven on by Him in darkness
and not in light.
³Against me does He turn His hand,
over and over again all the day.
⁴By Him are wasted all my flesh and skin,
Broken by Him are my bones.
⁵Built up against me, He has set poison and hardship.
⁶Black are the places where He makes me dwell,
like unto those long dead.
⁷Closely He fences me, so that I cannot get out; He
has made my fetters heavy.
⁸Calling, crying for help—
And He rejects my prayers.
⁹Cut stones He uses to enclose my ways,
He has made my paths crooked.
¹⁰Darkly He waits for me: as bear,
As lion in a secret place.
¹¹Desolate has He made me, has turned my way,
has pulled me into pieces.
¹²Deeply He bent His bow, and set me
As the target for the arrow.
¹³Even into my vitals
Has He shot the arrows of His quiver.
¹⁴Ever a derision have I become to all my people,
Their song all of the day.
¹⁵Enclosed within me has He bitterness, He has sated me
with wormwood.

טז וַיַּגְרֵס בֶּחָצָץ שִׁנָּי
הִכְפִּישַׁנִי בָּאֵפֶר:
יז וַתִּזְנַח מִשָּׁלוֹם נַפְשִׁי נָשִׁיתִי טוֹבָה:
יח וָאֹמַר אָבַד נִצְחִי
וְתוֹחַלְתִּי מֵיְהוָה:
יט זְכָר־עָנְיִי וּמְרוּדִי לַעֲנָה וָרֹאשׁ:
כ זָכוֹר תִּזְכּוֹר
וְתָשׁוֹחַ* עָלַי נַפְשִׁי:
כא זֹאת אָשִׁיב אֶל־לִבִּי עַל־כֵּן אוֹחִיל:
כב חַסְדֵי יְהוָה כִּי לֹא־תָמְנוּ
כִּי לֹא־כָלוּ רַחֲמָיו*:
כג חֲדָשִׁים לַבְּקָרִים
רַבָּה אֱמוּנָתֶךָ:
כד חֶלְקִי יְהוָה אָמְרָה נַפְשִׁי
עַל־כֵּן אוֹחִיל לוֹ:
כה טוֹב יְהוָה לְקֹוָו
לְנֶפֶשׁ תִּדְרְשֶׁנּוּ:
כו טוֹב וְיָחִיל וְדוּמָם
לִתְשׁוּעַת יְהוָה:
כז טוֹב לַגֶּבֶר
כִּי־יִשָּׂא עֹל בִּנְעוּרָיו:
כח יֵשֵׁב בָּדָד וְיִדֹּם
כִּי נָטַל עָלָיו:

(וְתָשִׁיחַ כתיב)   (רַחֲמוֹ כתיב)

¹⁶Full into the dust has He ground me,
He has broken my teeth with gravel stones.
¹⁷Far off from peace is now my soul removed:
I forgot prosperity.
¹⁸"Forsaken is my strength," I said,
"My hope has perished before the Lord."
¹⁹Giving remembrance to my affliction and anguish
is wormwood now, and poison.
²⁰Ground low within me are
The recollections of my soul.
²¹Giving reply to my heart, I do have hope:
²²How can the Lord's mercies be consumed?
Surely, His compassion does not fail.
²³Has not each dawn new hope?
Great is Your faithfulness!
²⁴Has not my soul said: The Lord is my portion,
Therefore, I hope in Him.
²⁵Is not the Lord good to those who trust in Him,
To the soul that seeks Him?
²⁶It is good that a man should quietly wait
For the salvation of the Lord.
²⁷It is good for a man
To bear the yoke in his youth.
²⁸Just let him sit alone and keep silence,
Because it is laid upon him.

"...the prisoners of the earth..."   3:34

כט יִתֵּן בֶּעָפָר פִּיהוּ
אוּלַי יֵשׁ תִּקְוָה:
ל יִתֵּן לְמַכֵּהוּ לֶחִי יִשְׂבַּע בְּחֶרְפָּה:
לא כִּי לֹא יִזְנַח לְעוֹלָם אֲדֹנָי:
לב כִּי אִם־הוֹגָה
וְרִחַם כְּרֹב חֲסָדָיו*:
לג כִּי לֹא עִנָּה מִלִּבּוֹ
וַיַּגֶּה בְּנֵי־אִישׁ:
לד לְדַכֵּא תַּחַת רַגְלָיו
כֹּל אֲסִירֵי אָרֶץ:
לה לְהַטּוֹת מִשְׁפַּט־גָּבֶר
נֶגֶד פְּנֵי עֶלְיוֹן:
לו לְעַוֵּת* אָדָם בְּרִיבוֹ
אֲדֹנָי לֹא רָאָה:
לז מִי זֶה אָמַר וַתֶּהִי
אֲדֹנָי לֹא צִוָּה:
לח מִפִּי עֶלְיוֹן לֹא תֵצֵא
הָרָעוֹת וְהַטּוֹב:
לט מַה־יִּתְאוֹנֵן אָדָם חָי
גֶּבֶר עַל־חֲטָאָיו*:
מ נַחְפְּשָׂה דְרָכֵינוּ וְנַחְקֹרָה
וְנָשׁוּבָה עַד־יְהוָה:
מא נִשָּׂא לְבָבֵנוּ אֶל־כַּפָּיִם

²⁹Joyous hope may yet be his,
If he puts his mouth in the dust.
³⁰Jowl, cheek to smiter let him turn, let him receive
full measure of abuse.
³¹Kept from the Lord forever is not His intent.
³²Kindness is His, although He will cause grief,
But many are His mercies.
³³Kindling pain is not what He desires,
Nor does He want to grieve the sons of man.
³⁴Letting the prisoners of the earth
Be crushed under His feet,
³⁵Leading defiance against the Most High,
By turning aside the rights of man,
³⁶Learning to subvert a man's just cause:
The Lord will not approve of this.
³⁷May there be any word which comes to pass,
When the Lord has not commanded it?
³⁸Must evil and the good not both proceed
Out of the mouth of the Most High?
³⁹May any living man therefore complain,
May any who has sinned?
⁴⁰Now let us search and try our ways,
And return to the Lord.
⁴¹Next, let us lift up our hearts with our hands,
Unto God in heaven.

אֶל־אֵל בַּשָּׁמָֽיִם:
מב נַחְנוּ פָשַׁעְנוּ וּמָרִינוּ
אַתָּה לֹא סָלָֽחְתָּ:
מג סַכֹּתָה בָאַף וַתִּרְדְּפֵנוּ
הָרַגְתָּ לֹא חָמָֽלְתָּ:
מד סַכֹּתָה בֶעָנָן לָךְ
מֵעֲבוֹר תְּפִלָּה:
מה סְחִי וּמָאוֹס תְּשִׂימֵנוּ בְּקֶרֶב הָעַמִּים:
מו פָּצוּ עָלֵינוּ פִּיהֶם כָּל־אֹיְבֵינוּ:
מז פַּחַד וָפַחַת הָיָה לָנוּ הַשֵּׁאת וְהַשָּׁבֶר:
מח פַּלְגֵי־מַיִם תֵּרַד עֵינִי
עַל־שֶׁבֶר בַּת־עַמִּי:
מט עֵינִי נִגְּרָה וְלֹא תִדְמֶה מֵאֵין הֲפֻגוֹת:
נ עַד־יַשְׁקִיף וְיֵרֶא
יְהוָה מִשָּׁמָֽיִם:
נא עֵינִי עוֹלְלָה לְנַפְשִׁי
מִכֹּל בְּנוֹת עִירִי:
נב צוֹד צָדוּנִי כַּצִּפּוֹר אֹיְבַי חִנָּם:
נג צָמְתוּ בַבּוֹר חַיָּי
וַיַּדּוּ־אֶבֶן בִּי:
נד צָפוּ־מַיִם עַל־רֹאשִׁי אָמַרְתִּי נִגְזָֽרְתִּי:
נה קָרָאתִי שִׁמְךָ יְהוָה
מִבּוֹר תַּחְתִּיּוֹת:
נו קוֹלִי שָׁמָֽעְתָּ
אַל־תַּעְלֵם אָזְנְךָ לְרַוְחָתִי לְשַׁוְעָתִֽי:

⁴²No, we have trespassed and we have rebelled,
You have not pardoned.
⁴³On us is placed Your anger and pursuit,
You have slain, You have not pitied.
⁴⁴Over Yourself You have now wrapped a cloud
So that no prayer can come through.
⁴⁵Offscouring and refuse have You made of us
in the midst of the peoples.
⁴⁶Pulled wide have our enemies their mouths, wide,
wide against us.
⁴⁷Pit and terror have now come upon us,
desolation and destruction.
⁴⁸Poured streams of water issue from my eyes,
For the breach of the daughter of my people.
⁴⁹Quivering eyes pour out and do not cease,
refusing any comfort.
⁵⁰Quelled when the Lord looks out,
And sees from heaven.
⁵¹Questing eye tortures me,
With the fate of all the daughters of my city.
⁵²Relentlessly, they chased me like a bird, they are
my enemies without cause.
⁵³Rancor thrust me alive into the pit,
And closed it over me with a stone.
⁵⁴Rushing waters flowed over my head. I said: "I am
cut off!"
⁵⁵So I then called upon Your name, O Lord,
Out of the pit of the nether world.
⁵⁶Shut not Your ear to my groan, my cry:
O hear my plea.

נ֟קָרַ֙בְתָּ֙ בְּי֣וֹם אֶקְרָאֶ֔ךָ
אָמַ֖רְתָּ אַל־תִּירָֽא׃
נח רַ֧בְתָּ אֲדֹנָ֛י רִיבֵ֥י נַפְשִׁ֖י גָּאַ֥לְתָּ חַיָּֽי׃
נט רָאִ֤יתָה יְהֹוָה֙ עַוָּ֣תָתִ֔י
שָׁפְטָ֖ה מִשְׁפָּטִֽי׃
ס רָאִ֙יתָה֙ כָּל־נִקְמָתָ֔ם
כָּל־מַחְשְׁבֹתָ֖ם לִֽי׃
סא שָׁמַ֤עְתָּ חֶרְפָּתָם֙ יְהֹוָ֔ה
כָּל־מַחְשְׁבֹתָ֖ם עָלָֽי׃
סב שִׂפְתֵ֥י קָמַי֙ וְהֶגְיוֹנָ֔ם
עָלַ֖י כָּל־הַיּֽוֹם׃
סג שִׁבְתָּ֤ם וְקִֽימָתָם֙ הַבִּ֔יטָה
אֲנִ֖י מַנְגִּֽינָתָֽם׃
סד תָּשִׁ֤יב לָהֶם֙ גְּמ֣וּל יְהֹוָ֔ה כְּמַעֲשֵׂ֖ה יְדֵיהֶֽם׃
סה תִּתֵּ֤ן לָהֶם֙ מְגִנַּת־לֵ֔ב
תַּאֲלָֽתְךָ֖ לָהֶֽם׃
סו תִּרְדֹּ֤ף בְּאַף֙ וְתַשְׁמִידֵ֔ם
מִתַּ֖חַת שְׁמֵ֥י יְהֹוָֽה׃
ד א אֵיכָה֙ יוּעַ֣ם זָהָ֔ב
יִשְׁנֶ֖א הַכֶּ֣תֶם הַטּ֑וֹב
תִּשְׁתַּפֵּ֙כְנָה֙ אַבְנֵי־קֹ֔דֶשׁ
בְּרֹ֖אשׁ כָּל־חוּצֽוֹת׃
ב בְּנֵ֤י צִיּוֹן֙ הַיְקָרִ֔ים
הַמְסֻלָּאִ֖ים בַּפָּ֑ז
אֵיכָ֤ה נֶחְשְׁבוּ֙ לְנִבְלֵי־חֶ֔רֶשׂ

⁵⁷So near were You when I called upon You.
You said: "Fear not!"
⁵⁸The causes of my soul You championed, Lord.
You have redeemed my life.
⁵⁹The wrong done me, O Lord, You saw.
Judge You my cause.
⁶⁰Their vengeance in its fullness You have seen,
And all their devices against me.
⁶¹Utterings which they make You hear, O Lord,
And all their plots against me.
⁶²Upon the lips of all my adversaries are murmurs,
Mutterings all the day.
⁶³Uprising, downsitting of the enemy see, O Lord:
They sing their taunts to me.
⁶⁴Vow them a recompense, O Lord, according to
their deeds.
⁶⁵Vilify them with Your curse,
Give them hardness of heart.
⁶⁶Visit upon them anger and destruction,
Purge them from under the heavens of the Lord.

4 ¹Alas, the gold is dulled,
How tarnished is the finest gold.
The stones of the Sanctuary are poured out
At the top of every street.
²Behold the precious children of Zion,
Comparable to fine gold,
How are they thought of as earthen pitchers,

מַעֲשֵׂה יְדֵי יוֹצֵר:

גגַּם־תַּנִּים* חָלְצוּ שַׁד

הֵינִיקוּ גּוּרֵיהֶן

בַּת־עַמִּי לְאַכְזָר

כַּיְעֵנִים* בַּמִּדְבָּר:

דדָּבַק לְשׁוֹן יוֹנֵק אֶל־חִכּוֹ בַּצָּמָא

עוֹלָלִים שָׁאֲלוּ לֶחֶם

פֹּרֵשׂ אֵין לָהֶם:

ההָאֹכְלִים לְמַעֲדַנִּים

נָשַׁמּוּ בַּחוּצוֹת

הָאֱמֻנִים עֲלֵי תוֹלָע

חִבְּקוּ אַשְׁפַּתּוֹת:

ווַיִּגְדַּל עֲוֺן בַּת־עַמִּי

מֵחַטַּאת סְדֹם

הַהֲפוּכָה כְמוֹ־רָגַע

וְלֹא־חָלוּ בָהּ יָדָיִם:

זזַכּוּ נְזִירֶיהָ מִשֶּׁלֶג

צַחוּ מֵחָלָב

אָדְמוּ עֶצֶם מִפְּנִינִים

סַפִּיר גִּזְרָתָם:

חחָשַׁךְ מִשְּׁחוֹר תָּאֳרָם

לֹא נִכְּרוּ בַּחוּצוֹת

צָפַד עוֹרָם עַל־עַצְמָם

(תנין כתיב)   (כי ענים)

The work of the potter's hands.
³Come see the jackals draw out the breast
As they suckle their young ones.
The daughter of my people is become cruel
Like the ostrich in the wilderness.
⁴Does not the tongue of the suckling cleave to his palate
for thirst;
The young children ask bread,
And no one breaks it to them.
⁵Enfamished in the streets
Lie those who fed on dainties.
They that were brought up in scarlet
Embrace dunghills.
⁶For the iniquity of the daughter of my people is greater
Than the sin of Sodom,
That was overthrown as in a moment,
and no hands stayed on her.
⁷Given to greater pureness than the snow,
Her crowned princes were whiter than milk.
Redder were they than coral,
Their form was that of sapphire.
⁸How blacker than coal is their face,
They are not known in the streets.
Their skin cleaves to their bones,

יָבֵשׁ הָיָה כָעֵץ:
ט טוֹבִים הָיוּ חַלְלֵי־חֶרֶב
מֵחַלְלֵי רָעָב
שֶׁהֵם יָזֻבוּ מְדֻקָּרִים
מִתְּנוּבֹת שָׂדָי:
י יְדֵי נָשִׁים רַחֲמָנִיּוֹת
בִּשְּׁלוּ יַלְדֵיהֶן
הָיוּ לְבָרוֹת לָמוֹ
בְּשֶׁבֶר בַּת־עַמִּי:
יא כִּלָּה יְהֹוָה אֶת־חֲמָתוֹ
שָׁפַךְ חֲרוֹן אַפּוֹ
וַיַּצֶּת־אֵשׁ בְּצִיּוֹן
וַתֹּאכַל יְסֹדֹתֶיהָ:
יב לֹא הֶאֱמִינוּ מַלְכֵי־אֶרֶץ
כֹּל* יֹשְׁבֵי תֵבֵל
כִּי יָבֹא צַר וְאוֹיֵב
בְּשַׁעֲרֵי יְרוּשָׁלָ͏ִם:
יג מֵחַטֹּאת נְבִיאֶיהָ
עֲוֹנֹת כֹּהֲנֶיהָ
הַשֹּׁפְכִים בְּקִרְבָּהּ דַּם צַדִּיקִים:
יד נָעוּ עִוְרִים בַּחוּצוֹת
נְגֹאֲלוּ בַּדָּם
בְּלֹא יוּכְלוּ

(וכל כתיב)

It is withered, is become like a stick.
⁹It was better to be slain by the sword,
Than those who were slain by hunger.
For these pine away, stricken through,
For want of the produce of the field.
¹⁰Just see the hands of tender women
Cooking their own children.
They were their meat
In the destruction of the daughter of my people.
¹¹Kindled a fire has the Lord in Zion
Which has destroyed its foundations.
The Lord has accomplished His fury;
He has poured out His fierce anger.
¹²Little believed the kings of the earth,
Nor all the inhabitants of the world,
That an adversary and an enemy would have entered
The gates of Jerusalem.
¹³Must it not be for the sins of the prophets,
And for the iniquity of her priests,
For those who have shed the blood of the just
within her walls?
¹⁴Now they wander as blind men in the streets;
They have polluted themselves with blood
So that men could not

Eagle of Heaven   4:19

יִגְּעוּ בִּלְבֻשֵׁיהֶם:

ט״ סוּרוּ טָמֵא קָרְאוּ לָמוֹ סוּרוּ סוּרוּ אַל־תִּגָּעוּ

כִּי נָצוּ גַּם־נָעוּ

אָמְרוּ בַּגּוֹיִם

לֹא יוֹסִפוּ לָגוּר:

ט״ז פְּנֵי יְהֹוָה חִלְּקָם

לֹא יוֹסִיף לְהַבִּיטָם

פְּנֵי כֹהֲנִים לֹא נָשָׂאוּ

וּזְקֵנִים* לֹא חָנָנוּ:

י״ז עוֹדֵינוּ* תִּכְלֶינָה עֵינֵינוּ

אֶל־עֶזְרָתֵנוּ הָבֶל

בְּצִפִּיָּתֵנוּ צִפִּינוּ

אֶל־גּוֹי לֹא יוֹשִׁעַ:

י״ח צָדוּ צְעָדֵינוּ

מִלֶּכֶת בִּרְחֹבֹתֵינוּ

קָרַב קִצֵּנוּ מָלְאוּ יָמֵינוּ כִּי־בָא קִצֵּנוּ:

י״ט קַלִּים הָיוּ רֹדְפֵינוּ

מִנִּשְׁרֵי שָׁמָיִם

עַל־הֶהָרִים דְּלָקֻנוּ

בַּמִּדְבָּר אָרְבוּ לָנוּ:

כ׳ רוּחַ אַפֵּינוּ מְשִׁיחַ יְהֹוָה

נִלְכַּד בִּשְׁחִיתוֹתָם

אֲשֶׁר אָמַרְנוּ

(עוֹדִינָה כתיב)   (זְקֵנִים כתיב)

Touch their garments.
[15]"Oh, away, away! Unclean!" men cried to them.
"Away, do not come!"
So they fled away, they wandered;
And it was said among the nations:
"They shall no more dwell here!"
[16]Parted are they by the anger of the Lord;
He will no more regard them.
They respected not the person of the priests,
They favored not the elders.
[17]Quenched is vain help for which our eyes still strain.
Watching,
We watched a nation that could not save us.
[18]Restrained from going into our broad places,
We find they hunt our steps.
Our end is near, our days are fulfilled;
Our end has come.
[19]Swifter than eagles of heaven
Were our pursuers.
They pursued us upon the mountains,
They laid in wait for us in the desert.
[20]The Lord's anointed, the breath of life to us,
Was taken in their pits.
Of him we had said:

בְּצִלּוֹ נִחְיֶה בַגּוֹיִם:

כֹּא שִׂישִׂי וְשִׂמְחִי בַּת־אֱדֹום

יוֹשֶׁבְתְּ* בְּאֶרֶץ עוּץ

גַּם־עָלַיִךְ תַּעֲבָר־כֹּוס

תִּשְׁכְּרִי וְתִתְעָרִי:

כֹּב תַּם־עֲוֹנֵךְ בַּת־צִיּוֹן

לֹא יוֹסִיף לְהַגְלוֹתֵךְ

פָּקַד עֲוֹנֵךְ בַּת־אֱדֹום

גִּלָּה עַל־חַטֹּאתָיִךְ:

ה א זְכֹר יְהוָה מֶה־הָיָה לָנוּ

הַבִּיטָה* וּרְאֵה אֶת־חֶרְפָּתֵנוּ:

ב נַחֲלָתֵנוּ נֶהֶפְכָה לְזָרִים

בָּתֵּינוּ לְנָכְרִים:

ג יְתוֹמִים הָיִינוּ וְאֵין* אָב

אִמֹּתֵינוּ כְּאַלְמָנֹות:

ד מֵימֵינוּ בְּכֶסֶף שָׁתִינוּ

עֵצֵינוּ בִּמְחִיר יָבֹאוּ:

ה עַל צַוָּארֵנוּ נִרְדָּפְנוּ

יָגַעְנוּ וְלֹא* הוּנַח־לָנוּ:

ו מִצְרַיִם נָתַנּוּ יָד

אַשּׁוּר לִשְׂבֹּעַ לָחֶם:

(אין כתיב)   (הביט כתיב)   (יושבתי כתיב)

(לא כתיב)

"Under his shadow we shall live among the nations!"
²¹Uz is the land where Edom's daughter dwells.
Rejoice there and be glad.
The cup will also pass to you.
You will be drunk, you will expose your nudity.
²²Verily, the punishment of your iniquity is done,
daughter of Zion.
No longer will He take you into exile.
But you, daughter of Edom, your sin He will discover;
And He will punish your iniquity.

5   ¹Remember, O Lord, what is come upon us.
Consider and behold our disgrace.
²Our inheritance has been turned over to strangers,
Our houses to aliens.
³We are orphans, fatherless,
Our mothers are as widows.
⁴We must buy our water to drink;
Our wood is sold to us.
⁵Upon our neck are our persecutors;
We labor, and have no rest.
⁶We have stretched out our hand to Egypt,
To Assyria, to provide us with bread.

יֹ אֲבֹתֵ֤ינוּ חָטְאוּ֙ וְאֵינָ֔ם*

וַאֲנַ֖חְנוּ* עֲוֺנֹתֵיהֶ֥ם סָבָֽלְנוּ׃

חֹ עֲבָדִים֙ מָ֣שְׁלוּ בָ֔נוּ

פֹּרֵ֖ק אֵ֥ין מִיָּדָֽם׃

טֹ בְּנַפְשֵׁ֙נוּ֙ נָבִ֣יא לַחְמֵ֔נוּ

מִפְּנֵ֖י חֶ֥רֶב הַמִּדְבָּֽר׃

יֹ עוֹרֵ֙נוּ֙ כְּתַנּ֣וּר נִכְמָ֔רוּ

מִפְּנֵ֖י זַלְעֲפ֥וֹת רָעָֽב׃

יאֹ נָשִׁים֙ בְּצִיּ֣וֹן עִנּ֔וּ

בְּתֻלֹ֖ת בְּעָרֵ֥י יְהוּדָֽה׃

יבֹ שָׂרִים֙ בְּיָדָ֣ם נִתְל֔וּ

פְּנֵ֥י זְקֵנִ֖ים לֹ֥א נֶהְדָּֽרוּ׃

יגֹ בַּחוּרִים֙ טְח֣וֹן נָשָׂ֔אוּ

וּנְעָרִ֖ים בָּעֵ֥ץ כָּשָֽׁלוּ׃

ידֹ זְקֵנִים֙ מִשַּׁ֣עַר שָׁבָ֔תוּ

בַּחוּרִ֖ים מִנְּגִינָתָֽם׃

טוֹ שָׁבַת֙ מְשׂ֣וֹשׂ לִבֵּ֔נוּ

נֶהְפַּ֥ךְ לְאֵ֖בֶל מְחוֹלֵֽנוּ׃

טזֹ נָֽפְלָה֙ עֲטֶ֣רֶת רֹאשֵׁ֔נוּ

אֽוֹי־נָ֥א לָ֖נוּ כִּ֥י חָטָֽאנוּ׃

יזֹ עַל־זֶ֗ה הָיָ֤ה דָוֶה֙ לִבֵּ֔נוּ

עַל־אֵ֖לֶּה חָשְׁכ֥וּ עֵינֵֽינוּ׃

יחֹ עַ֤ל הַר־צִיּוֹן֙ שֶׁשָּׁמֵ֔ם

(אינם כתיב)   (אנחנו כתיב)

⁷Our fathers have sinned, and are no more;
And we have borne their iniquities.
⁸Slaves are ruling over us;
There is none to deliver us out of their hand.
⁹We get our bread with the peril of our lives,
Because of the sword of the desert.
¹⁰Our skin was hot like an oven
Because of the furious famine.
¹¹They ravished women in Zion,
And maids in the cities of Judah.
¹²Princes are hanged by their hands;
No respect has been shown to the elders.
¹³Young men carried the millstones,
And boys stumbled under the wood.
¹⁴Elders have ceased from the gate,
Young men from their song.
¹⁵The joy of our heart is ended,
Our dance is turned into mourning.
¹⁶The crown has fallen from our head:
Woe unto us, that we have sinned.
¹⁷For this our heart is sick;
For these things our eyes are dim.
¹⁸Because Mount Zion is desolate;

"Turn us unto You, O Lord."   5:21

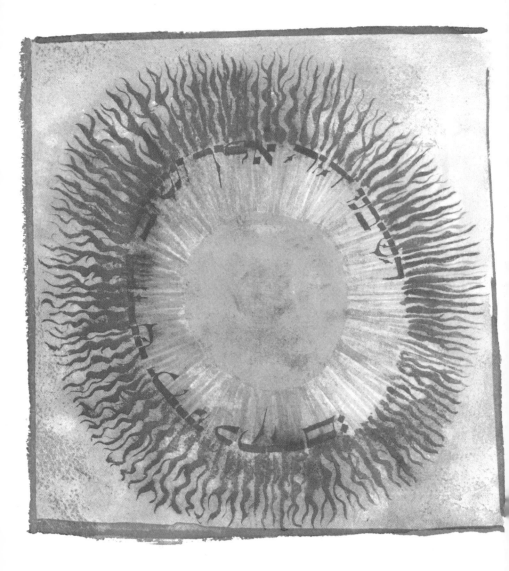

שׁוּעָלִים הִלְּכוּ־בְוֹ:

^{יט} אַתָּה יְהֹוָה לְעוֹלָם תֵּשֵׁב
כִּסְאֲךָ לְדוֹר וָדוֹר:

^כ לָמָּה לָנֶצַח תִּשְׁכָּחֵנוּ
תַּעַזְבֵנוּ לְאֹרֶךְ יָמִים:

^{כא} הֲשִׁיבֵנוּ יְהֹוָה אֵלֶיךָ וְנָשׁוּבָה*
חַדֵּשׁ יָמֵינוּ כְּקֶדֶם:

^{כב} כִּי אִם־מָאֹס מְאַסְתָּנוּ
קָצַפְתָּ עָלֵינוּ עַד־מְאֹד:

(וְנָשׁוּב כתיב)

Jackals walk upon it.
[19]O Lord, You remain forever,
Your throne is from generation to generation.
[20]Why will You forget us forever,
And forsake us for so long a time?
[21]Turn us unto You, O Lord, and we shall be turned;
Renew our days as of old.
[22]Can You have rejected us so utterly?
Can You be so greatly angry with us?

LITURGY FOR THE FESTIVALS

תְּפִלָּה לְיוֹם טוֹב

THE FESTIVAL SERVICE

And Moses proclaimed unto the Children of Israel
the appointed festivals of God.

וַיְדַבֵּר מֹשֶׁה אֶת־מֹעֲדֵי יְהֹוָה אֶל־בְּנֵי יִשְׂרָאֵל.

And God spoke unto Moses, saying:
"Speak unto the Children of Israel and say unto them:
'These are God's appointed festivals,
    especially sacred convocations,
which ye shall proclaim in their appointed seasons.
Three times in the year thou shalt observe a feast unto Me,
three times in the year all thy persons shall appear
    in the presence of God:
On the festival of Matzot,
on the festival of Shavuot,
and on the festival of Sukkot.'
And they shall not appear empty-handed before God;
everyone shall give as able, according to the blessing
    which יְהֹוָה, thy God, hath given unto thee."

וַיְדַבֵּר יְהֹוָה אֶל־מֹשֶׁה לֵּאמֹר,

דַּבֵּר אֶל־בְּנֵי יִשְׂרָאֵל וְאָמַרְתָּ אֲלֵהֶם:

אֵלֶּה מוֹעֲדֵי יְהֹוָה, מִקְרָאֵי קֹדֶשׁ

אֲשֶׁר־תִּקְרְאוּ אֹתָם בְּמוֹעֲדָם.

שָׁלוֹשׁ פְּעָמִים בַּשָּׁנָה יֵרָאֶה כָל־זְכוּרְךָ

אֶת־פְּנֵי יְהֹוָה אֱלֹהֶיךָ בַּמָּקוֹם אֲשֶׁר יִבְחָר:

בְּחַג הַמַּצוֹת,

וּבְחַג הַשָּׁבֻעוֹת

וּבְחַג הַסֻּכּוֹת.

וְלֹא יֵרָאֶה אֶת־פְּנֵי יְהֹוָה רֵיקָם,

אִישׁ כְּמַתְּנַת יָדוֹ, כְּבִרְכַּת יְהֹוָה אֱלֹהֶיךָ אֲשֶׁר נָתַן־לָךְ.

So did Moses proclaim the set festivals of God
unto the Children of Israel.

הָרִיעוּ לַיְיָ כָּל־הָאָרֶץ!

עִבְדוּ אֶת־יְהֹוָה בְּשִׂמְחָה!

בֹּאוּ לְפָנָיו בִּרְנָנָה!

Shout joyfully unto God, all the earth!
Serve יְהֹוָה with gladness!
Come into God's Presence with singing!

תהלים ק   Psalm 100

§   הָרִיעוּ לַיהֹוָה כָּל־הָאָרֶץ!

עִבְדוּ אֶת־יְהֹוָה בְּשִׂמְחָה!

בֹּאוּ לְפָנָיו בִּרְנָנָה!

דְּעוּ כִּי־יְהֹוָה הוּא אֱלֹהִים.

הוּא עָשָׂנוּ וְלוֹ אֲנַחְנוּ.

עַמּוֹ וְצֹאן מַרְעִיתוֹ.

בֹּאוּ שְׁעָרָיו בְּתוֹדָה,

חֲצֵרֹתָיו בִּתְהִלָּה;

הוֹדוּ לוֹ, בָּרְכוּ שְׁמוֹ!

כִּי־טוֹב יְהֹוָה,

לְעוֹלָם חַסְדּוֹ,

וְעַד־דֹּר וָדֹר אֱמוּנָתוֹ.

(Shout joyfully unto God, all the earth!
Serve God with gladness!
Come into God's Presence with singing!
Know that יְהֹוָה is God.
It is God who formed us, to God we belong,
as a people, a flock, divinely guided.
Now enter God's gates with thanksgiving,
into the courts of God with praise!
Giving thanks to God, praise God's Name!
For יְהֹוָה is good,
steadfast in love forever,
faithful to all generations!)

ON SUKKOT

And God spoke to Moses saying:
"Speak unto the Children of Israel, saying:
'On the fifteenth day of the seventh month
is the festival of Sukkot. . . .
When ye have gathered in the yield of your land,
ye shall observe the festival for seven days;
a complete rest on the first day,
and a complete rest on the seventh day. . . .
Ye shall take the product of *Hadar* trees,
branches of palm tree, boughs of leafy trees,
and willow of the brook,
and ye shall rejoice before God seven days, . . .
throughout the generations, . . .
in order that future generations may know
that I made the Israelite people to live in booths
when I brought them out of the land of Egypt,
and ye shall rejoice before God.'"

Thus Moses declared unto the Children of Israel
the appointed seasons unto God:
זְמַן שִׂמְחָתֵנוּ הוּא.
It is the season for our rejoicing.

אַשְׁרֵינוּ, מַה־טּוֹב חֶלְקֵנוּ,
וּמַה־נָּעִים גּוֹרָלֵנוּ,
וּמַה־יָּפָה יְרוּשָׁתֵנוּ.

How fortunate we are,
How good is our portion,
How pleasant our lot,
And how beautiful our heritage.

ON PESACH

The festival of Matzot shalt thou observe,
seven days thou shalt eat Matzot, unleavened bread,
as I have commanded thee,
at the time appointed in the month of Aviv,
for that was when ye went forth from Egypt . . . ;
On the first day ye shall have a sacred convocation,
and on the seventh day ye shall have a sacred convocation.
Ye shall do no manner of servile work . . .
that all the days of thy life thou mayest remember
the day when ye came forth out of the land of Egypt!

Thus Moses declared unto the Israelite people
the appointed seasons unto God:
זְמַן חֵרוּתֵנוּ הוּא.
It is the season for marking our liberation!

אֱלֹהֵינוּ וֵאלֹהֵי אֲבוֹתֵינוּ,

בְּטַלְלֵי אוֹרָה תָּאִיר אֲדָמָה,

בְּטַלְלֵי בְּרָכָה תְּבָרֵךְ אֲדָמָה,

בְּטַלְלֵי גִילָה תָּגִיל אֲדָמָה,

בְּטַלְלֵי דִיצָה תְּדַשֵּׁן אֲדָמָה,

בְּטַלְלֵי זִמְרָה תְּזַמֵּר אֲדָמָה,

בְּטַלְלֵי חַיִּים תְּחַיֶּה אֲדָמָה,

בְּטַלְלֵי טוֹבָה תֵּטִיב אֲדָמָה,

בְּטַלְלֵי יְשׁוּעָה תּוֹשִׁיעַ אֲדָמָה,
בְּטַלְלֵי כַלְכָּלָה תְּכַלְכֵּל אֲדָמָה.

Our God, and God of our ancestors:
Bring the dew of light to shine on the earth,
Bring the dew of benediction to bless the earth,
Bring the dew of rejoicing to gladden the earth,
Bring the dew of happiness to enrich the earth,
Bring the dew of song to make the earth sprout with song,
Bring the dew of life to vitalize the earth,
Bring the dew of goodness that makes the earth beneficent,
Bring the dew of deliverance that redeems the earth,
Bring the dew of sustenance to sustain the earth!

ON SHAVUOT

And God spoke unto Moses saying:
"Speak unto the Children of Israel and say unto them:
'When ye are come into the land which I am giving unto thee,
and shall reap the first harvests thereof,
then ye shall bring the sheaf of the *Bikurim,*
first fruits of thy harvest, unto the priest . . .
to be accepted for you. . . .
Seven weeks shalt thou number unto thee;
from the time the sickle is first put to the standing grain
shalt thou begin to number seven weeks.
And thou shalt observe the festival of Shavuot
unto יְהֹוָה thy God
according to the measure of the free-will offering of thy hand,
which thou shalt give,
according as יְהֹוָה thy God blesseth thee.
And thou shalt rejoice before יְהֹוָה thy God. . . .' "

Thus Moses proclaimed unto the Israelite people
the appointed seasons unto God:
זְמַן מַתַּן תּוֹרָתֵנוּ הוּא.
It is the season for marking God's gift to us of Torah!

We thank You, O God, for the Torah
which You give unto Your people.
May we ever learn it, observe it, protect it, cherish it,
for it is our life and the length of our days.

◆   ◆

FOR LIFE   בָּרוּךְ שֶׁאָמַר

בָּרוּךְ שֶׁאָמַר וְהָיָה הָעוֹלָם, בָּרוּךְ הוּא.

בָּרוּךְ עוֹשֶׂה בְרֵאשִׁית.

בָּרוּךְ אוֹמֵר וְעוֹשֶׂה, בָּרוּךְ גּוֹזֵר וּמְקַיֵּם.

בָּרוּךְ מְרַחֵם עַל הָאָרֶץ, בָּרוּךְ מְרַחֵם עַל־הַבְּרִיּוֹת.

בָּרוּךְ מְשַׁלֵּם שָׂכָר טוֹב לִירֵאָיו.

בָּרוּךְ חַי לָעַד וְקַיָּם לָנֶצַח, בָּרוּךְ פּוֹדֶה וּמַצִּיל, בָּרוּךְ שְׁמוֹ.

בִּשְׁבָחוֹת וּבִזְמִירוֹת נְגַדֶּלְךָ וּנְשַׁבֵּחֲךָ, וּנְפָאֶרְךָ, וְנַזְכִּיר שִׁמְךָ
וְנַמְלִיכְךָ, מַלְכֵּנוּ, אֱלֹהֵינוּ. יָחִיד, חֵי הָעוֹלָמִים, מֶלֶךְ, מְשֻׁבָּח
וּמְפֹאָר עֲדֵי־עַד שְׁמוֹ הַגָּדוֹל.

בָּרוּךְ אַתָּה, יְהֹוָה, מֶלֶךְ מְהֻלָּל בַּתִּשְׁבָּחוֹת.

Praised be our God who spoke and the world came into being.

Praise unto God!

Praised be the Maker of the creation.

Praised be our God whose word informs all Being!

Praised be God who decrees.

Praised be God who fulfills!

Praised be God who has mercy on all creatures.

Praised be God who has mercy on all the earth!

Praised be God who endows with the rewards of the spirit
the spirits of the reverent.

Praised be God, life of all existence, enduring forever!

Praised be God, enthroned in glory on our praises, Sovereign!
Life of the world!

Praised be God, Sovereign exalted in praise!

Psalm 19   תהלים י"ט

הַשָּׁמַיִם מְסַפְּרִים כְּבוֹד־אֵל,
וּמַעֲשֵׂה יָדָיו מַגִּיד הָרָקִיעַ.

The heavens are telling the glory of God;
the firmament declares God's handiwork.

יוֹם לְיוֹם יַבִּיעַ אֹמֶר, וְלַיְלָה לְּלַיְלָה יְחַוֶּה־דָּעַת.

Day after day gives forth a message,
night after night is revealing knowledge.

אֵין־אֹמֶר וְאֵין דְּבָרִים, בְּלִי נִשְׁמָע קוֹלָם,

There is no speech, there are no words, no sound is heard,

בְּכָל־הָאָרֶץ יָצָא קַוָּם, וּבִקְצֵה תֵבֵל מִלֵּיהֶם!

But the message goes out to all the earth,
and the utterance to the ends of the universe!

Psalm 150   תהלים ק"נ

הַלְלוּיָהּ!
הַלְלוּ־אֵל בְּקָדְשׁוֹ,
הַלְלוּהוּ בִּרְקִיעַ עֻזּוֹ.
הַלְלוּהוּ בִגְבוּרֹתָיו,
הַלְלוּהוּ כְּרֹב גֻּדְלוֹ.
הַלְלוּהוּ בְּתֵקַע שׁוֹפָר,
הַלְלוּהוּ בְּנֵבֶל וְכִנּוֹר.

הַלְלוּהוּ בְּתֹף וּמָחוֹל,

הַלְלוּהוּ בְּמִנִּים וְעֻגָב.

הַלְלוּהוּ בְּצִלְצְלֵי־שָׁמַע,

הַלְלוּהוּ בְּצִלְצְלֵי תְרוּעָה.

כֹּל הַנְּשָׁמָה תְּהַלֵּל יָהּ.

הַלְלוּיָהּ!

Halleluyah!
Praise God in the holy place.
Praise God whose power the heavens proclaim.
Praise the God of mighty acts;
Praise the God of surpassing greatness.
Praise God with shofar blast;
Praise God with harp and lute;
Praise God with drum and dance;
Praise God with strings and pipe;
Praise God with cymbals sounding praise;
Praise God with cymbals resounding praise,
Let every soul praise God.
Halleluyah!

ALL PRAISE   נשמת

נִשְׁמַת כָּל־חַי תְּבָרֵךְ אֶת־שִׁמְךָ, יְיָ אֱלֹהֵינוּ, וְרוּחַ כָּל־בָּשָׂר
תְּפָאֵר וּתְרוֹמֵם זִכְרְךָ, מַלְכֵּנוּ, תָּמִיד. מִן־הָעוֹלָם וְעַד־הָעוֹלָם
אַתָּה אֵל, וּמִבַּלְעָדֶיךָ אֵין לָנוּ מֶלֶךְ גּוֹאֵל וּמוֹשִׁיעַ, פּוֹדֶה וּמַצִּיל
וּמְפַרְנֵס וּמְרַחֵם בְּכָל־עֵת צָרָה וְצוּקָה. אֵין לָנוּ מֶלֶךְ אֶלָּא אָתָּה.
אֱלֹהֵי הָרִאשׁוֹנִים וְהָאַחֲרוֹנִים, אֱלוֹהַּ כָּל־בְּרִיּוֹת, אֲדוֹן כָּל־
תּוֹלָדוֹת, הַמְהֻלָּל בְּרֹב הַתִּשְׁבָּחוֹת, הַמְנַהֵג עוֹלָמוֹ בְּחֶסֶד וּבְרִיּוֹתָיו
בְּרַחֲמִים. וַיְיָ לֹא יָנוּם וְלֹא־יִישָׁן, הַמְעוֹרֵר יְשֵׁנִים וְהַמֵּקִיץ
נִרְדָּמִים וְהַמֵּשִׂיחַ אִלְּמִים וְהַמַּתִּיר אֲסוּרִים וְהַסּוֹמֵךְ נוֹפְלִים
וְהַזּוֹקֵף כְּפוּפִים. לְךָ לְבַדְּךָ אֲנַחְנוּ מוֹדִים.

אִלּוּ פִינוּ מָלֵא שִׁירָה כַּיָּם, וּלְשׁוֹנֵנוּ רִנָּה כַּהֲמוֹן גַּלָּיו, וְשִׂפְתוֹתֵינוּ
שֶׁבַח כְּמֶרְחֲבֵי רָקִיעַ, וְעֵינֵינוּ מְאִירוֹת כַּשֶּׁמֶשׁ וְכַיָּרֵחַ, וְיָדֵינוּ
פְרוּשׂוֹת כְּנִשְׁרֵי שָׁמָיִם, וְרַגְלֵינוּ קַלּוֹת כָּאַיָּלוֹת — אֵין אֲנַחְנוּ
מַסְפִּיקִים לְהוֹדוֹת לָךְ, יְיָ אֱלֹהֵינוּ וֵאלֹהֵי אֲבוֹתֵינוּ, וּלְבָרֵךְ אֶת־
שְׁמֶךָ עַל־אַחַת מֵאֶלֶף, אֶלֶף אַלְפֵי אֲלָפִים וְרִבֵּי רְבָבוֹת פְּעָמִים
הַטּוֹבוֹת שֶׁעָשִׂיתָ עִם־אֲבוֹתֵינוּ וְעִמָּנוּ.

The breath of all the living is praise of You, O God.
The spirit of all flesh is Your eternal glory, O our Sovereign.
From everlasting to everlasting You are God.
And besides You, we have no sovereign, no redeemer.

Were our mouths as full of song as the sea
and our tongues with melody as the multitude of its waves;
our eyes shining like the sun and the moon,
our arms like soaring eagles' pinions,
our limbs like those of the swift gazelle—
still our power would be naught to show
the thousand myriad bounties You have bestowed
upon our parents and on us.

But, O God, limbs and tongue and heart and mind
join now to praise Your Name,
as every tongue will yet avow You
and every soul give You allegiance.

As it is written: All my bones shall shout in joy;
O God, who is like You?
And as David sang:
Praise יְהֹוָה, my whole being!
All that is within me,
Praise God's holy Name!

O our God, Source of life and blessing,
we give thanks for the festivals, for the meaning
with which they endow our lives.

For the freedom to serve You that gives dignity to our being,
for the Torah that gives direction to our lives,
and for the harvest that sustains our bodies.

As our ancestors made pilgrimage to Jerusalem,
there to give thanks to You and to praise Your Name,
so are we now pilgrims toward You,
as heart and spirit rise to praise You.

◆ ◆

יִתְגַּדַּל וְיִתְקַדַּשׁ שְׁמֵהּ רַבָּא בְּעָלְמָא דִּי־בְרָא כִרְעוּתֵהּ, וְיַמְלִיךְ
מַלְכוּתֵהּ בְּחַיֵּיכוֹן וּבְיוֹמֵיכוֹן וּבְחַיֵּי דְכָל־בֵּית יִשְׂרָאֵל, בַּעֲגָלָא
וּבִזְמַן קָרִיב, וְאִמְרוּ: אָמֵן.

יְהֵא שְׁמֵהּ רַבָּא מְבָרַךְ לְעָלַם וּלְעָלְמֵי עָלְמַיָּא.

יִתְבָּרַךְ וְיִשְׁתַּבַּח, וְיִתְפָּאַר וְיִתְרוֹמַם וְיִתְנַשֵּׂא, וְיִתְהַדָּר וְיִתְעַלֶּה
וְיִתְהַלַּל שְׁמֵהּ דְּקוּדְשָׁא, בְּרִיךְ הוּא, לְעֵלָּא מִן כָּל־בִּרְכָתָא
וְשִׁירָתָא, תֻּשְׁבְּחָתָא וְנֶחֱמָתָא דַּאֲמִירָן בְּעָלְמָא, וְאִמְרוּ: אָמֵן.

Let the glory of God be extolled, let God's great Name be hallowed
throughout the creation born of God's will. May God's sovereignty soon
prevail, in our own day, our own lives, the life of all Israel, and let us
say: Amen.

Let God's great Name be blessed for ever and ever.

Let the Name of the Holy One, above all praises, be glorified, exalted,
and honored, though God is beyond all the songs and adorations that we
can utter, and let us say: Amen.

All rise

בָּרְכוּ אֶת־יְהֹוָה הַמְבֹרָךְ!

Praise God, to whom our praise is due!

בָּרוּךְ יְהֹוָה הַמְבֹרָךְ לְעוֹלָם וָעֶד!

Praise God, to whom our praise is due for ever and ever!

CREATION   יוֹצֵר

Evening   Morning

בָּרוּךְ אַתָּה, יְהֹוָה אֱלֹהֵינוּ, מֶלֶךְ
הָעוֹלָם, יוֹצֵר אוֹר וּבוֹרֵא חֹשֶׁךְ,
עֹשֶׂה שָׁלוֹם וּבוֹרֵא אֶת־הַכֹּל.
הַמֵּאִיר לָאָרֶץ וְלַדָּרִים עָלֶיהָ
בְּרַחֲמִים, וּבְטוּבוֹ מְחַדֵּשׁ בְּכָל־
יוֹם תָּמִיד מַעֲשֵׂה בְרֵאשִׁית.

מָה רַבּוּ מַעֲשֶׂיךָ, יְהֹוָה! כֻּלָּם
בְּחָכְמָה עָשִׂיתָ, מָלְאָה הָאָרֶץ
קִנְיָנֶךָ.

תִּתְבָּרַךְ, יְהֹוָה אֱלֹהֵינוּ, עַל־
שֶׁבַח מַעֲשֵׂה יָדֶיךָ, וְעַל־
מְאוֹרֵי־אוֹר שֶׁעָשִׂיתָ: יְפָאֲרוּךְ.
סֶלָה.

בָּרוּךְ אַתָּה, יְהֹוָה, יוֹצֵר
הַמְּאוֹרוֹת.

בָּרוּךְ אַתָּה, יְהֹוָה אֱלֹהֵינוּ, מֶלֶךְ
הָעוֹלָם, אֲשֶׁר בִּדְבָרוֹ מַעֲרִיב
עֲרָבִים. בְּחָכְמָה פּוֹתֵחַ שְׁעָרִים.
וּבִתְבוּנָה מְשַׁנֶּה עִתִּים, וּמַחֲלִיף
אֶת־הַזְּמַנִּים, וּמְסַדֵּר אֶת־
הַכּוֹכָבִים בְּמִשְׁמְרוֹתֵיהֶם
בָּרָקִיעַ כִּרְצוֹנוֹ. בּוֹרֵא יוֹם
וָלַיְלָה, גּוֹלֵל אוֹר מִפְּנֵי חֹשֶׁךְ
וְחֹשֶׁךְ מִפְּנֵי אוֹר, וּמַעֲבִיר יוֹם
וּמֵבִיא לַיְלָה, וּמַבְדִּיל בֵּין יוֹם
וּבֵין לַיְלָה, יְהֹוָה צְבָאוֹת שְׁמוֹ.
אֵל חַי וְקַיָּם, תָּמִיד יִמְלוֹךְ
עָלֵינוּ, לְעוֹלָם וָעֶד.

בָּרוּךְ אַתָּה, יְהֹוָה, הַמַּעֲרִיב
עֲרָבִים.

We praise You, O God, Sovereign of all existence, who forms
light and creates darkness, who ordains peace and creates all
Being; with compassion giving light to the earth and all who
dwell upon it, with goodness renewing the work of creation continually, day by day.

How manifold are Your works, O God; in wisdom have You
made them all; all existence is of Your fashioning.

We evoke a praise that is beyond whatever words of praise we,
the work of Your hands, could speak; beyond the luminaries of
light of Your own fashioning. We praise You, O God, who forms
the very sources of the light.

REVELATION   אהבה

אַהֲבָה רַבָּה אֲהַבְתָּנוּ, יְהוָה אֱלֹהֵינוּ, חֶמְלָה גְדוֹלָה וִיתֵרָה חָמַלְתָּ
עָלֵינוּ. אָבִינוּ מַלְכֵּנוּ, בַּעֲבוּר אֲבוֹתֵינוּ שֶׁבָּטְחוּ בְךָ וַתְּלַמְּדֵם חֻקֵּי
חַיִּים, כֵּן תְּחָנֵּנוּ וּתְלַמְּדֵנוּ.

אָבִינוּ, הָאָב הָרַחֲמָן, הַמְרַחֵם, רַחֵם עָלֵינוּ וְתֵן בְּלִבֵּנוּ לְהָבִין
וּלְהַשְׂכִּיל, לִשְׁמֹעַ לִלְמֹד וּלְלַמֵּד, לִשְׁמֹר וְלַעֲשׂוֹת וּלְקַיֵּם אֶת־כָּל־
דִּבְרֵי תַלְמוּד תּוֹרָתֶךָ בְּאַהֲבָה.

וְהָאֵר עֵינֵינוּ בְּתוֹרָתֶךָ, וְדַבֵּק לִבֵּנוּ בְּמִצְוֹתֶיךָ, וְיַחֵד לְבָבֵנוּ לְאַהֲבָה
וּלְיִרְאָה אֶת־שְׁמֶךָ. וְלֹא־נֵבוֹשׁ לְעוֹלָם וָעֶד, כִּי בְשֵׁם קָדְשְׁךָ הַגָּדוֹל
וְהַנּוֹרָא בָּטָחְנוּ. נָגִילָה וְנִשְׂמְחָה בִּישׁוּעָתֶךָ, כִּי אֵל פּוֹעֵל יְשׁוּעוֹת
אָתָּה. וּבָנוּ בָחַרְתָּ וְקֵרַבְתָּנוּ לְשִׁמְךָ הַגָּדוֹל סֶלָה בֶּאֱמֶת, לְהוֹדוֹת לְךָ
וּלְיַחֶדְךָ בְּאַהֲבָה. בָּרוּךְ אַתָּה, יְהוָה, הַבּוֹחֵר בְּעַמּוֹ יִשְׂרָאֵל
בְּאַהֲבָה.

Manifold has been Your love for us, יְהוָה, our God; with great
and exceeding compassion have You had mercy upon us.

Avinu Malkeinu, Parent and Sovereign, through the virtue of our
ancestors who trusted in You, and to whom You did teach the
statutes of life, so be gracious to us and teach us. As a loving
parent, have mercy upon us. Put it into our hearts to perceive, to
hearken, to learn and to teach, to observe in love, to do and perform the principles of the teaching of Your Torah.

Enlighten us through Your teaching; cause our hearts to cleave
unto Your commandments, and unite our hearts both to love and
revere Your Name.

And we will never be ashamed that we have had confidence in
all the greatness and awe that we have perceived in You. And we
will rejoice in Your deliverance because You, O God, are a
worker of many deliverances, and have chosen us and brought us
near unto You to serve You in truth, in thanksgiving, and in love
to proclaim Your unity.

We praise You, O God, who is still calling unto Your people
Israel in love.

שְׁמַע יִשְׂרָאֵל: יְהֹוָה אֱלֹהֵינוּ, יְהֹוָה אֶחָד!

Hear, O Israel: יְהֹוָה *is our God,* יְהֹוָה *is One!*

בָּרוּךְ שֵׁם כְּבוֹד מַלְכוּתוֹ לְעוֹלָם וָעֶד!

Praised be the Name of the glory of God's sovereignty for ever and ever.

All are seated

וְאָהַבְתָּ אֵת יְהֹוָה אֱלֹהֶיךָ בְּכָל־לְבָבְךָ וּבְכָל־נַפְשְׁךָ וּבְכָל־מְאֹדֶךָ.
וְהָיוּ הַדְּבָרִים הָאֵלֶּה, אֲשֶׁר אָנֹכִי מְצַוְּךָ הַיּוֹם, עַל־לְבָבֶךָ. וְשִׁנַּנְתָּם
לְבָנֶיךָ, וְדִבַּרְתָּ בָּם בְּשִׁבְתְּךָ בְּבֵיתֶךָ, וּבְלֶכְתְּךָ בַדֶּרֶךְ, וּבְשָׁכְבְּךָ
וּבְקוּמֶךָ.

וּקְשַׁרְתָּם לְאוֹת עַל־יָדֶךָ, וְהָיוּ לְטֹטָפֹת בֵּין עֵינֶיךָ, וּכְתַבְתָּם עַל־
מְזֻזוֹת בֵּיתֶךָ, וּבִשְׁעָרֶיךָ.

And thou shalt love יְהֹוָה *thy God with all thy heart, with all thy soul,
with all thy being. And these words which I command thee this day shall
be upon thy heart. And thou shalt teach them unto thy children and shalt
speak of them when thou sittest in thy house, when thou walkest by the
way, when thou liest down, and when thou risest up.*

*And thou shalt bind them as a sign upon thy hand and they shall be for
frontlets between thine eyes, and thou shalt write them upon the doorposts
of thy house and upon thy gates.*

לְמַעַן תִּזְכְּרוּ וַעֲשִׂיתֶם אֶת־כָּל־מִצְוֹתָי, וִהְיִיתֶם קְדֹשִׁים לֵאלֹהֵיכֶם.
אֲנִי יְהֹוָה אֱלֹהֵיכֶם, אֲשֶׁר הוֹצֵאתִי אֶתְכֶם מֵאֶרֶץ מִצְרַיִם לִהְיוֹת
לָכֶם לֵאלֹהִים.

In order that ye may remember and do all My commandments
and be holy unto thy God. I am יְהֹוָה thy God who brought thee
out of the land of Egypt to be thy God. I am יְהֹוָה thy God.

אֲנִי יְהֹוָה אֱלֹהֵיכֶם.

REDEMPTION   גאולה

אֱמֶת וְיַצִּיב, וְאָהוּב וְחָבִיב, וְנוֹרָא וְאַדִּיר, וְטוֹב וְיָפֶה הַדָּבָר הַזֶּה
עָלֵינוּ לְעוֹלָם וָעֶד.
אֱמֶת, אֱלֹהֵי עוֹלָם מַלְכֵּנוּ, צוּר יַעֲקֹב מָגֵן יִשְׁעֵנוּ. לְדֹר וָדֹר הוּא
קַיָּם, וּשְׁמוֹ קַיָּם, וְכִסְאוֹ נָכוֹן, וּמַלְכוּתוֹ וֶאֱמוּנָתוֹ לָעַד קַיֶּמֶת.
וּדְבָרָיו חַיִּים וְקַיָּמִים, נֶאֱמָנִים וְנֶחֱמָדִים, לָעַד וּלְעוֹלְמֵי עוֹלָמִים.

True and established is this teaching for us, beloved and dear yet
awesome and dread, good and lovely forever.

*In truth, as the eternal God is our Sovereign, Rock of Jacob, Shield of
deliverance, abiding through all generations, so God's words are living and
enduring, inspiring in us confidence and love forever, as in our ancestors so
within us, and so for our children and generations to come, yes, within all of
the generations of the seed of Israel, Your servant.*

עַל אֲבוֹתֵינוּ וְעָלֵינוּ, עַל בָּנֵינוּ וְעַל דּוֹרוֹתֵינוּ
וְעַל כָּל דּוֹרוֹת זֶרַע יִשְׂרָאֵל עֲבָדֶךָ.
עֶזְרַת אֲבוֹתֵינוּ אַתָּה הוּא מֵעוֹלָם,
מָגֵן וּמוֹשִׁיעַ לִבְנֵיהֶם אַחֲרֵיהֶם בְּכָל־דּוֹר וָדוֹר.
מִמִּצְרַיִם גְּאַלְתָּנוּ, יְהֹוָה אֱלֹהֵינוּ, וּמִבֵּית עֲבָדִים פְּדִיתָנוּ.

You have been the Help of our ancestors of old, Shield and
Deliverer of their children after them throughout the generations.

*From Egypt You have redeemed us, from the house of bondage You have
delivered us.*

עַל־זֹאת שִׁבְּחוּ אֲהוּבִים וְרוֹמְמוּ אֵל, וְנָתְנוּ יְדִידִים זְמִירוֹת,
שִׁירוֹת וְתִשְׁבָּחוֹת, בְּרָכוֹת וְהוֹדָאוֹת לַמֶּלֶךְ, אֵל חַי וְקַיָּם.
רָם וְנִשָּׂא, גָּדוֹל וְנוֹרָא, מַשְׁפִּיל גֵּאִים וּמַגְבִּיהַּ שְׁפָלִים, מוֹצִיא
אֲסִירִים וּפוֹדֶה עֲנָוִים, וְעוֹזֵר דַּלִּים, וְעוֹנֶה לְעַמּוֹ בְּעֵת שַׁוְּעָם
אֵלָיו.

It is for this that Your beloved ones, praised and exalted God,
offered songs and hymns of praise and thanksgiving to the
sovereign God who lives and endures, the awesome and great.
You are present when the arrogant are cast down and the humble
are lifted up, present when the captives are freed from prison and
the meek redeemed, present in every help to the destitute; You
answer with deliverance the cry for deliverance.

Praises unto God most high, praise and blessing.

תְּהִלּוֹת לְאֵל עֶלְיוֹן, בָּרוּךְ הוּא וּמְבֹרָךְ.
מֹשֶׁה וּבְנֵי יִשְׂרָאֵל לְךָ עָנוּ שִׁירָה בְּשִׂמְחָה רַבָּה, וְאָמְרוּ כֻלָּם:
מִי־כָמֹכָה בָּאֵלִם, יְהֹוָה?
מִי כָּמֹכָה, נֶאְדָּר בַּקֹּדֶשׁ,
נוֹרָא תְהִלֹּת, עֹשֵׂה פֶלֶא?

Thus did Moses and the Children of Israel respond to God's
redemption with song and great rejoicing, and thus do we.

Who is like unto Thee, Eternal One, among gods that are worshiped?
Who is like unto Thee, awesome in holiness,
Revered in praises, doing wonders?

שִׁירָה חֲדָשָׁה שִׁבְּחוּ גְאוּלִים לְשִׁמְךָ עַל־שְׂפַת הַיָּם; יַחַד כֻּלָּם הוֹדוּ
וְהִמְלִיכוּ וְאָמְרוּ:

„יְהֹוָה יִמְלֹךְ לְעוֹלָם וָעֶד!"

A new song the redeemed sang unto Your Name. On the shore
of the sea, together as one, they gave thanks and proclaimed
God's sovereignty:

"The Eternal will reign for ever and ever!"

O Rock of Israel, arise to the help of Israel. Redeem Judah and
Israel according to Your promised word. Our Redeemer, יְהֹוָה
of Hosts is Your Name, Holy One of Israel! We praise You, O
God, Redeemer of Israel.

צוּר יִשְׂרָאֵל, קוּמָה בְּעֶזְרַת יִשְׂרָאֵל, וּפְדֵה כִנְאֻמֶךָ יְהוּדָה
וְיִשְׂרָאֵל. גֹּאֲלֵנוּ, יְהֹוָה צְבָאוֹת שְׁמוֹ, קְדוֹשׁ יִשְׂרָאֵל.
בָּרוּךְ אַתָּה, יְהֹוָה, גָּאַל יִשְׂרָאֵל.

תפלה

All rise

אֲדֹנָי, שְׂפָתַי תִּפְתָּח, וּפִי יַגִּיד תְּהִלָּתֶךָ.

Eternal God, open our lips,
    that our mouths may declare Your glory.

ANCESTORS   אבות

בָּרוּךְ אַתָּה, יְהֹוָה אֱלֹהֵינוּ וֵאלֹהֵי אֲבוֹתֵינוּ, אֱלֹהֵי אַבְרָהָם, אֱלֹהֵי
יִצְחָק, וֵאלֹהֵי יַעֲקֹב: הָאֵל הַגָּדוֹל, הַגִּבּוֹר וְהַנּוֹרָא, אֵל עֶלְיוֹן.
גּוֹמֵל חֲסָדִים טוֹבִים, וְקוֹנֵה הַכֹּל, וְזוֹכֵר חַסְדֵי אָבוֹת, וּמֵבִיא
גְאֻלָּה לִבְנֵי בְנֵיהֶם, לְמַעַן שְׁמוֹ, בְּאַהֲבָה.
מֶלֶךְ עוֹזֵר וּמוֹשִׁיעַ וּמָגֵן. בָּרוּךְ אַתָּה, יְהֹוָה, מָגֵן אַבְרָהָם.

We praise You, יְהֹוָה our God, God of our ancestors, God of the mothers of Israel, God of Abraham, God of Isaac, God of Jacob, great, mighty, and awesome God, God Most High. You are our God who establishes the recompense of all good deeds, even as You are the sole possessor of all; remembering the virtue of our ancestors, and bringing redemption to their children's children in love, for the sake of Your Name. O our Sovereign, Helper, Redeemer, and Shield, we praise You, יְהֹוָה, Shield of Abraham.

POWERS   גבורות

אַתָּה גִבּוֹר לְעוֹלָם, אֲדֹנָי, מְחַיֵּה הַכֹּל אַתָּה, רַב לְהוֹשִׁיעַ.

מְכַלְכֵּל חַיִּים בְּחֶסֶד, מְחַיֵּה הַכֹּל בְּרַחֲמִים רַבִּים. סוֹמֵךְ נוֹפְלִים,

וְרוֹפֵא חוֹלִים, וּמַתִּיר אֲסוּרִים, וּמְקַיֵּם אֱמוּנָתוֹ לִישֵׁנֵי עָפָר.

מִי כָמוֹךָ, בַּעַל גְּבוּרוֹת, וּמִי דּוֹמֶה לָּךְ, מֶלֶךְ מֵמִית וּמְחַיֵּה

וּמַצְמִיחַ יְשׁוּעָה?

וְנֶאֱמָן אַתָּה לְהַחֲיוֹת הַכֹּל. בָּרוּךְ אַתָּה, יְהֹוָה, מְחַיֵּה הַכֹּל.

Great is Your might, O God, in this world; great is Your power in worlds beyond.

Your love sustains the living. Your great compassion is the source of life. Your power is in the help that comes to the falling, in the healing that comes to the sick, in the freedom brought to the captive, in the faith we keep with those who sleep in the dust.

Who is like You, God of all powers? Who is Your equal, God of life and death, Source of salvation?

We trust in You to restore our life. We praise You, O God, Source of all life.

HOLINESS   קדושה

נְקַדֵּשׁ אֶת־שִׁמְךָ בָּעוֹלָם, כְּשֵׁם שֶׁמַּקְדִּישִׁים אוֹתוֹ בִּשְׁמֵי מָרוֹם,

כַּכָּתוּב עַל־יַד נְבִיאֶךָ: וְקָרָא זֶה אֶל־זֶה וְאָמַר:

We sanctify Your Name on earth, even as all things, to the ends of time and space, proclaim Your holiness; and in the words of the prophet we say:

קָדוֹשׁ, קָדוֹשׁ, קָדוֹשׁ יְהוָֹה צְבָאוֹת, מְלֹא כָל־הָאָרֶץ כְּבוֹדוֹ.

Holy, holy, holy is יְהוָֹה of Hosts;
the fullness of the whole earth is God's glory!

אַדִּיר אַדִּירֵנוּ, יְהוָֹה אֲדוֹנֵנוּ, מָה־אַדִּיר שִׁמְךָ בְּכָל־הָאָרֶץ!

Mighty Source of our strength, יְהוָֹה, our Sovereign, how overpowering is Your Presence throughout all existence!

בָּרוּךְ כְּבוֹד יְהוָֹה מִמְּקוֹמוֹ.

Praised be the glory of God far beyond!

אֶחָד הוּא אֱלֹהֵינוּ, הוּא אָבִינוּ, הוּא מַלְכֵּנוּ, הוּא מוֹשִׁיעֵנוּ; וְהוּא
יַשְׁמִיעֵנוּ בְּרַחֲמָיו לְעֵינֵי כָּל־חַי:

Our God is One, Sovereign over all; yet, caring for us and stirred by great mercy, God will justify our faith in the sight of all the living, in all revelations proclaiming:

„אֲנִי יְהוָֹה אֱלֹהֵיכֶם!"

I am יְהוָֹה, thy God!

יִמְלֹךְ יְהוָֹה לְעוֹלָם, אֱלֹהַיִךְ צִיּוֹן, לְדֹר וָדֹר הַלְלוּיָהּ!

יְהוָֹה shall reign forever, thy God, O Zion,
through all the generations. Halleluyah!

לְדוֹר וָדוֹר נַגִּיד גָּדְלֶךָ, וּלְנֵצַח נְצָחִים קְדֻשָּׁתְךָ נַקְדִּישׁ. וְשִׁבְחֲךָ,
אֱלֹהֵינוּ, מִפִּינוּ לֹא יָמוּשׁ לְעוֹלָם וָעֶד.

To all generations we will proclaim Your greatness, and throughout all eternity declare Your holiness. Your praise, our God, shall never cease from our lips.

בָּרוּךְ אַתָּה, יְהֹוָה, הָאֵל הַקָּדוֹשׁ.

We praise You, O God of holiness.

All are seated

THE HOLINESS OF YOM TOV   קדושת היום

אַתָּה בְחַרְתָּנוּ מִכָּל־הָעַמִּים, אָהַבְתָּ אוֹתָנוּ, וְרָצִיתָ בָּנוּ, וְרוֹמַמְתָּנוּ
מִכָּל־הַלְּשׁוֹנוֹת, וְקִדַּשְׁתָּנוּ בְּמִצְוֹתֶיךָ. וְקֵרַבְתָּנוּ, מַלְכֵּנוּ, לַעֲבוֹדָתֶךָ,
וְשִׁמְךָ הַגָּדוֹל וְהַקָּדוֹשׁ עָלֵינוּ קָרָאתָ.

וַתִּתֶּן לָנוּ, יְהֹוָה אֱלֹהֵינוּ, בְּאַהֲבָה (שַׁבָּתוֹת לִמְנוּחָה וּ) מוֹעֲדִים
לְשִׂמְחָה, חַגִּים וּזְמַנִּים לְשָׂשׂוֹן: אֶת־יוֹם (הַשַּׁבָּת הַזֶּה וְאֶת־יוֹם)

חַג הַסֻּכּוֹת הַזֶּה — זְמַן שִׂמְחָתֵנוּ,

הַשְּׁמִינִי חַג הָעֲצֶרֶת הַזֶּה — זְמַן שִׂמְחָתֵנוּ,

חַג הַמַּצּוֹת הַזֶּה — זְמַן חֵרוּתֵנוּ,

חַג הַשָּׁבֻעוֹת הַזֶּה — זְמַן מַתַּן תּוֹרָתֵנוּ,

מִקְרָא קֹדֶשׁ, זֵכֶר לִיצִיאַת מִצְרָיִם.

You, O God, have chosen us from among the peoples. You have
loved us. You have favored us with Your acceptance, exalting us
by hallowing our lives through Your commandments. You have
brought us nearer to Your service, so that we have become a
name for Your presence in all the earth.

*In Your love You have given to us, our God, among (sabbaths of rest
and) seasons of gladness, festivals for rejoicing, this (Sabbath day and)
festival of*

Sukkot — *season of our rejoicing,*
Atseret-Simchat Torah — *season of our gladness,*
Pesach — *season of our liberation,*
Shavuot — *season of Your revelation to us,*

this sacred assembly made possible for us through our Exodus from Egypt.

אֱלֹהֵינוּ וֵאלֹהֵי אֲבוֹתֵינוּ, יַעֲלֶה וְיָבֹא וְיַגִּיעַ וְיֵרָאֶה וְיֵרָצֶה וְיִשָּׁמַע וְיִפָּקֵד וְיִזָּכֵר זִכְרוֹנֵנוּ וְזִכְרוֹן
כָּל־עַמְּךָ בֵּית יִשְׂרָאֵל לְפָנֶיךָ, לְטוֹבָה לְחֵן לְחֶסֶד וּלְרַחֲמִים לְחַיִּים
וּלְשָׁלוֹם בְּיוֹם

חַג הַסֻּכּוֹת הַזֶּה.

הַשְּׁמִינִי חַג הָעֲצֶרֶת הַזֶּה.

חַג הַמַּצּוֹת הַזֶּה.

חַג הַשָּׁבֻעוֹת הַזֶּה.

Our God and God of our ancestors, may this, our worship, evoke Your grace upon Your people, the House of Israel, in behalf of goodness, of life, and of peace, on this day of the festival of

Sukkot.
Atseret-Simchat Torah.
Pesach.
Shavuot.

זָכְרֵנוּ, יְהֹוָה אֱלֹהֵינוּ, בּוֹ לְטוֹבָה. אָמֵן.

This day, our God, remember us for good.

וּפָקְדֵנוּ בוֹ לִבְרָכָה. אָמֵן.

This day help us to experience Your blessing.

וְהוֹשִׁיעֵנוּ בוֹ לְחַיִּים. אָמֵן.

This day help us to know the fullness of life.

וְהַשִּׂיאֵנוּ, יְהֹוָה אֱלֹהֵינוּ, אֶת־בִּרְכַּת מוֹעֲדֶיךָ לְחַיִּים וּלְשָׁלוֹם,
לְשִׂמְחָה וּלְשָׂשׂוֹן, כַּאֲשֶׁר רָצִיתָ, וְאָמַרְתָּ לְבָרְכֵנוּ. אֱלֹהֵי וֵאלֹהֵי
אֲבוֹתֵינוּ, (רְצֵה בִמְנוּחָתֵנוּ,) קַדְּשֵׁנוּ בְּמִצְוֹתֶיךָ, וְתֵן חֶלְקֵנוּ
בְּתוֹרָתֶךָ. שַׂבְּעֵנוּ מִטּוּבֶךָ, וְשַׂמְּחֵנוּ בִּישׁוּעָתֶךָ, וְטַהֵר לִבֵּנוּ לְעָבְדְּךָ
בֶּאֱמֶת. וְהַנְחִילֵנוּ, יְהֹוָה אֱלֹהֵינוּ, (בְּאַהֲבָה וּבְרָצוֹן,) בְּשִׂמְחָה
וּבְשָׂשׂוֹן (שַׁבָּת וּ) מוֹעֲדֵי קָדְשֶׁךָ, וְיִשְׂמְחוּ בְךָ יִשְׂרָאֵל, מְקַדְּשֵׁי
שְׁמֶךָ. בָּרוּךְ אַתָּה, יְהֹוָה, מְקַדֵּשׁ (הַשַּׁבָּת וְ) יִשְׂרָאֵל וְהַזְּמַנִּים.

Bestow upon us the blessing of Your holy festivals, and may we so celebrate them as to be worthy of the fullness of life and peace, and of joy in Your service.

As it is Your desire to bless us, our God and God of our ancestors, (may our rest on this Sabbath find favor in Your sight,) hallow our lives through Your commandments; help us to delight in our heritage of Torah. Satisfy us from the store of Your goodness; cause us to rejoice in Your work of redemption; refine our spirits that we may serve You in truth, that we may find again, our God, our inheritance in Your holy seasons. Help us to celebrate Your holy festivals with joy and gladness that all Israel, hallowing Your Name, may discover the joy of Your service. We praise You, O God, who sanctifies (the Sabbath and) Israel and the holy seasons.

ACCEPTANCE   עבודה

רְצֵה, יְיָ אֱלֹהֵינוּ, בְּעַמְּךָ יִשְׂרָאֵל, וּתְפִלָּתָם בְּאַהֲבָה תְקַבֵּל, וּתְהִי לְרָצוֹן תָּמִיד עֲבוֹדַת יִשְׂרָאֵל עַמֶּךָ.

בָּרוּךְ אַתָּה, יְיָ, שֶׁאוֹתְךָ לְבַדְּךָ בְּיִרְאָה נַעֲבֹד:

Look with favor, our God, upon us, and may our worship ever be acceptable in Your sight.

We praise You, O God, whom alone we serve in reverence.

THANKSGIVING   הודאה

מוֹדִים אֲנַחְנוּ לָךְ, שָׁאַתָּה הוּא יְיָ אֱלֹהֵינוּ וֵאלֹהֵי אֲבוֹתֵינוּ לְעוֹלָם וָעֶד. צוּר חַיֵּינוּ, מָגֵן יִשְׁעֵנוּ, אַתָּה הוּא לְדוֹר וָדוֹר. נוֹדֶה לְּךָ וּנְסַפֵּר תְּהִלָּתֶךָ, עַל־חַיֵּינוּ הַמְּסוּרִים בְּיָדֶךָ, וְעַל־נִשְׁמוֹתֵינוּ הַפְּקוּדוֹת לָךְ, וְעַל־נִסֶּיךָ שֶׁבְּכָל־יוֹם עִמָּנוּ, וְעַל־נִפְלְאוֹתֶיךָ וְטוֹבוֹתֶיךָ שֶׁבְּכָל־עֵת, עֶרֶב וָבֹקֶר וְצָהֳרָיִם. הַטּוֹב: כִּי לֹא־כָלוּ רַחֲמֶיךָ, וְהַמְרַחֵם: כִּי־לֹא תַמּוּ חֲסָדֶיךָ, מֵעוֹלָם קִוִּינוּ לָךְ:

We gratefully acknowledge that You are our God and God of our people, God of all generations, Rock of our lives, Shield of our deliverance, from generation unto generation. We give thanks unto You for our lives which are in Your hands, for our souls which are ever in Your keeping, for Your wonders which are daily with us, and for Your miracles, morning, noon and night. We will always hope in You, whom we link with all signs of goodness, whose Name we call Compassionate.

וְעַל כֻּלָּם יִתְבָּרַךְ וְיִתְרוֹמַם שִׁמְךָ, מַלְכֵּנוּ, תָּמִיד לְעוֹלָם וָעֶד. וְכֹל הַחַיִּים יוֹדוּךָ סֶּלָה, וִיהַלְלוּ שִׁמְךָ בֶּאֱמֶת, הָאֵל יְשׁוּעָתֵנוּ וְעֶזְרָתֵנוּ סֶּלָה.

For all these things, O Sovereign God, let Your Name be forever exalted and praised. For life itself the living thank You and praise Your Name. O God, we give You thanks and praise.

בָּרוּךְ אַתָּה, יְיָ, הַטּוֹב שִׁמְךָ וּלְךָ נָאֶה לְהוֹדוֹת.

PEACE   ברכת שלום

אֱלֹהֵינוּ וֵאלֹהֵי אֲבוֹתֵינוּ, בָּרְכֵנוּ בַּבְּרָכָה הַמְשֻׁלֶּשֶׁת הַכְּתוּבָה בַּתּוֹרָה:

Our God and God of our ancestors, bless us with the threefold benediction written in Your Torah:

יְבָרֶכְךָ יְיָ וְיִשְׁמְרֶךָ.

כֵּן יְהִי רָצוֹן!

May God bless thee and guard thee.
Be this God's will!

יָאֵר יְיָ פָּנָיו אֵלֶיךָ וִיחֻנֶּךָּ.

כֵּן יְהִי רָצוֹן!

May the light of God's Presence shine upon thee and may God be gracious unto thee.
Be this God's will!

יִשָּׂא יְיָ פָּנָיו אֵלֶיךָ וְיָשֵׂם לְךָ שָׁלוֹם.

כֵּן יְהִי רָצוֹן!

May God's Presence ever be with thee and give thee peace.
Be this God's will!

*Grant peace unto us, the people of Israel; and on behalf of all humanity,
blessing, favor, grace, compassion. Bless us, O God, all of us as one, with
the light of Your Presence. For in the light of Your Presence we have
found a teaching of life, the love of mercy, a way of righteousness, compassion, life itself and a vision of peace. May it be good in Your sight to
bless Israel and all the peoples, at all times, in every hour, with peace.
We praise You, O God, Source of peace.*

Evening

Morning

שָׁלוֹם רָב עַל־יִשְׂרָאֵל עַמְּךָ
תָּשִׂים לְעוֹלָם, כִּי אַתָּה הוּא
מֶלֶךְ אָדוֹן לְכָל הַשָּׁלוֹם. וְטוֹב
בְּעֵינֶיךָ לְבָרֵךְ אֶת־עַמְּךָ
יִשְׂרָאֵל, בְּכָל־עֵת וּבְכָל־שָׁעָה
בִּשְׁלוֹמֶךָ. בָּרוּךְ אַתָּה, יְיָ,
הַמְבָרֵךְ אֶת־עַמּוֹ יִשְׂרָאֵל
בַּשָּׁלוֹם.

שִׂים שָׁלוֹם, טוֹבָה וּבְרָכָה, חֵן
וָחֶסֶד וְרַחֲמִים, עָלֵינוּ וְעַל־כָּל־
יִשְׂרָאֵל עַמֶּךָ.
בָּרְכֵנוּ אָבִינוּ, כֻּלָּנוּ כְּאֶחָד,
בְּאוֹר פָּנֶיךָ, כִּי בְאוֹר פָּנֶיךָ נָתַתָּ
לָנוּ, יְיָ אֱלֹהֵינוּ, תּוֹרַת חַיִּים,
וְאַהֲבַת חֶסֶד, וּצְדָקָה וּבְרָכָה
וְרַחֲמִים, וְחַיִּים וְשָׁלוֹם.

וְטוֹב בְּעֵינֶיךָ לְבָרֵךְ אֶת־עַמְּךָ יִשְׂרָאֵל בְּכָל־עֵת וּבְכָל־שָׁעָה
בִּשְׁלוֹמֶךָ. בָּרוּךְ אַתָּה, יְיָ, הַמְבָרֵךְ אֶת־עַמּוֹ יִשְׂרָאֵל בַּשָּׁלוֹם.

SILENT PRAYER

אֱלֹהַי, נְצֹר לְשׁוֹנִי מֵרָע, וּשְׂפָתַי מִדַּבֵּר מִרְמָה, וְלִמְקַלְלַי נַפְשִׁי
תִדּוֹם, וְנַפְשִׁי כֶּעָפָר לַכֹּל תִּהְיֶה. פְּתַח לִבִּי בְּתוֹרָתֶךָ, וּבְמִצְוֹתֶיךָ
תִּרְדּוֹף נַפְשִׁי, וְכֹל הַחוֹשְׁבִים עָלַי רָעָה, מְהֵרָה הָפֵר עֲצָתָם וְקַלְקֵל

מַחֲשַׁבְתָּם. עֲשֵׂה לְמַעַן שְׁמֶךָ, עֲשֵׂה לְמַעַן יְמִינֶךָ, עֲשֵׂה לְמַעַן
קְדֻשָּׁתֶךָ, עֲשֵׂה לְמַעַן תּוֹרָתֶךָ. לְמַעַן יֵחָלְצוּן יְדִידֶיךָ. הוֹשִׁיעָה
יְמִינְךָ וַעֲנֵנִי.

O God, guard my tongue from evil and my lips from speaking
guile. Help me to be silent and patient in the face of hypocrisy
and derision; let my soul be humble in the presence of all. Rather,
open my heart unto Your Torah, and strengthen in me the desire
to pursue Your commandments, even in the face of the arrogance
and success of the evil and the harmful. Do this for the sake of
Your way on earth, for the sake of the preservation of the sanctity
of life, for the sake of Your teachings in this world. Thus, may all
those dear to You and Your way be strengthened.

◆ ◆

♪ May the words of my mouth and the meditations of my heart be
acceptable unto You, O God, our Rock and our Redeemer.

♪ יִהְיוּ לְרָצוֹן אִמְרֵי־פִי וְהֶגְיוֹן לִבִּי לְפָנֶיךָ, יְיָ, צוּרִי וְגוֹאֲלִי.

On Sukkot, holding the *Lulav* and *Etrog*

בָּרוּךְ אַתָּה, יְיָ אֱלֹהֵינוּ, מֶלֶךְ הָעוֹלָם, אֲשֶׁר קִדְּשָׁנוּ בְּמִצְוֹתָיו וְצִוָּנוּ
עַל־נְטִילַת לוּלָב.

We praise You, O God, our God, Sovereign of all existence, who
hallows our lives with commandments and has ordained for us the Mitz-
vah of the Lulav.

הַלֵּל

THE HALLEL
A SERVICE OF PRAISE

"It is good to sing unto God."   טוֹב לְהוֹדוֹת לַיְיָ.

This means: It is good if a person can bring it about that God
sings within.

—Rabbi Elimelech of Lizhensk

◆　◆

There are halls in the heavens above that open only to the sound
of song.

—The Zohar

◆　◆

O, tell us, poet, what do you do? — I praise.
But those dark, deadly, devastating ways,
How do you bear them, suffer them? — I praise.
And then the Nameless, beyond guess or gaze,
How do you call it, conjure it? — I praise.

—Rainer Maria Rilke

◆　◆

HALLEL, PRAISE!
This is the gate of God
By which the righteous enter.

Open up,
O gates of righteousness,
That we may enter
And praise our God.

פִּתְחוּ־לִי שַׁעֲרֵי־צֶדֶק אָבֹא־בָם אוֹדֶה יָהּ:
זֶה־הַשַּׁעַר לַיְיָ צַדִּיקִים יָבֹאוּ בוֹ:
אוֹדְךָ כִּי עֲנִיתָנִי וַתְּהִי־לִי לִישׁוּעָה:

We praise.

We are a people who praise.

In times of joy, in seasons of gladness, we praise.
In periods of sorrow, in hours of sadness, still we praise.

All our prayer is praise of God,
The Living God, Creator of all, Giver of life!

בָּרוּךְ אַתָּה יְיָ אֱלֹהֵינוּ מֶלֶךְ הָעוֹלָם, אֲשֶׁר קִדְּשָׁנוּ בְּמִצְוֹתָיו וְצִוָּנוּ
לִקְרֹא אֶת־הַהַלֵּל:

Ba-ruch a-ta, A-do-nai E-lo-hei-nu, me-lech ha-o-lam, a-sher ki-de-sha-nu be-mits-vo-tav, ve-tsi-va-nu lik-ro et ha-ha-leil.

> *We praise You, our God,*
> *Adonai,*
> *Sovereign Creator of all existence*
> *Who has hallowed us through commandments*
> *Summoning us to utter praise and affirmation.*

> We praise.
> In eternity our song is one
> With the chant of the Levites
> In the days of the Temple's glory.
> On every festival
> They sang their service of psalms of praise,
> The Hallel.

> *In eternity our song is one.*

> Our song is one
> With all the hymns of flesh and blood
> Which sing of the triumph of people together,
> Over the powers of destruction.

In eternity our song is one.

Our song is one, and will be one
With the praise songs of all peoples:
Praise for the earth restored to its goodness;
Praise for human beings restored to themselves,
For life fulfilled in sacred celebration.

הַלְלוּהוּ הַלְלוּהוּ
בְּצִלְצְלֵי־שָׁמַע.
הַלְלוּהוּ הַלְלוּהוּ
בְּצִלְצְלֵי תְרוּעָה.
כֹּל הַנְּשָׁמָה
תְּהַלֵּל יָהּ.
הַלְלוּיָהּ!

ON SUKKOT

God's Name is praised in every place
From the rising of the sun until its setting.

Psalm 113　　　　　　　　　　　　　　　　　　תהלים קי״ג

הַלְלוּיָהּ הַלְלוּ עַבְדֵי יְיָ הַלְלוּ אֶת־שֵׁם יְיָ: יְהִי שֵׁם יְיָ מְבֹרָךְ מֵעַתָּה
וְעַד־עוֹלָם: מִמִּזְרַח־שֶׁמֶשׁ עַד־מְבוֹאוֹ מְהֻלָּל שֵׁם יְיָ: רָם עַל־כָּל־
גּוֹיִם יְיָ עַל הַשָּׁמַיִם כְּבוֹדוֹ: מִי כַּיְיָ אֱלֹהֵינוּ הַמַּגְבִּיהִי לָשָׁבֶת:
הַמַּשְׁפִּילִי לִרְאוֹת בַּשָּׁמַיִם וּבָאָרֶץ: מְקִימִי מֵעָפָר דָּל מֵאַשְׁפֹּת
יָרִים אֶבְיוֹן: לְהוֹשִׁיבִי עִם־נְדִיבִים עִם נְדִיבֵי עַמּוֹ: מוֹשִׁיבִי
עֲקֶרֶת הַבַּיִת אֵם־הַבָּנִים שְׂמֵחָה הַלְלוּיָהּ:

Who is like Adonai our God
Enthroned in exaltation?

But whose gaze is lowered to earth
To raise the poor from the dirt

And from the ash-heap lifts the needy.

To set them with princes,
Yea, with the princes of our people.

Who makes the barren woman
A joyful mother of children.
Halleluyah.

ON PESACH

When Israel went out of Egypt,
the House of Jacob from a people of strange speech . . .

Psalm 114   תהלים קי"ד

בְּצֵאת יִשְׂרָאֵל מִמִּצְרָיִם בֵּית יַעֲקֹב מֵעַם לֹעֵז: הָיְתָה יְהוּדָה
לְקָדְשׁוֹ יִשְׂרָאֵל מַמְשְׁלוֹתָיו: הַיָּם רָאָה וַיָּנֹס הַיַּרְדֵּן יִסֹּב לְאָחוֹר:
הֶהָרִים רָקְדוּ כְאֵילִים גְּבָעוֹת כִּבְנֵי־צֹאן: מַה־לְּךָ הַיָּם כִּי תָנוּס
הַיַּרְדֵּן תִּסֹּב לְאָחוֹר: הֶהָרִים תִּרְקְדוּ כְאֵילִים גְּבָעוֹת כִּבְנֵי־צֹאן:
מִלִּפְנֵי אָדוֹן חוּלִי אָרֶץ מִלִּפְנֵי אֱלוֹהַּ יַעֲקֹב: הַהֹפְכִי הַצּוּר אֲגַם־
מָיִם חַלָּמִישׁ לְמַעְיְנוֹ־מָיִם:

When Israel went out of Egypt,
the House of Jacob from
A people of strange speech. . . .

Tremble, O Earth, at the Presence of our God,
At the Presence of the God of Jacob!

Judah became God's dwelling,
Israel God's dominion.

Tremble, O Earth, at the presence of our God,
At the Presence of the God of Jacob!

God turns the rock into a pool of water,
The flint into a fountain of water.

Tremble, O Earth, at the Presence of our God!

ON SHAVUOT

The loving-faithfulness of God
has been mighty with us.

Psalm 117   תהלים קי"ז

$\oint$ הַלְלוּ אֶת־יְיָ כָּל־גּוֹיִם
שַׁבְּחוּהוּ כָּל־הָאֻמִּים:
כִּי גָבַר עָלֵינוּ חַסְדּוֹ
וֶאֱמֶת־יְיָ לְעוֹלָם הַלְלוּיָהּ:

Praise God, all ye nations,
Sing praise unto God, all ye peoples,
For the loving-faithfulness of God
Has been mighty with us
And the truth of our God is forever.

Not to us belongs the praise, God,
Not to us;
All glory to Your Name,
For Your mercy and Your truth.

May God increase you,
You and your children;
God will bless you and your children,
The small and the great.

◆ ◆

PASSAGES FROM HALLEL FOR RECITATION AND SONG

Psalm 115   תהלים קט"ו

לֹא לָנוּ יְיָ לֹא לָנוּ כִּי־לְשִׁמְךָ תֵּן כָּבוֹד עַל־חַסְדְּךָ עַל־אֲמִתֶּךָ: לָמָּה
יֹאמְרוּ הַגּוֹיִם אַיֵּה־נָא אֱלֹהֵיהֶם: וֵאלֹהֵינוּ בַשָּׁמָיִם כֹּל אֲשֶׁר־חָפֵץ
עָשָׂה: עֲצַבֵּיהֶם כֶּסֶף וְזָהָב מַעֲשֵׂה יְדֵי אָדָם: פֶּה־לָהֶם וְלֹא יְדַבֵּרוּ

עֵינַיִם לָהֶם וְלֹא יִרְאוּ: אָזְנַיִם לָהֶם וְלֹא יִשְׁמָעוּ אַף לָהֶם וְלֹא
יְרִיחוּן: יְדֵיהֶם וְלֹא יְמִישׁוּן רַגְלֵיהֶם וְלֹא יְהַלֵּכוּ לֹא־יֶהְגּוּ בִּגְרוֹנָם:
כְּמוֹהֶם יִהְיוּ עֹשֵׂיהֶם כֹּל אֲשֶׁר־בֹּטֵחַ בָּהֶם: יִשְׂרָאֵל בְּטַח בַּייָ עֶזְרָם
וּמָגִנָּם הוּא: בֵּית אַהֲרֹן בִּטְחוּ בַייָ עֶזְרָם וּמָגִנָּם הוּא:
יִרְאֵי יְיָ בִּטְחוּ בַייָ עֶזְרָם וּמָגִנָּם הוּא:

Why should the nations say:
"Where now is their God?"

Not for our sake, Adonai, not for our sake,
But for Your renown bring glory,
And for Your steadfast love.

Why should the nations say:
"Where now is their God?"
"Where now is their God?"
Their idols are silver and gold.

Their idols are silver and gold;
The work of human hands.

Unseeing eyes they have;

And mouths, but no true speech;

Inert, without the vivid breath of life.

Those who make them will be as they,
Their worshipers become like them;
Yes, all who put their trust in them.

Israel! Trust in God!
God is our Help and Shield.
All who revere God, keep your trust.
God is our Help and Shield.

God is our Help and our Shield!

יְיָ זְכָרָנוּ יְבָרֵךְ יְבָרֵךְ אֶת־בֵּית יִשְׂרָאֵל יְבָרֵךְ אֶת־בֵּית אַהֲרֹן: יְבָרֵךְ
יִרְאֵי יְיָ הַקְּטַנִּים עִם־הַגְּדֹלִים: יֹסֵף יְיָ עֲלֵיכֶם עֲלֵיכֶם וְעַל־בְּנֵיכֶם:
בְּרוּכִים אַתֶּם לַיְיָ עֹשֵׂה שָׁמַיִם וָאָרֶץ: הַשָּׁמַיִם שָׁמַיִם לַיְיָ וְהָאָרֶץ
נָתַן לִבְנֵי־אָדָם: לֹא־הַמֵּתִים יְהַלְלוּ־יָהּ וְלֹא כָּל־יֹרְדֵי דוּמָה:
וַאֲנַחְנוּ נְבָרֵךְ יָהּ מֵעַתָּה וְעַד־עוֹלָם הַלְלוּיָהּ:

God has been mindful of us.
O may God bring blessing:

Blessing to the House of Israel,
Blessing for those who revere God,
The small and the great alike.

May God increase your numbers,

Yours and your children as well.

May you be blessed by God,

Maker of heaven and earth.

The heavens are the heavens of God,

But the earth has been given to humankind.

The dead praise not our God,

Nor any who have gone down into silence.

But we will praise God,

Now and always.

Halleluyah!

אָהַבְתִּי כִּי־יִשְׁמַע יְיָ אֶת־קוֹלִי תַּחֲנוּנָי: כִּי־הִטָּה אָזְנוֹ לִי וּבְיָמַי
אֶקְרָא: אֲפָפוּנִי חֶבְלֵי־מָוֶת וּמְצָרֵי שְׁאוֹל מְצָאוּנִי צָרָה וְיָגוֹן
אֶמְצָא: וּבְשֵׁם־יְיָ אֶקְרָא אָנָּה יְיָ מַלְּטָה נַפְשִׁי: חַנּוּן יְיָ וְצַדִּיק

וֵאלֹהֵֽינוּ מְרַחֵם: שֹׁמֵר פְּתָאִים יְיָ דַּלּֽוֹתִי וְלִי יְהוֹשִֽׁיעַ: שׁוּבִי נַפְשִׁי
לִמְנוּחָֽיְכִי כִּי־יְיָ גָּמַל עָלָֽיְכִי: כִּי חִלַּֽצְתָּ נַפְשִׁי מִמָּֽוֶת אֶת־עֵינִי מִן־
דִּמְעָה אֶת־רַגְלִי מִדֶּֽחִי: אֶתְהַלֵּךְ לִפְנֵי יְיָ בְּאַרְצוֹת הַחַיִּים:
הֶאֱמַֽנְתִּי כִּי אֲדַבֵּר אֲנִי עָנִֽיתִי מְאֹד: אֲנִי אָמַֽרְתִּי בְחָפְזִי כָּל־הָאָדָם
כֹּזֵב:

> In God's way will I walk
> In the land of the living will I walk
> In the way of God.
> For I trust and am faithful
> Though I have said:
> Crushed am I.
> Though I said in my haste, in my haste I said
> All that is human is deceit.
> Return, my soul, unto your tranquility
> For God has dealt well with you.

—Based on passages of Psalm 116

Psalm 118   תהלים קי״ח

כִּי לְעוֹלָם חַסְדּוֹ:   הוֹדוּ לַיְיָ כִּי־טוֹב
Ho-du la-do-nai ki tov, ki le-o-lam chas-do.

O give thanks unto God who is Good

For the truth of God is forever.

O give thanks unto God who is Good

For the faithfulness of God is forever.

O give thanks unto God who is Good

For the mercy of God is forever.

O give thanks unto God who is Good

For the steadfast law of God endures forever.

כִּי לְעוֹלָם חַסְדּוֹ:   הוֹדוּ לַיְיָ כִּי־טוֹב 𝄞

כִּי לְעוֹלָם חַסְדּוֹ:   יֹאמַר־נָא יִשְׂרָאֵל

יֹאמְרוּ־נָא בֵית אַהֲרֹן   כִּי לְעוֹלָם חַסְדּוֹ:
יֹאמְרוּ־נָא יִרְאֵי יְיָ   כִּי לְעוֹלָם חַסְדּוֹ:
הוֹדוּ לַיְיָ כִּי־טוֹב   כִּי לְעוֹלָם חַסְדּוֹ:

HALLEL: THE AFFIRMATION OF LIFE

מִן־הַמֵּצַר קָרָאתִי יָּה עָנָנִי בַמֶּרְחָב יָהּ:
לֹא־אָמוּת כִּי־אֶחְיֶה וַאֲסַפֵּר מַעֲשֵׂי יָהּ:

עָזִּי וְזִמְרָת יָהּ,
וַיְהִי־לִי לִישׁוּעָה.
קוֹל רִנָּה וִישׁוּעָה
בְּאָהֳלֵי צַדִּיקִים:

God is with me, in my aid;
I will gaze upon mine enemies.

We will not die but live.

It is better to take refuge in God
Than to trust in ourselves;
It is better to take refuge in God
Than to trust in princes.

We will praise our God forever.

The Eternal is for me; I will not fear.
What can humans do unto me?

We will not die but live.

Out of the depths I called upon God;
God answers me with liberation.

We will praise our God forever.

You have delivered my soul from death,
Mine eyes from tears.

We will not die but live.

The cords of death encompassed me
And the straits of the nether world seized me;
I was brought low and God saved me.

We will praise our God forever.

I shall walk before my God
In the land of the living.

We will not die but live.

The dead praise not our God,
Nor any that go down into silence.

We will praise our God forever.

God has chastened me sore
But has not given my soul over into death.

We will not die but live.

The stone which the builders rejected
Has become the chief cornerstone.

We will praise our God forever.

I lift up the cup of triumph
And call upon the Name of God.

We will not die but live.

God is my strength and my song
And has become my triumph.

We will praise our God forever.

We will not die but live!

We will praise our God forever.

ALL PRAISE נשמת

נִשְׁמַת כָּל־חַי תְּבָרֵךְ אֶת־שִׁמְךָ יְיָ אֱלֹהֵינוּ. וְרוּחַ כָּל־בָּשָׂר תְּפָאֵר
וּתְרוֹמֵם זִכְרְךָ מַלְכֵּנוּ תָּמִיד: מִן־הָעוֹלָם וְעַד־הָעוֹלָם אַתָּה אֵל.
וּמִבַּלְעָדֶיךָ אֵין לָנוּ מֶלֶךְ גּוֹאֵל וּמוֹשִׁיעַ פּוֹדֶה וּמַצִּיל. וּמְפַרְנֵס
וּמְרַחֵם. בְּכָל־עֵת צָרָה וְצוּקָה. אֵין לָנוּ מֶלֶךְ אֶלָּא אָתָּה: אֱלֹהֵי
הָרִאשׁוֹנִים וְהָאַחֲרוֹנִים. הַמְנַהֵג עוֹלָמוֹ בְּחֶסֶד וּבְרִיּוֹתָיו בְּרַחֲמִים.
לְךָ לְבַדְּךָ אֲנַחְנוּ מוֹדִים: אִלּוּ פִינוּ מָלֵא שִׁירָה כַּיָּם וּלְשׁוֹנֵנוּ רִנָּה
כַּהֲמוֹן גַּלָּיו. וְשִׂפְתוֹתֵינוּ שֶׁבַח כְּמֶרְחֲבֵי רָקִיעַ. אֵין אֲנַחְנוּ
מַסְפִּיקִים לְהוֹדוֹת לְךָ יְיָ אֱלֹהֵינוּ וֵאלֹהֵי אֲבוֹתֵינוּ. עַל־כָּל־
הַטּוֹבוֹת שֶׁעָשִׂיתָ עִם־אֲבוֹתֵינוּ וְעִמָּנוּ: מִמִּצְרַיִם גְּאַלְתָּנוּ יְיָ
אֱלֹהֵינוּ וּמִבֵּית עֲבָדִים פְּדִיתָנוּ. בְּרָעָב זַנְתָּנוּ. וּבְשָׂבָע כִּלְכַּלְתָּנוּ:
מֵחֶרֶב הִצַּלְתָּנוּ וּמִדֶּבֶר מִלַּטְתָּנוּ. וּמֵחֳלָיִם רָעִים וְנֶאֱמָנִים דִּלִּיתָנוּ:
עַד־הֵנָּה עֲזָרוּנוּ רַחֲמֶיךָ. וְלֹא־עֲזָבוּנוּ חֲסָדֶיךָ. וְאַל תִּטְּשֵׁנוּ־יְיָ
אֱלֹהֵינוּ לָנֶצַח: עַל־כֵּן נְהַלֵּךְ וּנְשַׁבֵּחַךְ וּנְפָאֶרְךָ וּנְבָרֵךְ אֶת־שֵׁם
קָדְשֶׁךָ: בָּרוּךְ אַתָּה יְיָ אֵל מֶלֶךְ גָּדוֹל בַּתִּשְׁבָּחוֹת. אֵל הַהוֹדָאוֹת
אֲדוֹן הַנִּפְלָאוֹת. הַבּוֹחֵר בְּשִׁירֵי זִמְרָה. מֶלֶךְ אֵל חֵי הָעוֹלָמִים:

The breath of all living is praise of You, O God.
The spirit of all flesh is Your eternal glory, our Sovereign.
From everlasting to everlasting You are God.
And beside You, we have no sovereign, no redeemer.

Were our mouths as full of song as the sea,
And our tongues with melody as the multitude of its waves,
Our eyes shining like the sun and the moon,
Our arms like soaring eagles' pinions,
Our limbs like those of the swift gazelle,
Still our power would be naught to show
The thousand myriad bounties You bestow.

But, O God, limbs and tongue and heart and mind,
Join now to praise Your Name
As every tongue will yet avow You
And every soul give You allegiance.

Praise God, my whole being!
All that is within me:
Praise God's holy Name!

פִּתְחוּ־לִי שַׁעֲרֵי־צֶדֶק אָבֹא־בָם 𝄞
זֶה־הַשַּׁעַר לַיְיָ צַדִּיקִים יָבֹאוּ בוֹ:
אֶבֶן מָאֲסוּ הַבּוֹנִים הָיְתָה לְרֹאשׁ פִּנָּה:
מֵאֵת יְיָ הָיְתָה זֹּאת הִיא נִפְלָאת בְּעֵינֵינוּ:
זֶה־הַיּוֹם עָשָׂה יְיָ נָגִילָה וְנִשְׂמְחָה בוֹ:
הוֹדוּ לַיְיָ כִּי־טוֹב כִּי לְעוֹלָם חַסְדּוֹ:

Open up, O gates of righteousness,
That we may enter and sing Your praise.
To You, O God, does Israel's song arise,
Wond'rous in our eyes.

This is the day which God has ordained for us
For we were destined of old.
We lift our voices, our souls within rejoice,
God's endless praise be told.

אָנָּא יְיָ, הוֹשִׁיעָה נָּא! 𝄞
אָנָּא יְיָ, הוֹשִׁיעָה נָּא!

O God, bring our deliverance!
O God, bring our deliverance!

THE TORAH READING

There is none like You, יְהֹוָה, among the gods that are worshiped. There are no deeds like Yours. Your dominion is everlasting, enduring through all generations.

God was Sovereign; God is Sovereign; God will be Sovereign forever. And in this sovereign power, may God bless the people with peace.

אֵין כָּמְוֹךָ בָאֱלֹהִים, יְיָ, וְאֵין כְּמַעֲשֶׂיךָ. מַלְכוּתְךָ מַלְכוּת כָּל־עוֹלָמִים וּמֶמְשַׁלְתְּךָ בְּכָל־דּוֹר וָדֹר.

יְיָ מֶלֶךְ, יְיָ מָלָךְ, יְיָ יִמְלֹךְ לְעוֹלָם וָעֶד. יְיָ עֹז לְעַמּוֹ יִתֵּן, יְיָ יְבָרֵךְ אֶת־עַמּוֹ בַשָּׁלוֹם.

The Ark is opened

All rise

אַב הָרַחֲמִים, הֵיטִיבָה בִרְצוֹנְךָ אֶת־צִיּוֹן; תִּבְנֶה חוֹמוֹת יְרוּשָׁלָיִם. כִּי בְךָ לְבַד בָּטָחְנוּ, מֶלֶךְ אֵל רָם וְנִשָּׂא, אֲדוֹן עוֹלָמִים.

(Source of mercy, let Your goodness be a blessing to Zion; let Jerusalem be built according to Your will.
In You alone do we trust, O Sovereign God, high and exalted, Sovereign of all the worlds.)

יְיָ, יְיָ, אֵל רַחוּם וְחַנּוּן, אֶרֶךְ אַפַּיִם וְרַב־חֶסֶד וֶאֱמֶת, נוֹצֵר חֶסֶד לַאֲלָפִים, נֹשֵׂא עָוֺן וָפֶשַׁע וְחַטָּאָה וְנַקֵּה.

יְהֹוָה, יְהֹוָה, God of mercy and grace, endlessly patient, of steadfast love and truth, keeping faith with thousands, forgiving iniquity, transgression and sin, and granting pardon.

הָבוּ גֹדֶל לֵאלֹהֵינוּ וּתְנוּ כָבוֹד לַתּוֹרָה.

Let us declare the greatness of our God
and render honor unto the Torah.

The Torah is taken from the Ark

For out of Zion shall go forth Torah,
and the word of God from Jerusalem.

כִּי מִצִיּוֹן תֵּצֵא תוֹרָה, וּדְבַר־יְיָ מִירוּשָׁלָיִם.

Praised be God who in holiness
has given the Torah to the people of Israel.

בָּרוּךְ שֶׁנָּתַן תּוֹרָה לְעַמּוֹ יִשְׂרָאֵל בִּקְדֻשָּׁתוֹ.

שְׁמַע יִשְׂרָאֵל: יְיָ אֱלֹהֵינוּ, יְיָ אֶחָד!

Hear, O Israel:
Adonai is our God, Adonai is One!

אֶחָד אֱלֹהֵינוּ, גָּדוֹל אֲדוֹנֵינוּ, קָדוֹשׁ שְׁמוֹ.

Our God is One; our God is great;
the Name of God is holy.

גַּדְּלוּ לַיהֹוָה אִתִּי וּנְרוֹמְמָה שְׁמוֹ יַחְדָּו.

O magnify God with me,
and let us exalt God's Name together.

♪ לְךָ, יְיָ, הַגְּדֻלָּה וְהַגְּבוּרָה וְהַתִּפְאֶרֶת וְהַנֵּצַח וְהַהוֹד, כִּי כֹל בַּשָּׁמַיִם
וּבָאָרֶץ, לְךָ יְיָ הַמַּמְלָכָה וְהַמִּתְנַשֵּׂא לְכֹל לְרֹאשׁ.

(Yours, God, is the greatness, the power, the glory, the victory, and the majesty; for all that is in heaven and earth is Yours. Yours is sovereignty, יְהֹוָה. You are supreme over all.)

All are seated

• •

The following verses may be read
before the reading of the Torah on Shavuot

AKDAMUT   אקדמות

א קַדְמוּת מִלִּין וְשָׁרָיוּת שׁוּתָא

א וְלָא שָׁקֵילְנָא הַרְמָן וּרְשׁוּתָא:

בְּ בָבֵי תְּרֵי וּתְלָת דְּאֶפְתַּח בְּנַקְשׁוּתָא

בְּ בָרֵי דְבָרֵי וְטָרֵי עֲדֵי לְקַשִּׁישׁוּתָא:

גְּ בּוּרָן עָלְמִין לֵהּ וְלָא סְפֵק פְּרִישׁוּתָא

גְּ וִיל אִלּוּ רְקִיעֵי קְנֵי כָּל־חֻרְשָׁתָא:

דְּ יוֹ אִלּוּ יַמֵּי וְכָל־מֵי כְנִישׁוּתָא

דְּ יְרֵי אַרְעָא סָפְרֵי וְרַשְׁמֵי רַשְׁוָתָא:

הֲ דַר מָרֵי שְׁמַיָּא וְשַׁלִּיט בְּיַבֶּשְׁתָּא

הֲ קֵם עָלְמָא יְחִידַי וְכַבְּשֵׁהּ בְּכַבְּשׁוּתָא:

וּ בְלָא לֵאוּ שַׁכְלְלֵהּ וּבְלָא תְשָׁשׁוּתָא

וּ בְאָתָא קַלִּילָא דְּלֵית בָּהּ מְשָׁשׁוּתָא:

זַ מִין כָּל עֲבִדְתֵּהּ בְּהַךְ יוֹמֵי שִׁתָּא

זַ הוֹר יְקָרֵהּ עֲלִי עֲלֵי כָּרְסְיֵהּ דְּאֶשָּׁתָא:

חָ יָל אֶלֶף אַלְפִין וְרִבּוֹא לְשַׁמְּשׁוּתָא

חַ דְתִּין נְבוֹט לְצַפְרִין סַגִּיאָה טְרָשׁוּתָא:

טְ פֵי יְקִידִין שָׂרָפִין כְּלוּל גַּפֵּי שִׁתָּא

טְ עֵם עַד יִתְיְהֵב לְהוֹן שְׁתִיקִין בְּאַדִּשְׁתָּא:

יְ קַבְּלוּן דֵּין מִן־דֵּין שָׁוֵי דְּלָא בְשַׁשְׁתָּא
יְ קַר מְלֵי כָל־אַרְעָא לְתִלוֹתֵי קַדְשָׁתָּא:

Before the words of God supreme
Today are read, for this my theme
Approbation will I seek
These my sentences to speak,

Just two or three,
While tremblingly
On God I meditate,

The Pure, who doth bear
The world for e'er;
God's power who can relate?

Were the sky of parchment made,
A quill each reed, each twig and blade,
Could we with ink fill sea and brook,
Were everyone to write a book,

The marvelous story
Of God's great glory
Would still remain untold.

For God, Most High,
The earth and sky
Created alone of old,

Without fatigue or weary hand.
God spoke the word, and breathed command.

The world and all that therein dwell,
Field and meadow, fen and fell,

Valley and mount,
The oceans' fount
With life did God inspire.

The work when ended,
God's glory ascended
Upon the throne of fire.

Before God myriad angels flash,
To do God's will they run and dash;

Each day new hosts gleam forth to praise
The Mighty One, Ancient of days.
Their song being done, they too are ended,
While ever new music aloft is blended.

But Israel's folk
Who bear God's yoke
In faith and troth well tried,

God's glory share,
And One declare
At morn and eventide.

God's portion they, God's will obey,
God's power declare by night and day;
A precious law, dearer than gold,
God bade them study, their life to enfold,
That God may be near,
Their prayer to hear,

Then perfect joy will our God bring,
In sacred rites our voices ring;
And day and night
Shall be God's light
A canopy of splendor.

◆　◆

Before the reading of the Torah

בָּרְכוּ אֶת־יְיָ הַמְבֹרָךְ!
בָּרוּךְ יְיָ הַמְבֹרָךְ לְעוֹלָם וָעֶד!

בָּרוּךְ אַתָּה, יְיָ אֱלֹהֵינוּ, מֶלֶךְ הָעוֹלָם, אֲשֶׁר בָּחַר־בָּנוּ מִכָּל־הָעַמִּים
וְנָתַן־לָנוּ אֶת־תּוֹרָתוֹ. בָּרוּךְ אַתָּה, יְיָ, נוֹתֵן הַתּוֹרָה.

Praised be God, to whom our praise is due!
Praised be God, to whom our praise is due, now and forever!
We praise our God, Sovereign of all existence, who has chosen us
from all peoples by giving us the Torah. We praise You, O God,
who gives us the Torah.

After the reading

בָּרוּךְ אַתָּה, יְיָ אֱלֹהֵינוּ, מֶלֶךְ הָעוֹלָם, אֲשֶׁר נָתַן לָנוּ תּוֹרַת אֱמֶת
וְחַיֵּי עוֹלָם נָטַע בְּתוֹכֵנוּ. בָּרוּךְ אַתָּה, יְיָ, נוֹתֵן הַתּוֹרָה.

We praise You, our God, Sovereign of all existence, who has
given us a teaching of truth, implanting within us everlasting life.
We praise You, O God, who gives us the Torah.

After the reading is completed, the Torah is held high while this is said:

וְזֹאת הַתּוֹרָה אֲשֶׁר־שָׂם מֹשֶׁה לִפְנֵי בְּנֵי יִשְׂרָאֵל, עַל־פִּי יְיָ
בְּיַד־מֹשֶׁה.

Now this is the Torah that Moses, at the word of God, placed
before the Children of Israel!

Before the reading of the Haftarah

בָּרוּךְ אַתָּה, יְיָ אֱלֹהֵינוּ, מֶלֶךְ הָעוֹלָם, אֲשֶׁר בָּחַר בִּנְבִיאִים טוֹבִים
וְרָצָה בְדִבְרֵיהֶם הַנֶּאֱמָרִים בֶּאֱמֶת. בָּרוּךְ אַתָּה, יְיָ, הַבּוֹחֵר בַּתּוֹרָה
וּבְמֹשֶׁה עַבְדּוֹ וּבְיִשְׂרָאֵל עַמּוֹ וּבִנְבִיאֵי הָאֱמֶת וָצֶדֶק.

We praise you, יְהֹוָה, our God, Sovereign of all existence, who
has chosen faithful prophets of truth and found favor in their
teachings. We praise You, our God, who reveals Your choice
through Torah as through Moses Your servant, Israel Your
people, and through prophets of truth and righteousness.

After the reading

בָּרוּךְ אַתָּה, יְיָ אֱלֹהֵינוּ, מֶלֶךְ הָעוֹלָם, צוּר כָּל־הָעוֹלָמִים, צַדִּיק בְּכָל־הַדּוֹרוֹת, הָאֵל הַנֶּאֱמָן, הָאוֹמֵר וְעוֹשֶׂה, הַמְדַבֵּר וּמְקַיֵּם, שֶׁכָּל דְּבָרָיו אֱמֶת וָצֶדֶק.

עַל־הַתּוֹרָה וְעַל־הָעֲבוֹדָה וְעַל־הַנְּבִיאִים וְעַל־יוֹם (הַשַּׁבָּת הַזֶּה, וְעַל־יוֹם)

חַג הַסֻּכּוֹת הַזֶּה

חַג הַמַּצוֹת הַזֶּה

חַג הַשָּׁבֻעוֹת הַזֶּה

שֶׁנָּתַתָּ־לָּנוּ, יְיָ אֱלֹהֵינוּ, (לִקְדֻשָׁה וְלִמְנוּחָה,) לְשָׂשׂוֹן וּלְשִׂמְחָה, לְכָבוֹד וּלְתִפְאָרֶת. עַל־הַכֹּל, יְיָ אֱלֹהֵינוּ, אֲנַחְנוּ מוֹדִים לָךְ, וּמְבָרְכִים אוֹתָךְ. יִתְבָּרַךְ שִׁמְךָ בְּפִי כָּל־חַי תָּמִיד לְעוֹלָם וָעֶד. בָּרוּךְ אַתָּה, יְיָ, מְקַדֵּשׁ (הַשַּׁבָּת וְ) יִשְׂרָאֵל וְהַזְּמַנִּים.

We praise You, our God, Sovereign of all existence, Rock of all creation, whose righteousness in all generations is unfailing, faithful God, who speaks and fulfills, whose commandments are just and true. For the Torah, for the privilege of worship, for the prophets, (for this Shabbat,) and for this festival of

Sukkot
Pesach
Shavuot

that You, יְהֹוָה *our God, have given us (for holiness and rest,) for joy and gladness, for honor and glory, we thank and bless You. May Your Name be blessed forever by every living being. We praise You, God, who hallows (the Sabbath,) the House of Israel and the festivals.*

(The Scrolls for the Holy Days may be read here.)

(For the Memorial Service, see page 365)

RETURNING THE TORAH TO THE ARK

All rise

יְהַלְלוּ אֶת־שֵׁם יְיָ, כִּי נִשְׂגָּב שְׁמוֹ לְבַדּוֹ.

Let us praise the Name of God, for God's Name alone is to be exalted.

הוֹדוֹ עַל אֶרֶץ וְשָׁמָיִם, וַיָּרֶם קֶרֶן לְעַמּוֹ, תְּהִלָּה לְכָל־חֲסִידָיו, לִבְנֵי
יִשְׂרָאֵל עַם קְרוֹבוֹ. הַלְלוּיָהּ.

God's splendor is over heaven and earth; through Torah, God exalts the dignity of the people! Praise to those faithful to God, to those of the Children of Israel whom God has drawn near in service. Halleluyah!

תּוֹרַת יְיָ תְּמִימָה, מְשִׁיבַת נָפֶשׁ;

The Torah, the teaching of God, is whole and brings
wholeness to the spirit.

עֵדוּת יְיָ נֶאֱמָנָה, מַחְכִּימַת פֶּתִי;

The testimony of God is reliable, giving wisdom to those without guile.

פִּקּוּדֵי יְיָ יְשָׁרִים, מְשַׂמְּחֵי־לֵב;

The statutes taught by God are right; they bring joy
into our lives.

מִצְוַת יְיָ בָּרָה, מְאִירַת עֵינָיִם;

The commandment of God is elemental, enlightening our minds.

יִרְאַת יְיָ טְהוֹרָה, עֹמֶדֶת לָעַד;

Reverence for God is pure; it stands forever.

מִשְׁפְּטֵי יְיָ אֱמֶת, צָדְקוּ יַחְדָּו.

The judgments of God are true; they are righteous altogether.

כִּי לֶקַח טוֹב נָתַתִּי לָכֶם, תּוֹרָתִי אַל־תַּעֲזְבוּ.

Behold, a good doctrine has been given unto you; forsake it not.
It is a tree of life to those who grasp hold of it,
and fortunate are those who support it.
Its ways are ways of pleasantness, and all its paths are peace.

Return us unto You, our God, and we will return.
Renew our days as of old.

עֵץ חַיִּים הִיא לַמַּחֲזִיקִים בָּהּ, וְתֹמְכֶיהָ מְאֻשָּׁר.
דְּרָכֶיהָ דַּרְכֵי־נֹעַם, וְכָל נְתִיבוֹתֶיהָ שָׁלוֹם.
הֲשִׁיבֵנוּ, יְיָ, אֵלֶיךָ, וְנָשׁוּבָה. חַדֵּשׁ יָמֵינוּ כְּקֶדֶם.

The Ark is closed

All are seated

הַזְכָּרַת נְשָׁמוֹת

THE MEMORIAL SERVICE

For the seventh day of Pesach, Shavuot, and Atseret-Simchat Torah.

Psalm 23   תהלים כג

♭ מִזְמוֹר לְדָוִד.

יְיָ רֹעִי, לֹא אֶחְסָר.

בִּנְאוֹת דֶּשֶׁא יַרְבִּיצֵנִי, עַל־מֵי מְנֻחוֹת יְנַהֲלֵנִי.

נַפְשִׁי יְשׁוֹבֵב, יַנְחֵנִי בְמַעְגְּלֵי־צֶדֶק לְמַעַן שְׁמוֹ.

גַּם כִּי אֵלֵךְ בְּגֵיא צַלְמָוֶת לֹא אִירָא רָע, כִּי אַתָּה עִמָּדִי;

שִׁבְטְךָ וּמִשְׁעַנְתֶּךָ, הֵמָּה יְנַחֲמֻנִי.

תַּעֲרֹךְ לְפָנַי שֻׁלְחָן נֶגֶד צֹרְרָי.

דִּשַּׁנְתָּ בַשֶּׁמֶן רֹאשִׁי, כּוֹסִי רְוָיָה.

אַךְ טוֹב וָחֶסֶד יִרְדְּפוּנִי כָּל־יְמֵי חַיָּי,

וְשַׁבְתִּי בְּבֵית־יְיָ לְאֹרֶךְ יָמִים.

The Lord is my Shepherd; I shall not want.
He maketh me to lie down in green pastures;
He leadeth me beside the still waters.
He restoreth my soul;
He guideth me in straight paths for His Name's sake.
Yea, though I walk through the valley of the shadow of death,
I will fear no evil, for Thou art with me;
Thy rod and Thy staff, they comfort me.
Thou preparest a table before me in the presence of mine enemies;
Thou hast anointed my head with oil; my cup runneth over.
Surely goodness and mercy shall follow me all the days of my life;
and I shall dwell in the House of the Lord forever.

◆ ◆

In nature's ebb and flow, God's eternal law abides. When tears dim our vision and grief clouds our understanding, we often lose sight of God's eternal plan. Yet we know that growth and decay, life and death, all reveal God's purpose. Our support in the struggles of life is also our hope in death. We have set God before us and shall not despair. In God's hands are the souls of all the living and the spirits of all flesh. Under God's protection we abide, and by God's love are we comforted. O Life of our life, Soul of our soul, cause Your light to shine into our hearts, and fill our spirit with abiding trust in You.

◆ ◆

God, Thou hast been our dwelling-place in all generations. Before the mountains were brought forth, before Thou hadst formed the universe, this world, even from everlasting to everlasting, Thou art God.

But, as for us, Thy children, Thou turnest us all unto contrition;
and sayest: Return, you human children.

The days of our years are, at the round, threescore years and ten, or even by reason of special strength fourscore years. But a thousand years in Thy sight are but as yesterday when it is past, and as a watch in the night.

Teach us, therefore, to number our days with a heart of wisdom.
As for us, may Thy favor, O God, be upon us,
establish for us the work of our hands.
Yea, the work of our spirits, establish it, O God.

שִׁוִּיתִי יְיָ לְנֶגְדִּי תָמִיד; ♪
כִּי מִימִינִי בַּל־אֶמּוֹט.
לָכֵן שָׂמַח לִבִּי וַיָּגֶל כְּבוֹדִי;
אַף־בְּשָׂרִי יִשְׁכֹּן לָבֶטַח.

כִּי לֹא־תַעֲזֹב נַפְשִׁי לִשְׁאוֹל,

לֹא־תִתֵּן חֲסִידְךָ לִרְאוֹת שָׁחַת.

תּוֹדִיעֵנִי אֹרַח חַיִּים;

שֹׂבַע שְׂמָחוֹת אֶת־פָּנֶיךָ;

נְעִמוֹת בִּימִינְךָ נֶצַח.

I have set the Eternal before me;
God is at my side, I shall not be moved.
My heart exults, my soul rejoices;
my being dwells in confidence.
For Thou will not abandon me to death
nor let Thy faithful ones see destruction.
Make me to know the path of life;
a satiety of joy is in Thy Presence;
loveliness at Thy right hand forever.

O God, this hour revives in us memories of loved ones who are no more. What happiness we shared when they walked among us! What joy, when, loving and loved, we lived our lives together!

Their memory is a blessing forever.

Months or years may have passed, yet we feel near to them. Our hearts yearn for them. Though the bitter grief has softened, a duller pain abides, for the place where once they stood is empty now forever. The links of life are broken. But the links of love and longing cannot break.

Their souls are bound up with ours forever.

We see them now with the eye of memory, their faults forgiven, their virtues grown larger. So does goodness live, and weakness fade from sight. We remember them with gratitude and bless their names.

Their memory is a blessing forever.

And we remember as well the men and women who but yesterday were part of our congregation and community. To all who cared for us and labored for the well-being of our people and of humanity, we pay tribute. May we prove worthy of carrying on the tradition of our people and our faith, for now the task is ours.

Their souls are bound up with ours forever.

We think, too, of the whole household of Israel and its martyrs. The tragedy of our own age is still a fresh wound within us. And we recall how often in ages past our people walked through the flames of the furnace. Merciful God, let the memory never fade of the faithful and upright of our people who have given their lives to hallow Your Name. Even in death they continue to speak to us of faith and courage. They rest in nameless graves, but their deeds endure, and their sacrifices will not be forgotten. Their souls are bound up in the bond of eternal life. No evil shall touch them; they are at peace.

We will remember, and never forget them.

In gratitude for all the blessings our loved ones, our friends, our teachers, and the martyrs of our people have brought to us, to our people, and to humanity, we dedicate ourselves anew to the sacred faith for which they lived and died, and to the tasks they have bequeathed to us. Let them be remembered for blessing, O God, together with the righteous of all peoples, and let us say: *Amen.*

SILENT REMEMBRANCE · יזכור

יִזְכּוֹר אֱלֹהִים נִשְׁמוֹת יַקִּירַי ·/· · · · · שֶׁהָלְכוּ לְעוֹלָמָם. אָנָּא
תִּהְיֶינָה נַפְשׁוֹתֵיהֶם צְרוּרוֹת בִּצְרוֹר הַחַיִּים וּתְהִי מְנוּחָתָם כָּבוֹד.
שֹׂבַע שְׂמָחוֹת אֶת־פָּנֶיךָ, נְעִימוֹת בִּימִינְךָ נֶצַח. אָמֵן.

May God remember forever my dear ones . . . . . who have gone to their eternal rest. May they be at one with the One who is life eternal. May the beauty of their lives shine for evermore, and may my life always bring honor to their memory.

יִזְכּוֹר אֱלֹהִים נִשְׁמוֹת כָּל־אַחֵינוּ בְּנֵי יִשְׂרָאֵל שֶׁמָּסְרוּ
אֶת־נַפְשׁוֹתֵיהֶם עַל קִדּוּשׁ הַשֵּׁם. אָנָּא תִּהְיֶינָה נַפְשׁוֹתֵיהֶם צְרוּרוֹת
בִּצְרוֹר הַחַיִּים וּתְהִי מְנוּחָתָם כָּבוֹד. שֶׁבַע שְׂמָחוֹת אֶת־פָּנֶיךָ,
נְעִימוֹת בִּימִינְךָ נֶצַח. אָמֵן.

May God remember forever our brothers and sisters of the House
of Israel who gave their lives for the sanctification of the Divine
Name. May they be at one with the One who is life eternal.
May the beauty of their lives shine for evermore, and may my life
always bring honor to their memory.

> In the rising of the sun and in its going down,
> we remember them.
>
> *In the blowing of the wind and in the chill of winter,*
> *we remember them.*
>
> In the opening of buds and in the rebirth of spring,
> we remember them.
>
> *In the blueness of the sky and in the warmth of summer,*
> *we remember them.*
>
> In the rustling of leaves and in the splendor of autumn,
> we remember them.
>
> *In the beginning of the year and when it ends,*
> *we remember them.*
>
> When we are weary and in need of strength,
> we remember them.
>
> *When we are lost and sick at heart,*
> *we remember them.*
>
> When we have joys we yearn to share,
> we remember them.

So long as we live, they too shall live,
for they are now a part of us, as we remember them.

All rise

אֵל מָלֵא רַחֲמִים, שׁוֹכֵן בַּמְּרוֹמִים, הַמְצֵא מְנוּחָה נְכוֹנָה תַּחַת
כַּנְפֵי הַשְּׁכִינָה עִם קְדוֹשִׁים וּטְהוֹרִים כְּזֹהַר הָרָקִיעַ מַזְהִירִים
לְנִשְׁמוֹת יַקִּירֵינוּ שֶׁהָלְכוּ לְעוֹלָמָם. בַּעַל הָרַחֲמִים יַסְתִּירֵם בְּסֵתֶר
כְּנָפָיו לְעוֹלָמִים, וְיִצְרוֹר בִּצְרוֹר הַחַיִּים אֶת־נִשְׁמָתָם. יְיָ הוּא
נַחֲלָתָם. וְיָנוּחוּ בְּשָׁלוֹם עַל מִשְׁכָּבָם, וְנֹאמַר: אָמֵן.

Our God full of compassion, whom we image forth as dwelling
on high, grant perfect rest in Thy Presence to the holy and pure,
who shine more brightly than the brightness of the firmament,
the souls of our dear ones who have gone with Thee into eternity. God of mercy, let them find refuge in the shadow of Thy
wings, and let their souls be bound up in a bond of ongoing and
everlasting life. May God be their possession, may their repose be
peace, and may their memory inspire us to noble and consecrated
living, and let us say: *Amen.*

(The prayers for the returning of the Torah to the Ark begin on page 362)

עָלֵינוּ

CONCLUSION OF WORSHIP

All rise

It is our destined calling to praise the God of all existence, to render honor unto the Sovereign of all eternity who has called us to an appointed purpose among all the families of the earth.
We therefore bow in awe and thanksgiving before the One who is Sovereign over all, the Holy One, whose Name we reverence.

עָלֵינוּ לְשַׁבֵּחַ לַאֲדוֹן הַכֹּל, לָתֵת גְּדֻלָּה לְיוֹצֵר בְּרֵאשִׁית,
שֶׁלֹּא עָשָׂנוּ כְּגוֹיֵי הָאֲרָצוֹת, וְלֹא שָׂמָנוּ כְּמִשְׁפְּחוֹת הָאֲדָמָה,
שֶׁלֹּא שָׂם חֶלְקֵנוּ כָּהֶם, וְגוֹרָלֵנוּ כְּכָל־הֲמוֹנָם.
וַאֲנַחְנוּ כּוֹרְעִים וּמִשְׁתַּחֲוִים וּמוֹדִים
לִפְנֵי מֶלֶךְ מַלְכֵי הַמְּלָכִים, הַקָּדוֹשׁ בָּרוּךְ הוּא.

All are seated

שֶׁהוּא נוֹטֶה שָׁמַיִם וְיֹסֵד אָרֶץ, וּמוֹשַׁב יְקָרוֹ בַּשָּׁמַיִם מִמַּעַל,
וּשְׁכִינַת עֻזּוֹ בְּגָבְהֵי מְרוֹמִים. הוּא אֱלֹהֵינוּ, אֵין עוֹד; אֱמֶת מַלְכֵּנוּ,
אֶפֶס זוּלָתוֹ, כַּכָּתוּב בְּתוֹרָתוֹ: „וְיָדַעְתָּ הַיּוֹם וַהֲשֵׁבֹתָ אֶל־לְבָבֶךָ, כִּי
יְיָ הוּא הָאֱלֹהִים בַּשָּׁמַיִם מִמַּעַל וְעַל־הָאָרֶץ מִתָּחַת, אֵין עוֹד."

עַל־כֵּן נְקַוֶּה לְּךָ, יְיָ אֱלֹהֵינוּ לִרְאוֹת מְהֵרָה בְּתִפְאֶרֶת עֻזֶּךָ, לְהַעֲבִיר
גִּלּוּלִים מִן־הָאָרֶץ, וְהָאֱלִילִים כָּרוֹת יִכָּרֵתוּן, לְתַקֵּן עוֹלָם בְּמַלְכוּת
שַׁדַּי. וְכָל־בְּנֵי בָשָׂר יִקְרְאוּ בִשְׁמֶךָ, לְהַפְנוֹת אֵלֶיךָ כָּל־רִשְׁעֵי
אָרֶץ.

יַכִּירוּ וְיֵדְעוּ כָּל־יוֹשְׁבֵי תֵבֵל כִּי לְךָ תִּכְרַע כָּל־בֶּרֶךְ, תִּשָּׁבַע

371

כָּל־לָשׁוֹן. לְפָנֶיךָ, יְיָ אֱלֹהֵינוּ, יִכְרְעוּ וְיִפְּלוּ, וְלִכְבוֹד שִׁמְךָ יְקָר
יִתֵּנוּ, וִיקַבְּלוּ כֻלָּם אֶת־עֹל מַלְכוּתֶךָ, וְתִמְלוֹךְ עֲלֵיהֶם מְהֵרָה
לְעוֹלָם וָעֶד.

כִּי הַמַּלְכוּת שֶׁלְּךָ הִיא, וּלְעוֹלְמֵי עַד תִּמְלוֹךְ בְּכָבוֹד, כַּכָּתוּב
בְּתוֹרָתֶךָ: „יְיָ יִמְלֹךְ לְעֹלָם וָעֶד."

It is God who stretched forth the heavens and laid the foundations of the earth. God's glorious Presence is in the heavens above; the dominion of God's might in transcendent heights. Adonai is our God; there is none else. God is our Sovereign; there is none other. As it is written in the Torah, "And thou shalt know this day and meditate in thy heart that God is the Sovereign in the heavens above and on the earth beneath; there is none else."

We therefore hope, our God, that we shall soon behold the triumph of Your might, when idolatry will be uprooted from the earth and falsehood be destroyed. We hope for the day when the world will be perfected under the sovereignty of the Almighty, and all humankind learn to revere Your Name, when the wicked of the earth will be drawn in penitence unto You.

O God, fervently we pray that the day may come when all shall turn to You in love, when corruption and evil shall give way to integrity and goodness, when superstition shall no longer enslave the mind, nor idolatry blind the eyes, when all who dwell on earth shall know that You alone are God. Before You, O God, may they bow in worship, and give honor to Your glorious Name. May all created in Your image become one in spirit and one in fellowship, forever united in Your service. May they all acknowledge Your sovereignty, and may Your dominion be established speedily.

For the sovereignty is Yours, and to all eternity You will reign in glory. As it is written in Your Torah, "Adonai will reign for ever and ever."

And it is further written, "Adonai will be acknowledged as Sovereign over all the earth. On that day God will be One and God's Name will be One."

וְנֶאֱמַר: „וְהָיָה יְיָ לְמֶלֶךְ עַל־כָּל־הָאָרֶץ; בַּיּוֹם הַהוּא יִהְיֶה יְיָ אֶחָד וּשְׁמוֹ אֶחָד.‟

MOURNER'S KADDISH   קדיש יתום

Our parents taught us to praise the name of God, to praise God who created us into life. Not only in hours of joy and times of gladness did our people arise to praise God's Name, but also in times of sadness and hours of pain. Through the long round of the centuries we have learned to rise in the face of every storm, out of the abyss of anguish, on the ashes of every destruction, to praise God's Name, to maintain a stance of human dignity and to affirm our consecration to the tasks of life. In confronting death we still can utter a hymn to life. We speak those words which bind our generations each to each and in whose spirit we triumph over death.

                       ◆   ◆

When cherished ties are broken and fond hopes shattered, only faith and confidence can lighten the heaviness of the heart. The pang of separation is hard to bear, but to brood over our sorrow is to embitter our grief. The Psalmist said that in his affliction he learned the law of God. Indeed, not unavailing will be our grief, if it send us back to serve and bless the living. We learn how to counsel and comfort those who, like ourselves, are sorrow-stricken. Though absent, the departed still minister to our spirits, teaching us patience, faithfulness, and devotion. Within the circle of daily association, we often failed to discern their worth and their loveliness. In the remembrance of their virtues and affections, the best and purest part of their nature lies eternally enshrined. Let us lift our head in hope, and summon our strength for duty. We dwell in the shelter of the Almighty; God is our Refuge and our Fortress.

יִתְגַּדַּל וְיִתְקַדַּשׁ שְׁמֵהּ רַבָּא בְּעָלְמָא דִּי־בְרָא כִרְעוּתֵהּ, וְיַמְלִיךְ מַלְכוּתֵהּ בְּחַיֵּיכוֹן וּבְיוֹמֵיכוֹן וּבְחַיֵּי דְכָל־בֵּית יִשְׂרָאֵל, בַּעֲגָלָא

וּבִזְמַן קָרִיב, וְאִמְרוּ אָמֵן:

יְהֵא שְׁמֵהּ רַבָּא מְבָרַךְ לְעָלַם וּלְעָלְמֵי עָלְמַיָּא:

יִתְבָּרַךְ וְיִשְׁתַּבַּח, וְיִתְפָּאַר וְיִתְרוֹמַם וְיִתְנַשֵּׂא, וְיִתְהַדָּר וְיִתְעַלֶּה
וְיִתְהַלָּל שְׁמֵהּ דְּקוּדְשָׁא, בְּרִיךְ הוּא, לְעֵלָּא מִן כָּל־בִּרְכָתָא
וְשִׁירָתָא, תֻּשְׁבְּחָתָא וְנֶחֱמָתָא, דַּאֲמִירָן בְּעָלְמָא, וְאִמְרוּ: אָמֵן.

יְהֵא שְׁלָמָא רַבָּא מִן־שְׁמַיָּא וְחַיִּים עָלֵינוּ וְעַל־כָּל־יִשְׂרָאֵל,
וְאִמְרוּ: אָמֵן.

עֹשֶׂה שָׁלוֹם בִּמְרוֹמָיו, הוּא יַעֲשֶׂה שָׁלוֹם עָלֵינוּ וְעַל־כָּל־יִשְׂרָאֵל,
וְאִמְרוּ: אָמֵן.

Yit-ga-dal ve-yit-ka-dash she-meih ra-ba be-a-le-ma di ve-ra chi-re-u-teih, ve-yam-lich mal-chu-teih be-cha-yei-chon u-ve-yo-mei-chon u-ve-cha-yei de-chol beit Yis-ra-eil, ba-a-ga-la u-vi-ze-man ka-riv, ve-i-me-ru: A-mein.

Ye-hei she-meih ra-ba me-va-rach le-a-lam u-le-a-le-mei a-le-ma-ya.

Yit-ba-rach ve-yish-ta-bach, ve-yit-pa-ar ve-yit-ro-mam ve-yit-na-sei, ve-yit-ha-dar ve-yit-a-leh ve-yit-ha-lal she-meih de-kud-sha, be-rich hu, le-ei-la min kol bi-re-cha-ta ve-shi-ra-ta, tush-be-cha-ta ve-ne-che-ma-ta, da-a-mi-ran be-a-le-ma, ve-i-me-ru: A-mein.

Ye-hei she-la-ma ra-ba min she-ma-ya ve-cha-yim a-lei-nu ve-al kol Yis-ra-eil, ve-i-me-ru: A-mein.

O-seh sha-lom bi-me-ro-mav, hu ya-a-seh sha-lom a-lei-nu ve-al kol Yis-ra-eil, ve-i-me-ru: A-mein.

Let the glory of God be extolled, let God's great Name be hallowed in the world whose creation God willed. May God's sovereignty soon prevail in our own day, our own lives, the life of all the people of Israel, and let us say: *Amen.*

Let God's great Name be praised for ever and ever.

Let the Name of the Holy One be glorified, exalted, and honored, though God is beyond all the praises, songs, and adorations that we can utter, and let us say: *Amen.*

For us, for all the people of Israel, may the blessing of peace and the promise of life come true, and let us say: *Amen.*

May God, whose will is harmony throughout existence, bring peace to us, to all Israel, to all the world, and let us say: *Amen.*

May the Source of peace bring peace to all who mourn. May God comfort the bereaved here among us, and let us all say: *Amen.*

ADON OLAM · אדון עולם

אֲדוֹן עוֹלָם, אֲשֶׁר מָלַךְ בְּטֶרֶם כָּל־יְצִיר נִבְרָא,

לְעֵת נַעֲשָׂה בְחֶפְצוֹ כֹּל, אֲזַי מֶלֶךְ שְׁמוֹ נִקְרָא.

וְאַחֲרֵי כִּכְלוֹת הַכֹּל, לְבַדּוֹ יִמְלוֹךְ נוֹרָא.

וְהוּא הָיָה, וְהוּא הֹוֶה, וְהוּא יִהְיֶה בְּתִפְאָרָה.

וְהוּא אֶחָד, וְאֵין שֵׁנִי לְהַמְשִׁיל לוֹ, לְהַחְבִּירָה,

בְּלִי רֵאשִׁית, בְּלִי תַכְלִית, וְלוֹ הָעֹז וְהַמִּשְׂרָה.

וְהוּא אֵלִי, וְחַי גּוֹאֲלִי, וְצוּר חֶבְלִי בְּעֵת צָרָה,

וְהוּא נִסִּי וּמָנוֹס לִי, מְנָת כּוֹסִי בְּיוֹם אֶקְרָא.

בְּיָדוֹ אַפְקִיד רוּחִי בְּעֵת אִישַׁן וְאָעִירָה,

וְעִם־רוּחִי גְּוִיָּתִי: יְיָ לִי, וְלֹא אִירָא.

A-don o-lam, a-sher ma-lach be-te-rem kol ye-tsir niv-ra,
le-eit na-a-sa ve-chef-tso kol, a-zai me-lech she-mo nik-ra.
Ve-a-cha-rei ki-che-lot ha-kol, le-va-do yim-loch no-ra,
ve-hu ha-ya, ve-hu ho-veh, ve-hu yih-yeh be-tif-a-ra.
Ve-hu e-chad, ve-ein shei-ni le-ham-shil lo, le-hach-bi-ra,
be-li rei-shit, be-li tach-lit, ve-lo ha-oz ve-ha-mis-ra.
Ve-hu Ei-li, ve-chai go-a-li, ve-tsur chev-li be-eit tsa-ra,

ve-hu ni-si u-ma-nos li, me-nat ko-si be-yom ek-ra.
Be-ya-do af-kid ru-chi be-eit i-shan ve-a-i-ra,
ve-im ru-chi ge-vi-ya-ti: A-do-nai li, ve-lo i-ra.

(God is the Eternal One, who reigned before any being had yet been created; when all was done according to God's will, already then God's Name was Sovereign.

And after all has ceased to be, still will God reign in solitary majesty; God was, God is, God shall be in glory.

And God is One, without compare, without beginning, without end; to God belongs power and dominion.

And the Sovereign of all is my own God, my living Redeemer, my Rock in time of trouble and distress; my Banner and my Refuge, my Benefactor to whom, in anguish, I can call.

Into God's hands I entrust my spirit, both when I sleep as when I wake; and with my spirit, my body also: God is with me, I will not fear.)

BENEDICTION

A GUIDE FOR FURTHER READING

ACKNOWLEDGMENTS

A GUIDE FOR FURTHER READING

We can read the Bible in a secular manner and in a religious manner. In the secular, we attempt to understand the text and its message, re-creating as best we can what it meant to ancient Israelites. In the religious, we read classic rabbinic commentaries to learn what our ancestors knew and believed about these books and how these books shaped their Jewish identity and inspired them as Jews. These two approaches can be, but need not be, mutually exclusive. For there are those who have tried to integrate them in order to create commentaries which are historically accurate and spiritually uplifting.

An example of the secular is the *Anchor Bible* (Garden City, NY: Doubleday), a multi-volume work which has been coming out piece-meal for many years. Each book is prepared by a scholar of Bible and Old Testament studies: *Song of Songs* was prepared by Marvin Pope (1977), *Ruth*, by Edward F. Campbell, Jr. (1975), *Lamentations*, by Delbert Hiller (1972), *Ecclesiastes*, by R.B.Y. Scott (1965), and *Esther*, by Carey Moore (1971).

Other examples of the secular approach are Marcia Falk's study of Song of Songs, *Love Lyrics from the Bible* (Sheffield, England: Almond Press, 1982), Jack M. Sasson's *Ruth: A New Translation with a Philological and Formalist-Folklorist Interpretation* (Baltimore: Johns Hopkins University Press, 1979), and Sandra B. Berg's *The Book of Esther: Motifs, Themes, and Structures* (Chico, California: Scholars Press, 1979).

The most classic example of a Jewish interpretation of the Five Scrolls is included in the English translation of *Midrash Rabba* (London: Soncino, 1971). For those who read Yiddish, there is a charming translation-commentary by Samson Dunsky: *Song of Songs* (Montreal, 1973), *Lamentations* (Montreal, 1956), *Ecclesiastes* (Montreal, 1967), and *Esther and Ruth* (Montreal, 1962).

The commentary of the most famous Jewish Bible commentator,

Rashi, is available in English: *The Megillot and Rashi's Commentary with Linear Translation*, translated by Avraham Schwartz and Yisroel Schwartz (New York: Hebrew Linear Classics, 1983).

Raphael Chiyya Pontremoli was a nineteenth century Turkish rabbi whose *Book of Esther* was very popular among Sephardic Jews. Translated by Aryeh Kaplan, it is part of the Sephardic anthology, *Me'am Lo'ez* (New York: Maznayim, 1978).

Modern commentaries which use classical sources are *The Five Scrolls*, edited by Israel Bettan (New York: Union of American Hebrew Congregations, 1950) and *The Five Megilloth*, edited by A. Cohen (London: Soncino, 1961).

Robert Gordis is a Conservative rabbi who has combined the secular and religious approaches. Among his works are *The Song of Songs and Lamentations* (revised and augmented edition, New York: KTAV, 1974), and *Kohelet: The Man and His World* (3rd edition, New York: Schocken, 1968).

ACKNOWLEDGMENTS

The Central Conference of American Rabbis wishes to express its profound gratitude and admiration to the following individuals, whose devotion to this project has been truly selfless. Whether the number of hours of labor turned out to be few or many hundreds, all have given of themselves, and have made this truly a work of love.

We thank:

Rabbi Herbert Bronstein, co-editor, who is senior rabbi of North Shore Congregation Israel, Glencoe, Illinois. He is the editor of the new Haggadah of the CCAR, and has published many articles in many journals, including the *Journal of Reform Judaism, Moment,* and the *Shakespeare Quarterly*;

Rabbi Albert H. Friedlander, co-editor, for sharing overall supervision of the project, whose translations represent a significant contribution for their aptness, spirit, and clarity. Rabbi Friedlander is Dean and Senior Lecturer in History and Theology at the Leo Baeck College, London, England. He is senior rabbi of the Westminster Synagogue in London, and the author of *Out of the Whirlwind, Leo Baeck: Teacher of Theresienstadt,* and other works in English and German;

Leonard Baskin, our illustrator, for his unique and powerful series of new interpretations. His work constitutes a commentary and makes its own contribution to the study of the Five Scrolls. For Mr. Baskin—water colorist, engraver, illustrator, designer, essayist, and sculptor—the primary focus of his art is the human being in the light of the ultimate questions of existence and the inevitability of death. He has held to a figurative style as the most forceful conveyor of his humanist themes. His work, winner of many awards, is displayed in leading museums throughout the world;

Rabbi Joseph B. Glaser, whose initial vision of how festival and

holy day worship services might be enhanced was matched throughout this entire project by his dedicated and gentle, yet insistent prodding toward quality and efficiency. Without his steady guidance, the work would never have begun;

Rabbi Elliot L. Stevens, whose masterful coordination of the myriad production details from typesetting through promotion was never overwhelmed by "author's alterations" or printer's gremlins. Without his supervision the work would not have progressed so smoothly;

Rabbi Jordan Pearlson, spiritual leader of Temple Sinai of Toronto, who deserves a special word of thanks in his role as chair of the CCAR Publications Committee, which first recognized and promoted the important contribution to Jewish life represented by this volume;

Dr. Yehiel Hayon, a meticulous, knowledgeable, and very concerned copy editor whose profound learning in Hebrew linguistics and style are directly responsible for many substantial improvements, and who devoted countless hours beyond his commission without losing his sense of humor. Without his capacities and efficiency the work would not yet have been concluded;

Rabbi A. Stanley Dreyfus, whose expertise in matters of liturgy and rabbinics is equalled by the elegance of his style and the sensitivity with which his comments and criticisms were shared. He was always more generous with his time than we had any hope to expect;

Rabbi Lawrence A. Hoffman, who chaired the Liturgy Committee at the genesis of this project and provided that fundamental guidance and support necessary to launch a work of such complexity;

Rabbi Elyse D. Frishman, a poetic soul who willingly accepted the difficult task of emending sexist language constructions;

Rabbi Henry A. Bamberger, who assisted in the early work of proofreading the biblical megillot in Hebrew;

Cantor Edward Graham, for his early involvement in choosing and reviewing the English translation;

Barry N. Sher and his colleagues at Nostradamus Advertising, for their professional yet loving attention to all the details of production;

Dr. Philip E. Miller, librarian at Hebrew Union College–Jewish Institute of Religion in New York, who willingly prepared the Guide for Further Reading.

In preparing the liturgies which accompany each scroll, committees were invited to convene in different parts of the country, each for a different scroll, and asked to submit suggested liturgies to the editors. The editors wish to record their profound gratitude to these colleagues, whose thinking and insights have made this the work it is: Avram Arian, Henry Bamberger, Bernard Baskin, Herman Blumberg, Gerald S. Brieger, Lawrence A. Englander, Adam Fisher, Elyse Frishman, Marc Gellman, Irwin Goldenberg, Gerald A. Goldman, Hirshel L. Jaffe, Lawerence Kushner, Jerome R. Malino, Bernard Mehlman, Fred J. Neulander, Peter J. Rubinstein, William Sajowitz, Marc Saperstein, Herman E. Schaalman, Mark Shapiro, Rav A. Soloff, Ned J. Soltz, Samuel M. Stahl, Chaim Stern, Edward S. Treister, Roy Walter.